ENDLESS SUMMER

VOL. 1

DEAD MAN'S CURVE

ENDLESS SUMMER

VOL. 1

DEAD MAN'S CURVE

WRITTEN BY **B. CLAY MOORE**

ILLUSTRATED BY **SHANE PATRICK WHITE**

INSIGHT COMICS

SAN RAFAEL · LOS ANGELES · LONDON

PART 1

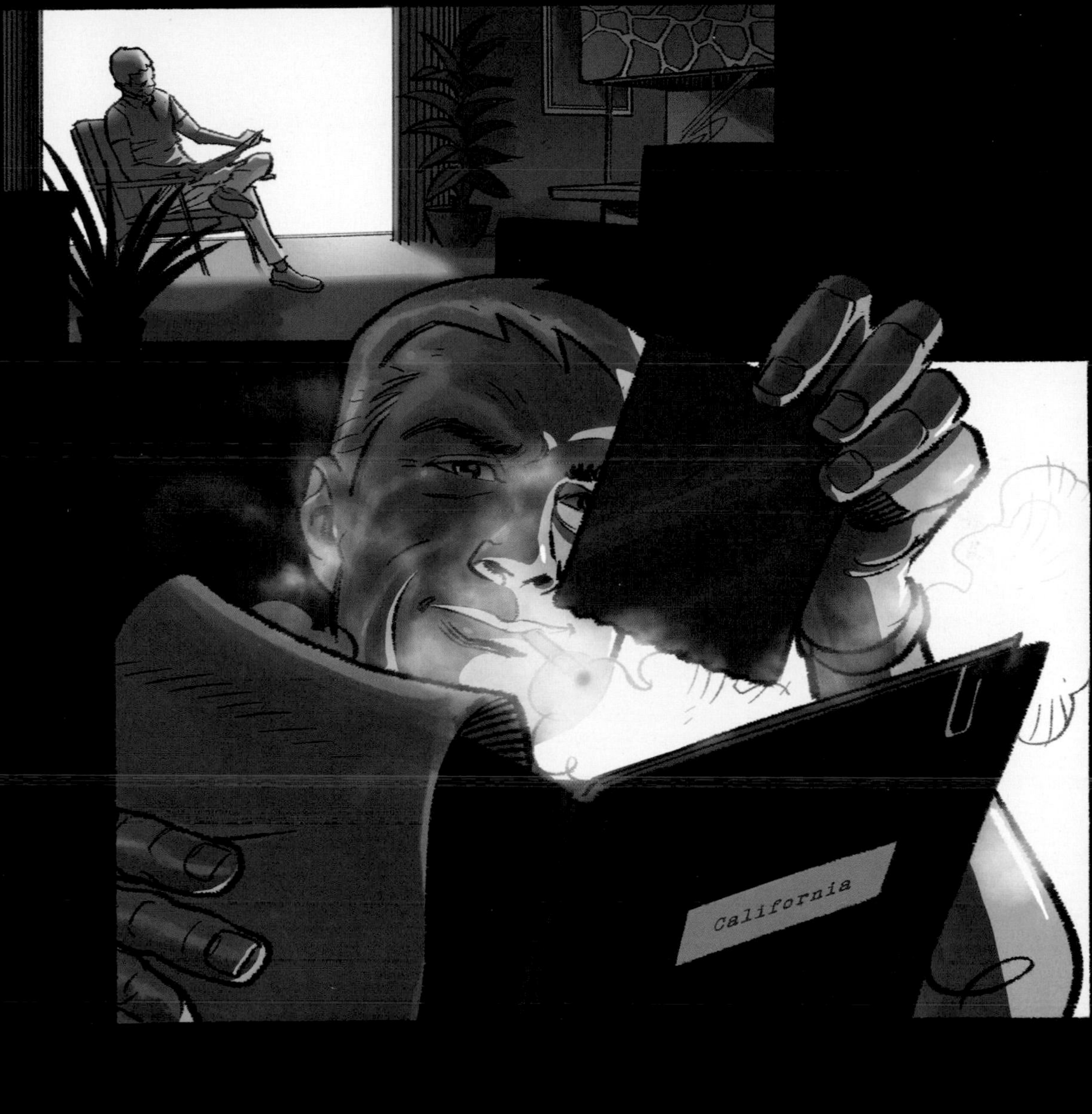
California

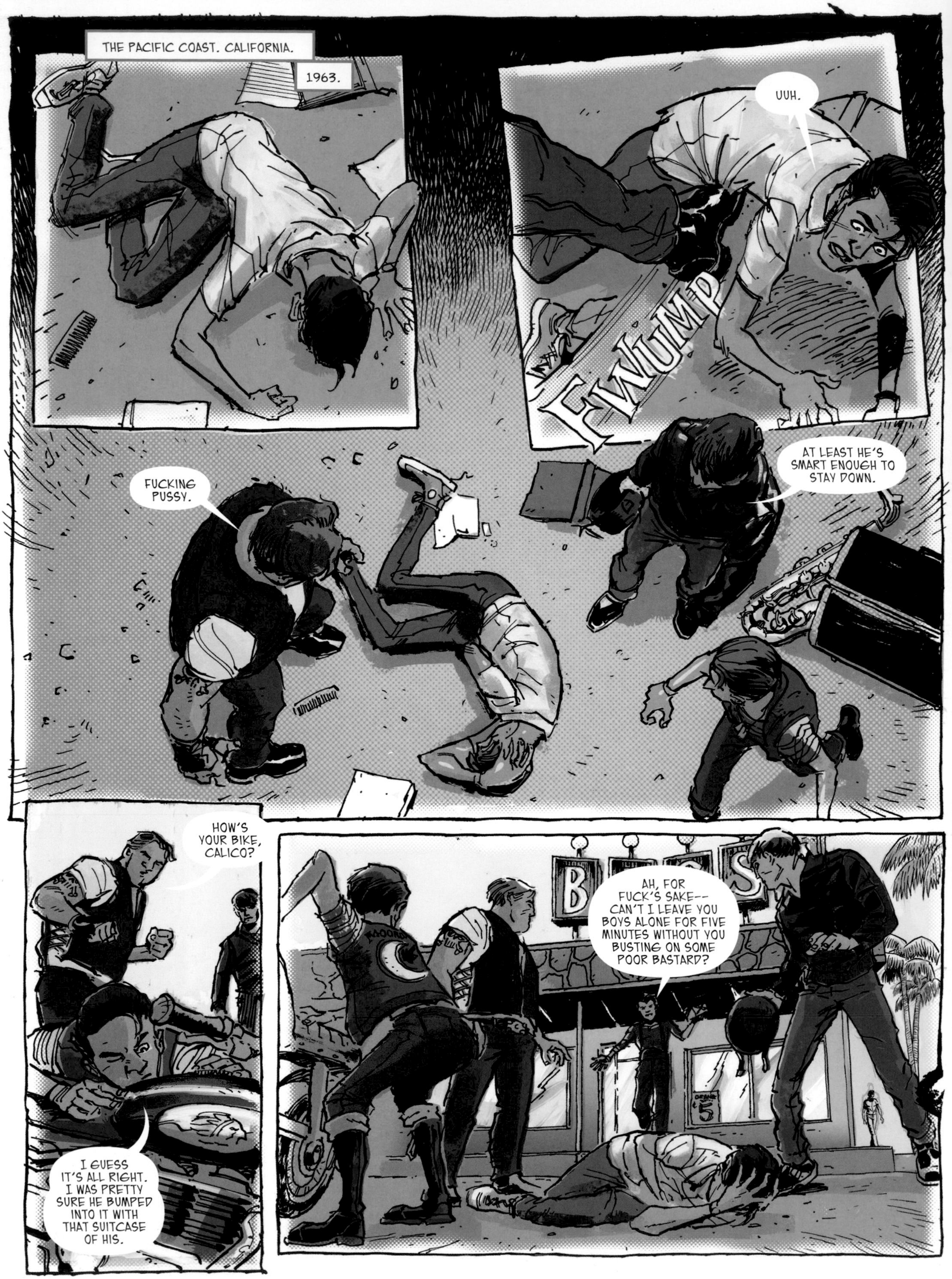
THE PACIFIC COAST. CALIFORNIA.
1963.
UUH.
FWUMP
FUCKING PUSSY.
AT LEAST HE'S SMART ENOUGH TO STAY DOWN.
HOW'S YOUR BIKE, CALICO?
I GUESS IT'S ALL RIGHT. I WAS PRETTY SURE HE BUMPED INTO IT WITH THAT SUITCASE OF HIS.
AH, FOR FUCK'S SAKE-- CAN'T I LEAVE YOU BOYS ALONE FOR FIVE MINUTES WITHOUT YOU BUSTING ON SOME POOR BASTARD?

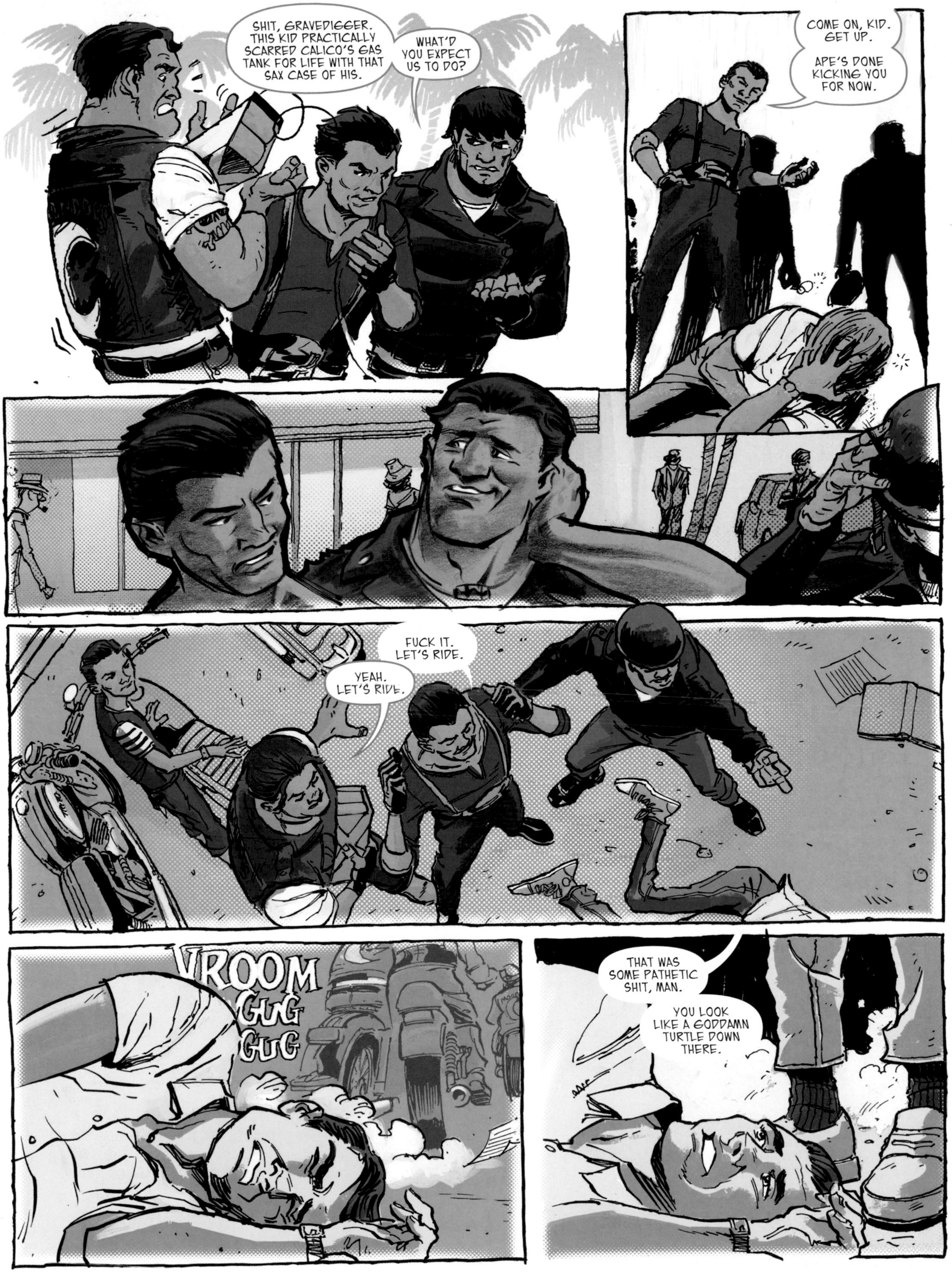
SHIT, GRAVEDIGGER. THIS KID PRACTICALLY SCARRED CALICO'S GAS TANK FOR LIFE WITH THAT SAX CASE OF HIS.
WHAT'D YOU EXPECT US TO DO?
COME ON, KID. GET UP.
APE'S DONE KICKING YOU FOR NOW.
FUCK IT. LET'S RIDE.
YEAH. LET'S RIDE.
VROOM
GUG
GUG
THAT WAS SOME PATHETIC SHIT, MAN.
YOU LOOK LIKE A GODDAMN TURTLE DOWN THERE.

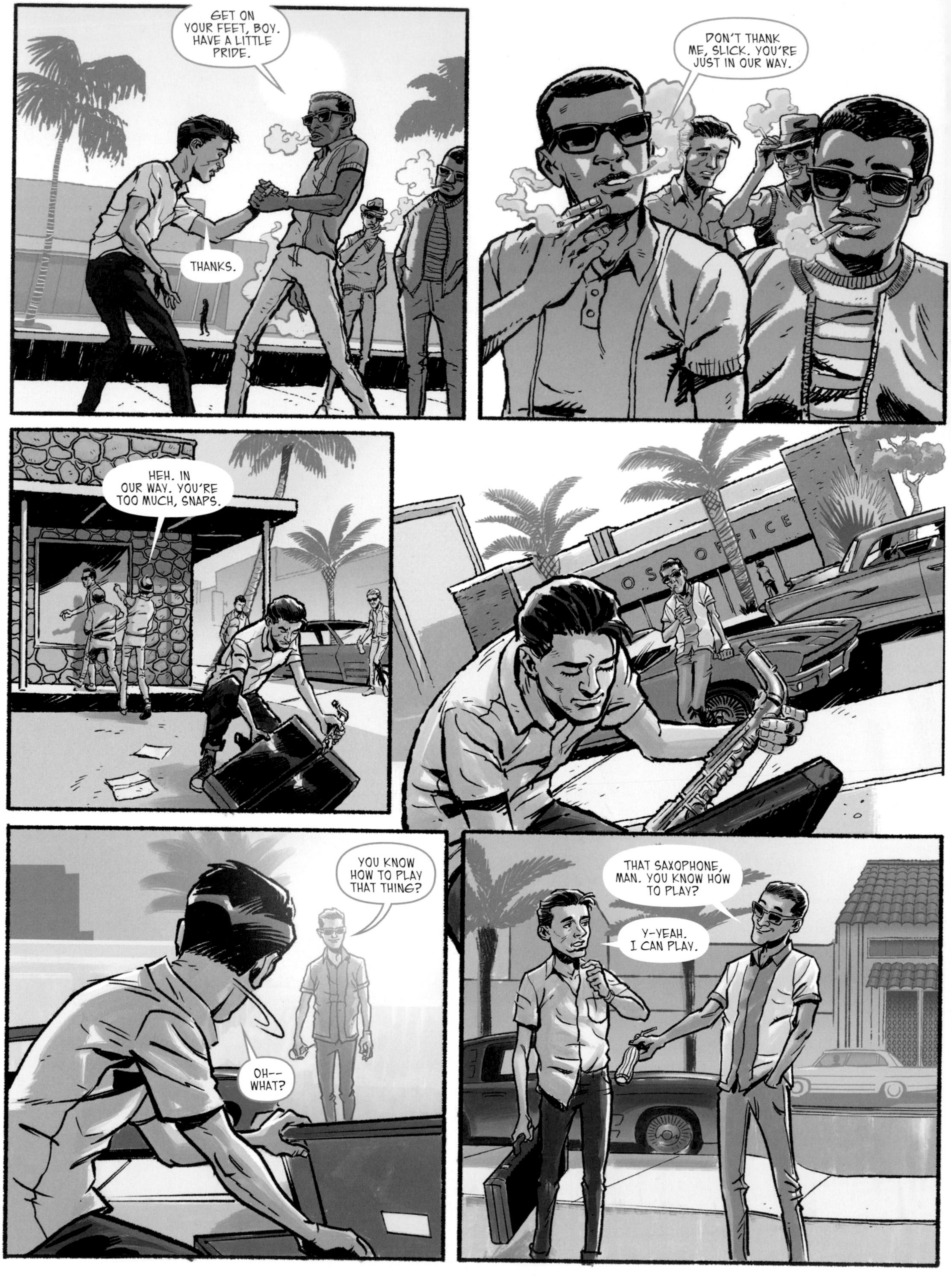
GET ON YOUR FEET, BOY. HAVE A LITTLE PRIDE.
THANKS.
DON'T THANK ME, SLICK. YOU'RE JUST IN OUR WAY.
HEH. IN OUR WAY. YOU'RE TOO MUCH, SNAPS.
POST OFFICE
YOU KNOW HOW TO PLAY THAT THING?
OH-- WHAT?
THAT SAXOPHONE, MAN. YOU KNOW HOW TO PLAY?
Y-YEAH. I CAN PLAY.

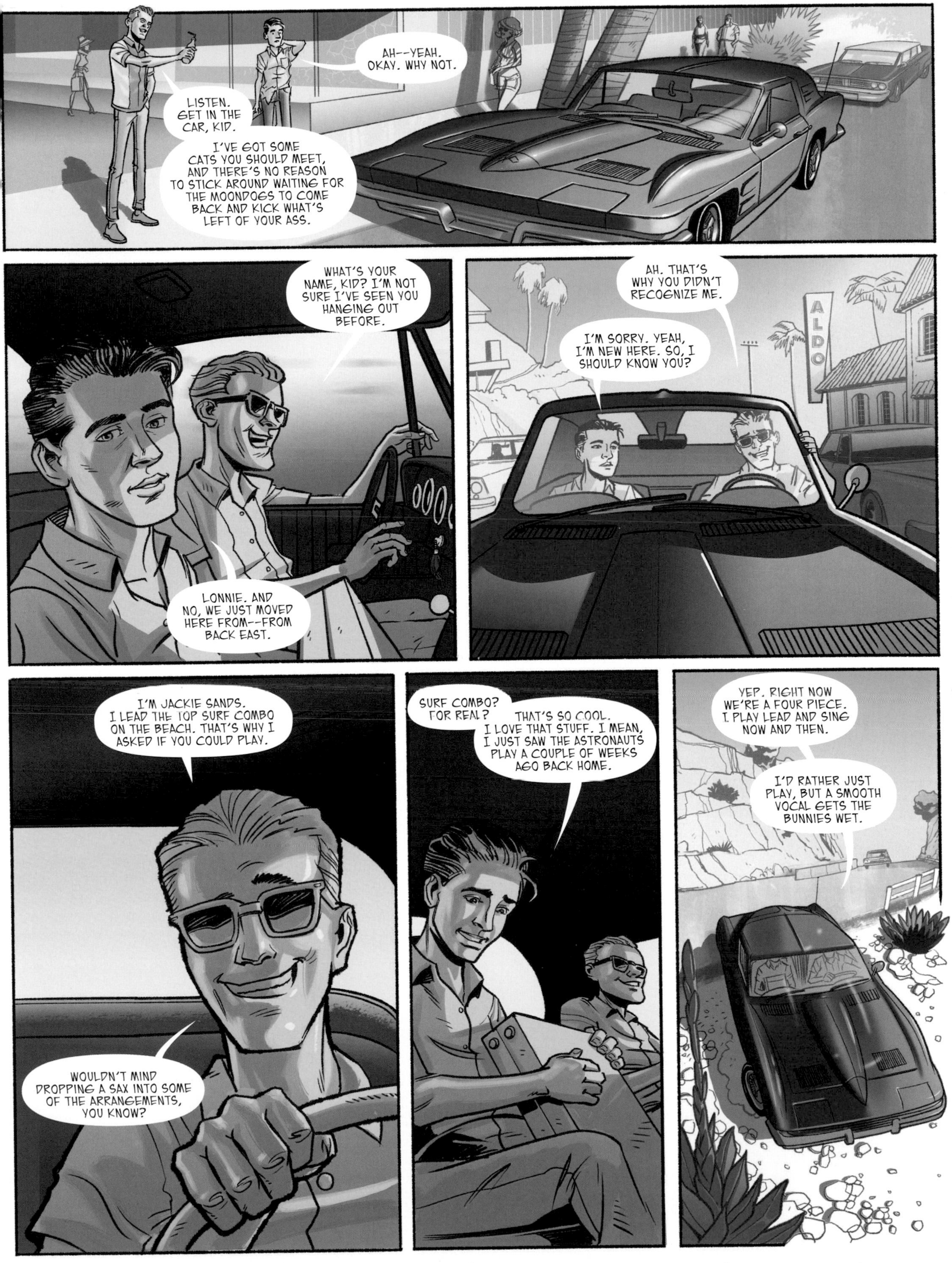
AH--YEAH. OKAY. WHY NOT.
LISTEN. GET IN THE CAR, KID.
I'VE GOT SOME CATS YOU SHOULD MEET, AND THERE'S NO REASON TO STICK AROUND WAITING FOR THE MOONDOGS TO COME BACK AND KICK WHAT'S LEFT OF YOUR ASS.
WHAT'S YOUR NAME, KID? I'M NOT SURE I'VE SEEN YOU HANGING OUT BEFORE.
LONNIE. AND NO, WE JUST MOVED HERE FROM--FROM BACK EAST.
AH. THAT'S WHY YOU DIDN'T RECOGNIZE ME.
I'M SORRY. YEAH, I'M NEW HERE. SO, I SHOULD KNOW YOU?
ALDO
I'M JACKIE SANDS. I LEAD THE TOP SURF COMBO ON THE BEACH. THAT'S WHY I ASKED IF YOU COULD PLAY.
WOULDN'T MIND DROPPING A SAX INTO SOME OF THE ARRANGEMENTS, YOU KNOW?
SURF COMBO? FOR REAL?
THAT'S SO COOL. I LOVE THAT STUFF. I MEAN, I JUST SAW THE ASTRONAUTS PLAY A COUPLE OF WEEKS AGO BACK HOME.
YEP. RIGHT NOW WE'RE A FOUR PIECE. I PLAY LEAD AND SING NOW AND THEN.
I'D RATHER JUST PLAY, BUT A SMOOTH VOCAL GETS THE BUNNIES WET.

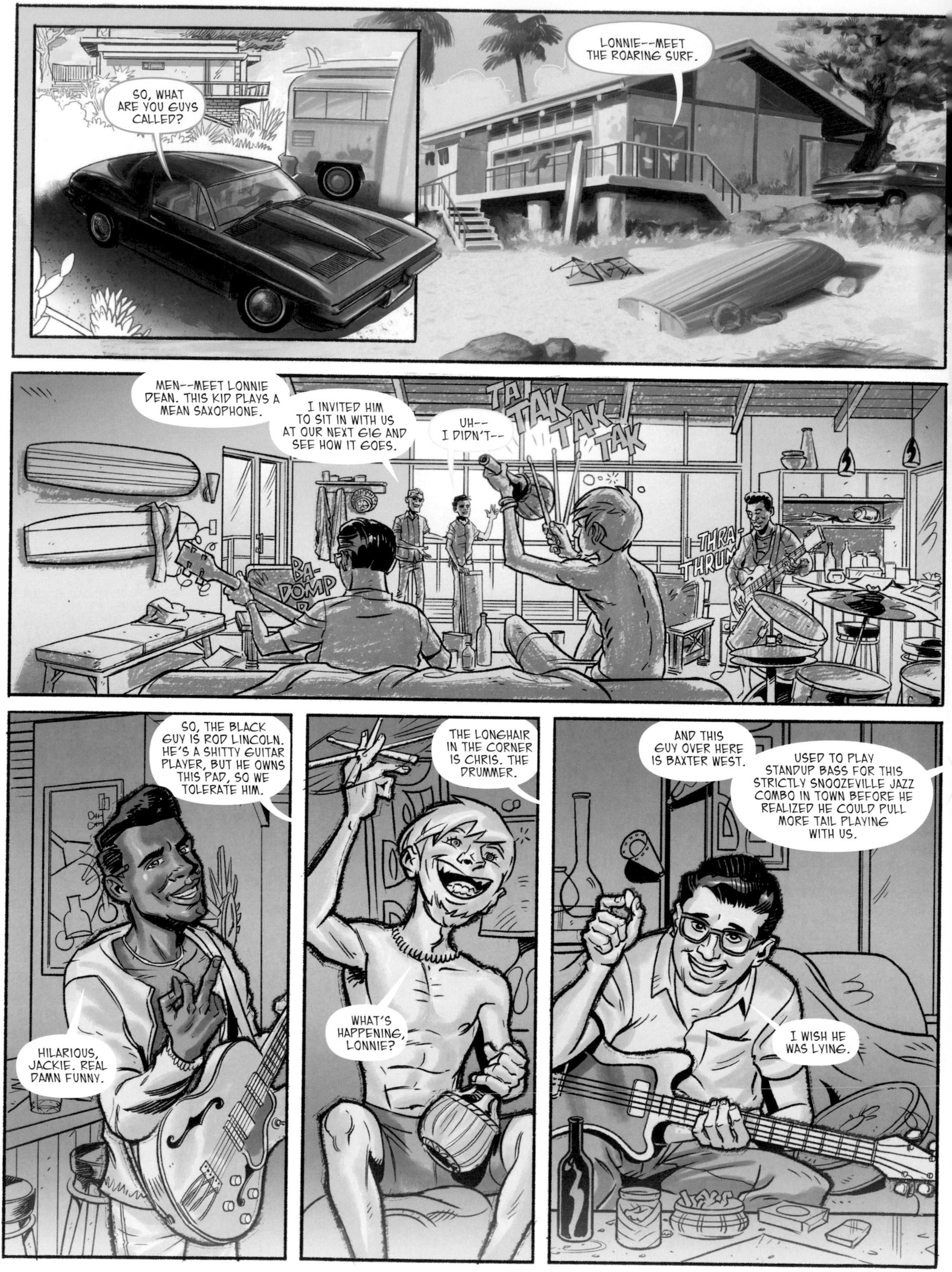
SO, WHAT ARE YOU GUYS CALLED?
LONNIE--MEET THE ROARING SURF.
MEN--MEET LONNIE DEAN. THIS KID PLAYS A MEAN SAXOPHONE.
I INVITED HIM TO SIT IN WITH US AT OUR NEXT GIG AND SEE HOW IT GOES.
UH-- I DIDN'T--
TA! TAK TAK TAK
BA-DOMP
THRA-THRUM
SO, THE BLACK GUY IS ROD LINCOLN. HE'S A SHITTY GUITAR PLAYER, BUT HE OWNS THIS PAD, SO WE TOLERATE HIM.
HILARIOUS, JACKIE. REAL DAMN FUNNY.
THE LONGHAIR IN THE CORNER IS CHRIS. THE DRUMMER.
WHAT'S HAPPENING, LONNIE?
AND THIS GUY OVER HERE IS BAXTER WEST.
USED TO PLAY STANDUP BASS FOR THIS STRICTLY SNOOZEVILLE JAZZ COMBO IN TOWN BEFORE HE REALIZED HE COULD PULL MORE TAIL PLAYING WITH US.
I WISH HE WAS LYING.

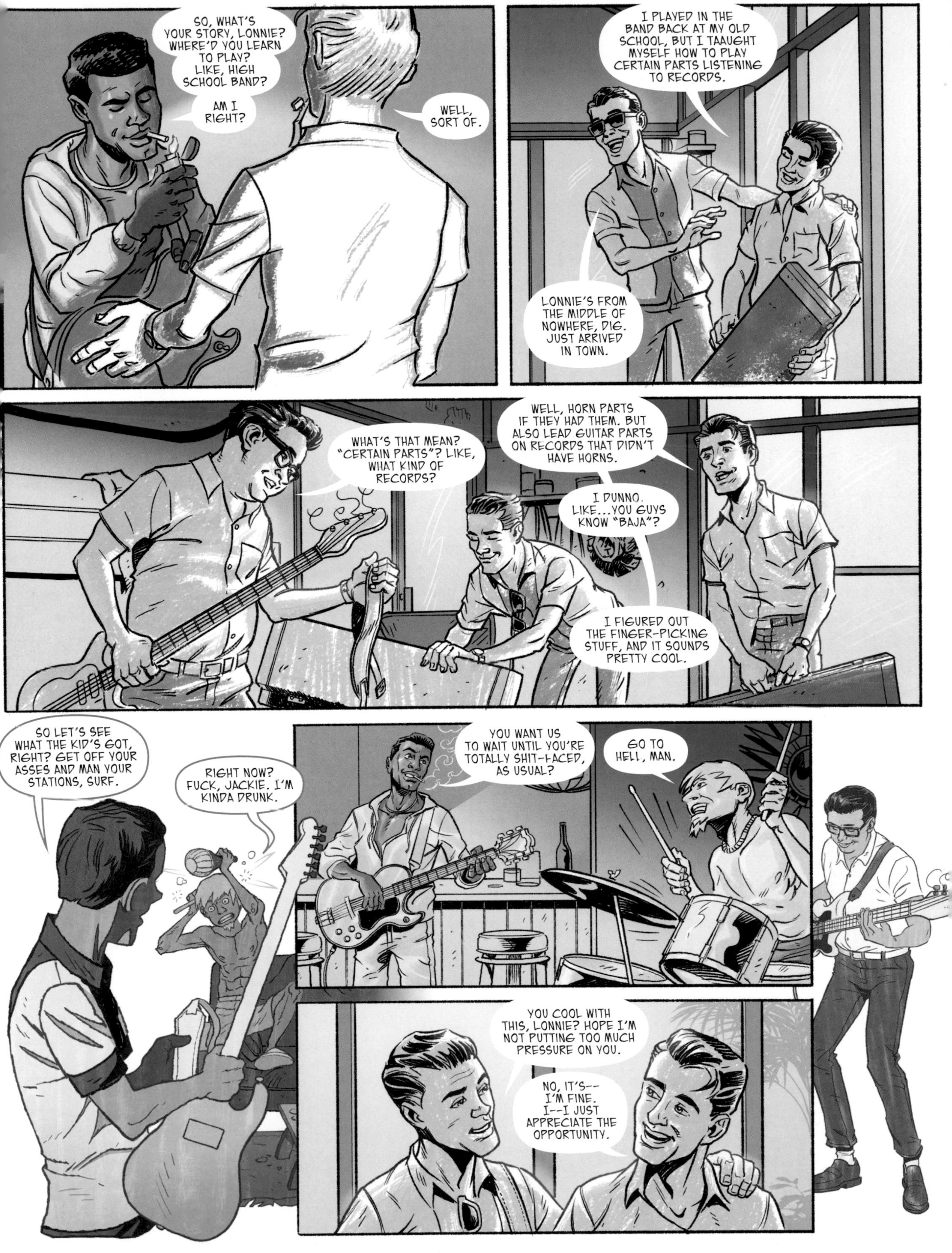

SO, WHAT'S YOUR STORY, LONNIE? WHERE'D YOU LEARN TO PLAY? LIKE, HIGH SCHOOL BAND?
AM I RIGHT?
WELL, SORT OF.
I PLAYED IN THE BAND BACK AT MY OLD SCHOOL, BUT I TAAUGHT MYSELF HOW TO PLAY CERTAIN PARTS LISTENING TO RECORDS.
LONNIE'S FROM THE MIDDLE OF NOWHERE, DIG. JUST ARRIVED IN TOWN.
WHAT'S THAT MEAN? "CERTAIN PARTS"? LIKE, WHAT KIND OF RECORDS?
WELL, HORN PARTS IF THEY HAD THEM. BUT ALSO LEAD GUITAR PARTS ON RECORDS THAT DIDN'T HAVE HORNS.
I DUNNO. LIKE...YOU GUYS KNOW "BAJA"?
I FIGURED OUT THE FINGER-PICKING STUFF, AND IT SOUNDS PRETTY COOL.
SO LET'S SEE WHAT THE KID'S GOT, RIGHT? GET OFF YOUR ASSES AND MAN YOUR STATIONS, SURF.
RIGHT NOW? FUCK, JACKIE. I'M KINDA DRUNK.
YOU WANT US TO WAIT UNTIL YOU'RE TOTALLY SHIT-FACED, AS USUAL?
GO TO HELL, MAN.
YOU COOL WITH THIS, LONNIE? HOPE I'M NOT PUTTING TOO MUCH PRESSURE ON YOU.
NO, IT'S-- I'M FINE. I--I JUST APPRECIATE THE OPPORTUNITY.

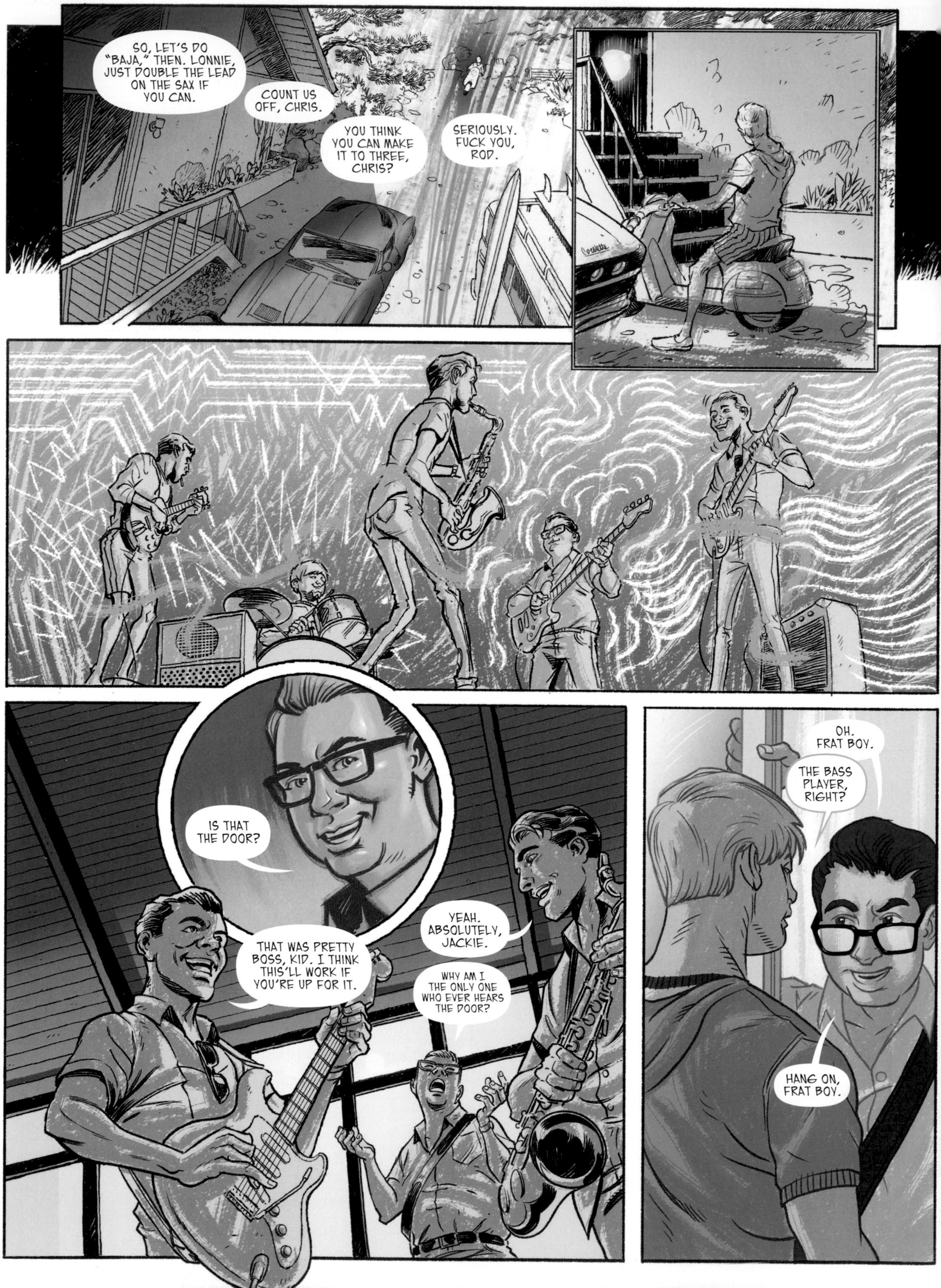
SO, LET'S DO "BAJA," THEN. LONNIE, JUST DOUBLE THE LEAD ON THE SAX IF YOU CAN.
COUNT US OFF, CHRIS.
YOU THINK YOU CAN MAKE IT TO THREE, CHRIS?
SERIOUSLY. FUCK YOU, ROD.
IS THAT THE DOOR?
THAT WAS PRETTY BOSS, KID. I THINK THIS'LL WORK IF YOU'RE UP FOR IT.
YEAH. ABSOLUTELY, JACKIE.
WHY AM I THE ONLY ONE WHO EVER HEARS THE DOOR?
OH. FRAT BOY.
THE BASS PLAYER, RIGHT?
HANG ON, FRAT BOY.

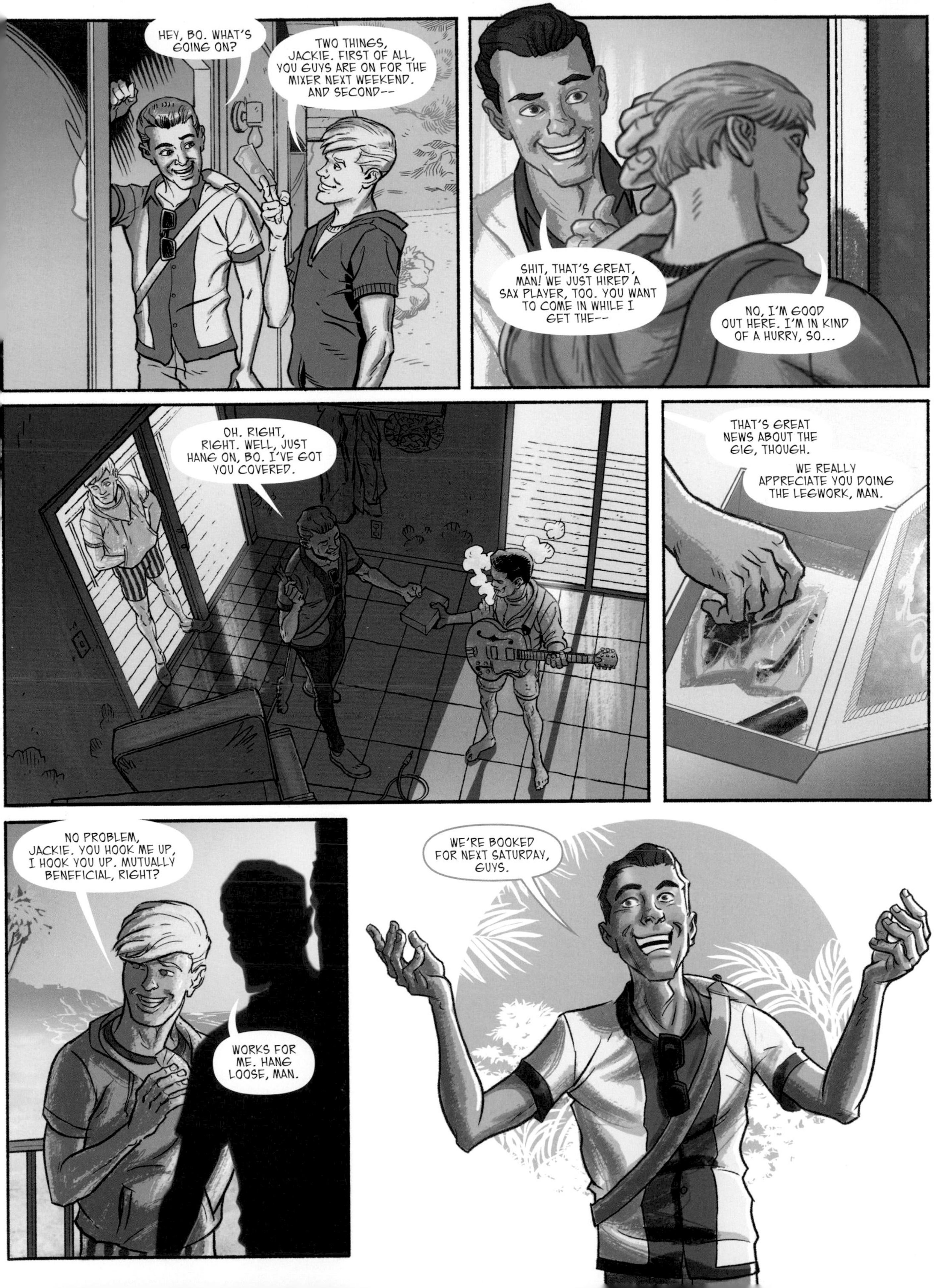
HEY, BO. WHAT'S GOING ON?
TWO THINGS, JACKIE. FIRST OF ALL, YOU GUYS ARE ON FOR THE MIXER NEXT WEEKEND. AND SECOND--
SHIT, THAT'S GREAT, MAN! WE JUST HIRED A SAX PLAYER, TOO. YOU WANT TO COME IN WHILE I GET THE--
NO, I'M GOOD OUT HERE. I'M IN KIND OF A HURRY, SO...
OH. RIGHT, RIGHT. WELL, JUST HANG ON, BO. I'VE GOT YOU COVERED.
THAT'S GREAT NEWS ABOUT THE GIG, THOUGH.
WE REALLY APPRECIATE YOU DOING THE LEGWORK, MAN.
NO PROBLEM, JACKIE. YOU HOOK ME UP, I HOOK YOU UP. MUTUALLY BENEFICIAL, RIGHT?
WORKS FOR ME. HANG LOOSE, MAN.
WE'RE BOOKED FOR NEXT SATURDAY, GUYS.

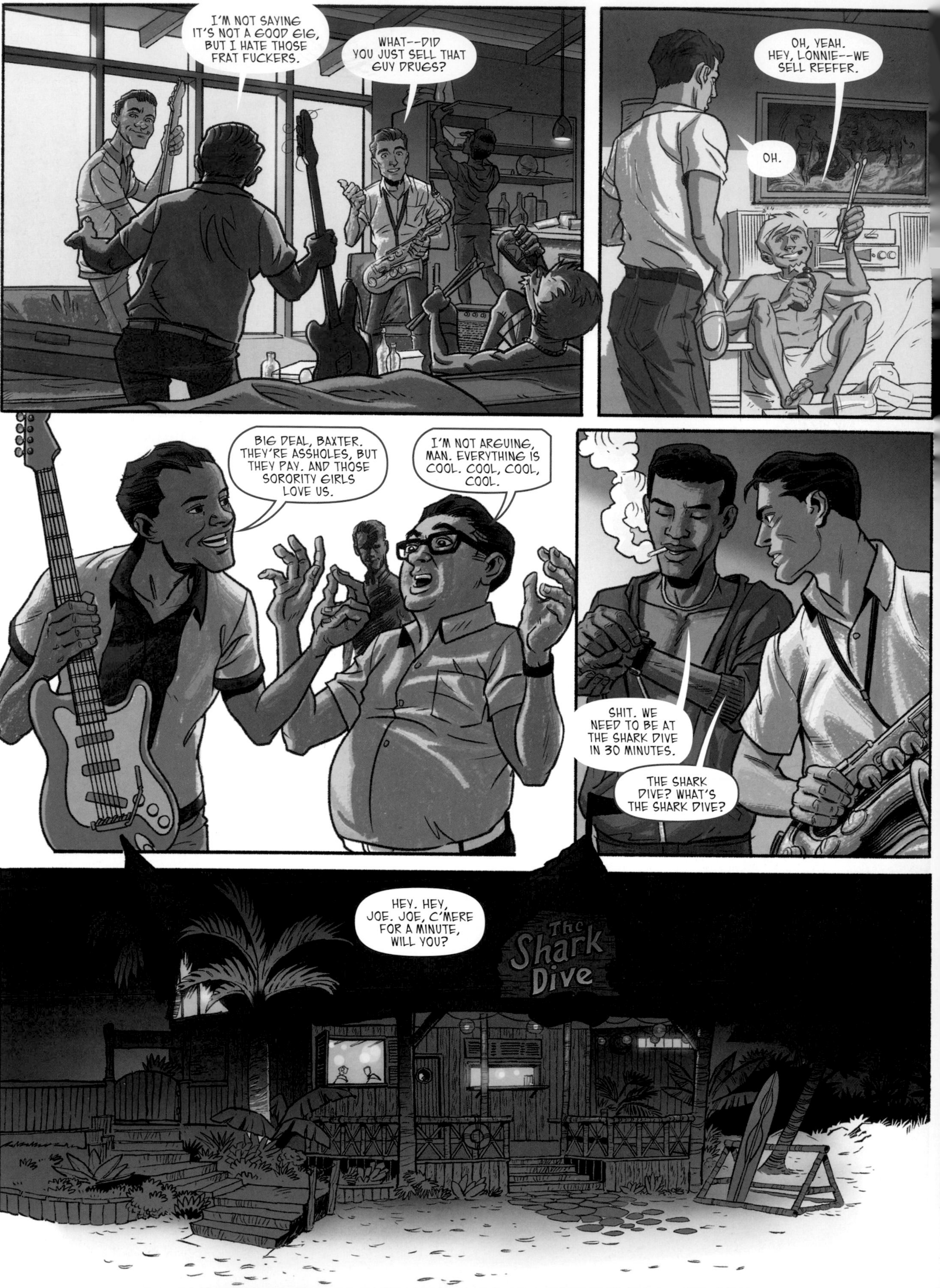
I'M NOT SAYING IT'S NOT A GOOD GIG, BUT I HATE THOSE FRAT FUCKERS.
WHAT--DID YOU JUST SELL THAT GUY DRUGS?
OH, YEAH. HEY, LONNIE--WE SELL REEFER.
OH.
BIG DEAL, BAXTER. THEY'RE ASSHOLES, BUT THEY PAY. AND THOSE SORORITY GIRLS LOVE US.
I'M NOT ARGUING, MAN. EVERYTHING IS COOL. COOL, COOL, COOL.
SHIT. WE NEED TO BE AT THE SHARK DIVE IN 30 MINUTES.
THE SHARK DIVE? WHAT'S THE SHARK DIVE?
HEY. HEY, JOE. JOE, C'MERE FOR A MINUTE, WILL YOU?
The Shark Dive

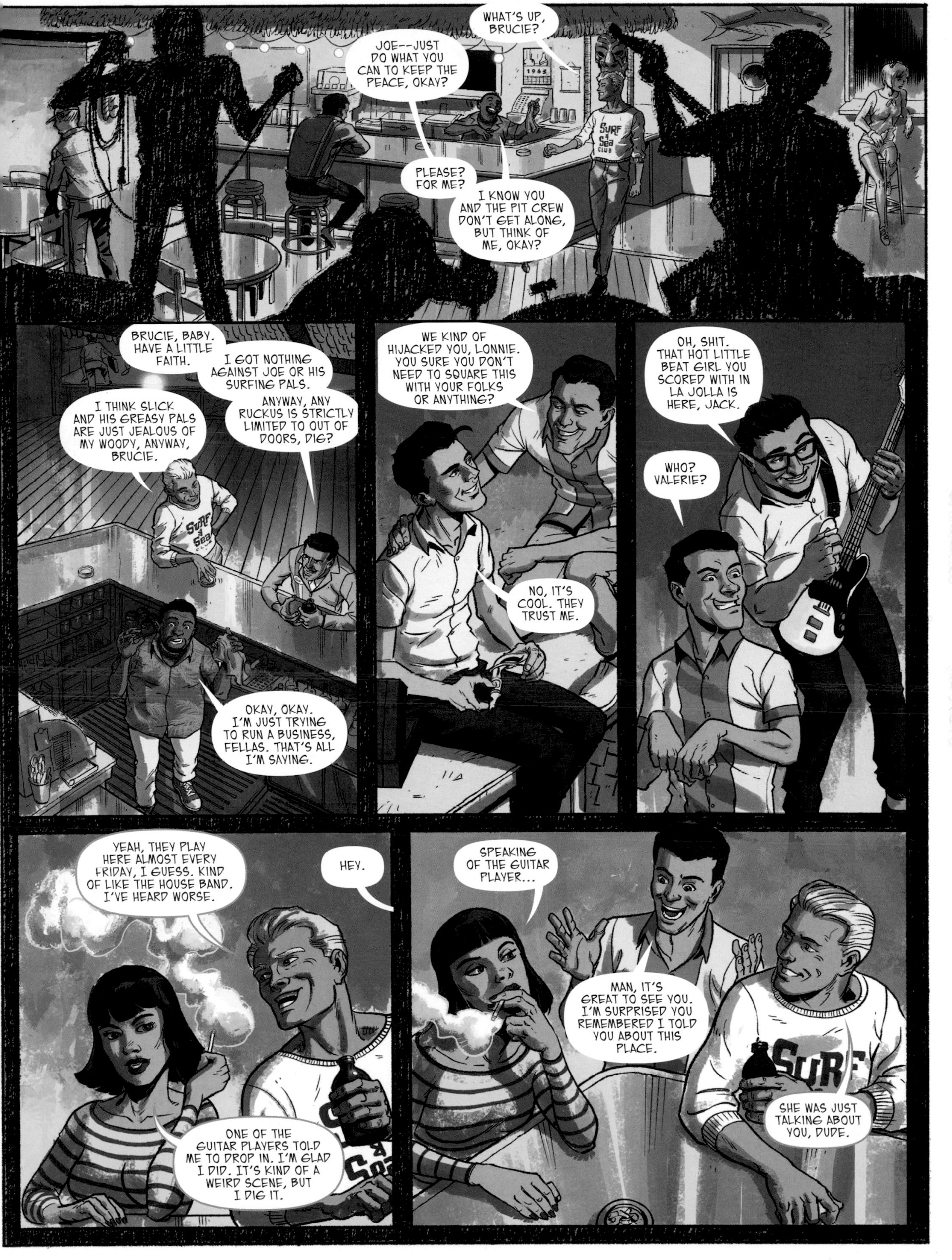

WHAT'S UP, BRUCIE?
JOE--JUST DO WHAT YOU CAN TO KEEP THE PEACE, OKAY?
PLEASE? FOR ME?
I KNOW YOU AND THE PIT CREW DON'T GET ALONG, BUT THINK OF ME, OKAY?
1965
SURF & SEA CLUB
BRUCIE, BABY. HAVE A LITTLE FAITH.
I GOT NOTHING AGAINST JOE OR HIS SURFING PALS.
I THINK SLICK AND HIS GREASY PALS ARE JUST JEALOUS OF MY WOODY, ANYWAY, BRUCIE.
ANYWAY, ANY RUCKUS IS STRICTLY LIMITED TO OUT OF DOORS, DIG?
OKAY, OKAY. I'M JUST TRYING TO RUN A BUSINESS, FELLAS. THAT'S ALL I'M SAYING.
WE KIND OF HIJACKED YOU, LONNIE. YOU SURE YOU DON'T NEED TO SQUARE THIS WITH YOUR FOLKS OR ANYTHING?
NO, IT'S COOL. THEY TRUST ME.
OH, SHIT. THAT HOT LITTLE BEAT GIRL YOU SCORED WITH IN LA JOLLA IS HERE, JACK.
WHO? VALERIE?
YEAH, THEY PLAY HERE ALMOST EVERY FRIDAY, I GUESS. KIND OF LIKE THE HOUSE BAND. I'VE HEARD WORSE.
HEY.
ONE OF THE GUITAR PLAYERS TOLD ME TO DROP IN. I'M GLAD I DID. IT'S KIND OF A WEIRD SCENE, BUT I DIG IT.
SPEAKING OF THE GUITAR PLAYER...
MAN, IT'S GREAT TO SEE YOU. I'M SURPRISED YOU REMEMBERED I TOLD YOU ABOUT THIS PLACE.
SHE WAS JUST TALKING ABOUT YOU, DUDE.

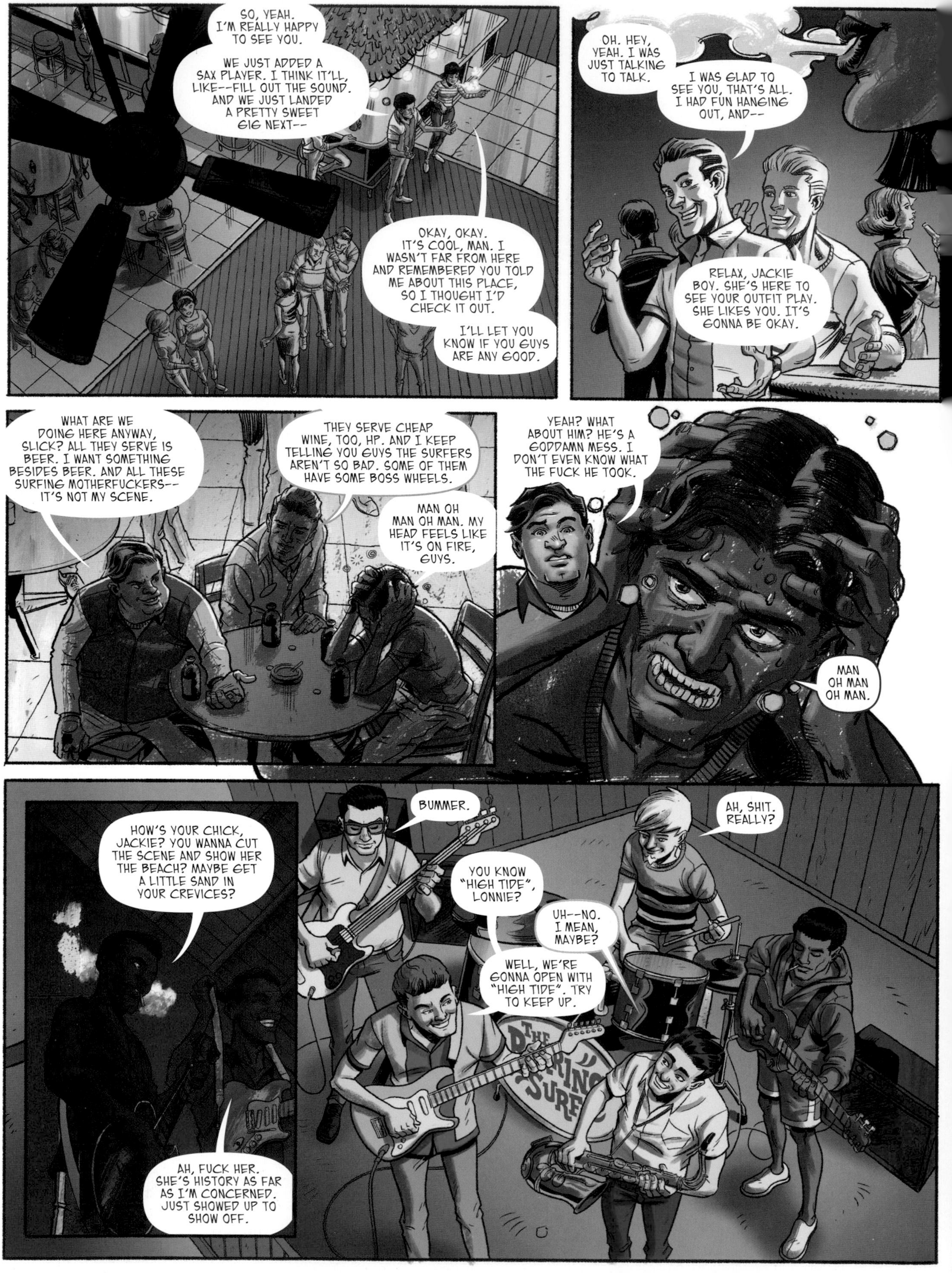
SO, YEAH. I'M REALLY HAPPY TO SEE YOU.
WE JUST ADDED A SAX PLAYER. I THINK IT'LL, LIKE--FILL OUT THE SOUND. AND WE JUST LANDED A PRETTY SWEET GIG NEXT--
OKAY, OKAY. IT'S COOL, MAN. I WASN'T FAR FROM HERE AND REMEMBERED YOU TOLD ME ABOUT THIS PLACE, SO I THOUGHT I'D CHECK IT OUT.
I'LL LET YOU KNOW IF YOU GUYS ARE ANY GOOD.
OH. HEY, YEAH. I WAS JUST TALKING TO TALK.
I WAS GLAD TO SEE YOU, THAT'S ALL. I HAD FUN HANGING OUT, AND--
RELAX, JACKIE BOY. SHE'S HERE TO SEE YOUR OUTFIT PLAY. SHE LIKES YOU. IT'S GONNA BE OKAY.
WHAT ARE WE DOING HERE ANYWAY, SLICK? ALL THEY SERVE IS BEER. I WANT SOMETHING BESIDES BEER. AND ALL THESE SURFING MOTHERFUCKERS--IT'S NOT MY SCENE.
THEY SERVE CHEAP WINE, TOO, HP. AND I KEEP TELLING YOU GUYS THE SURFERS AREN'T SO BAD. SOME OF THEM HAVE SOME BOSS WHEELS.
MAN OH MAN OH MAN. MY HEAD FEELS LIKE IT'S ON FIRE, GUYS.
YEAH? WHAT ABOUT HIM? HE'S A GODDAMN MESS. I DON'T EVEN KNOW WHAT THE FUCK HE TOOK.
MAN OH MAN OH MAN.
HOW'S YOUR CHICK, JACKIE? YOU WANNA CUT THE SCENE AND SHOW HER THE BEACH? MAYBE GET A LITTLE SAND IN YOUR CREVICES?
AH, FUCK HER. SHE'S HISTORY AS FAR AS I'M CONCERNED. JUST SHOWED UP TO SHOW OFF.
BUMMER.
AH, SHIT. REALLY?
YOU KNOW "HIGH TIDE", LONNIE?
UH--NO. I MEAN, MAYBE?
WELL, WE'RE GONNA OPEN WITH "HIGH TIDE". TRY TO KEEP UP.

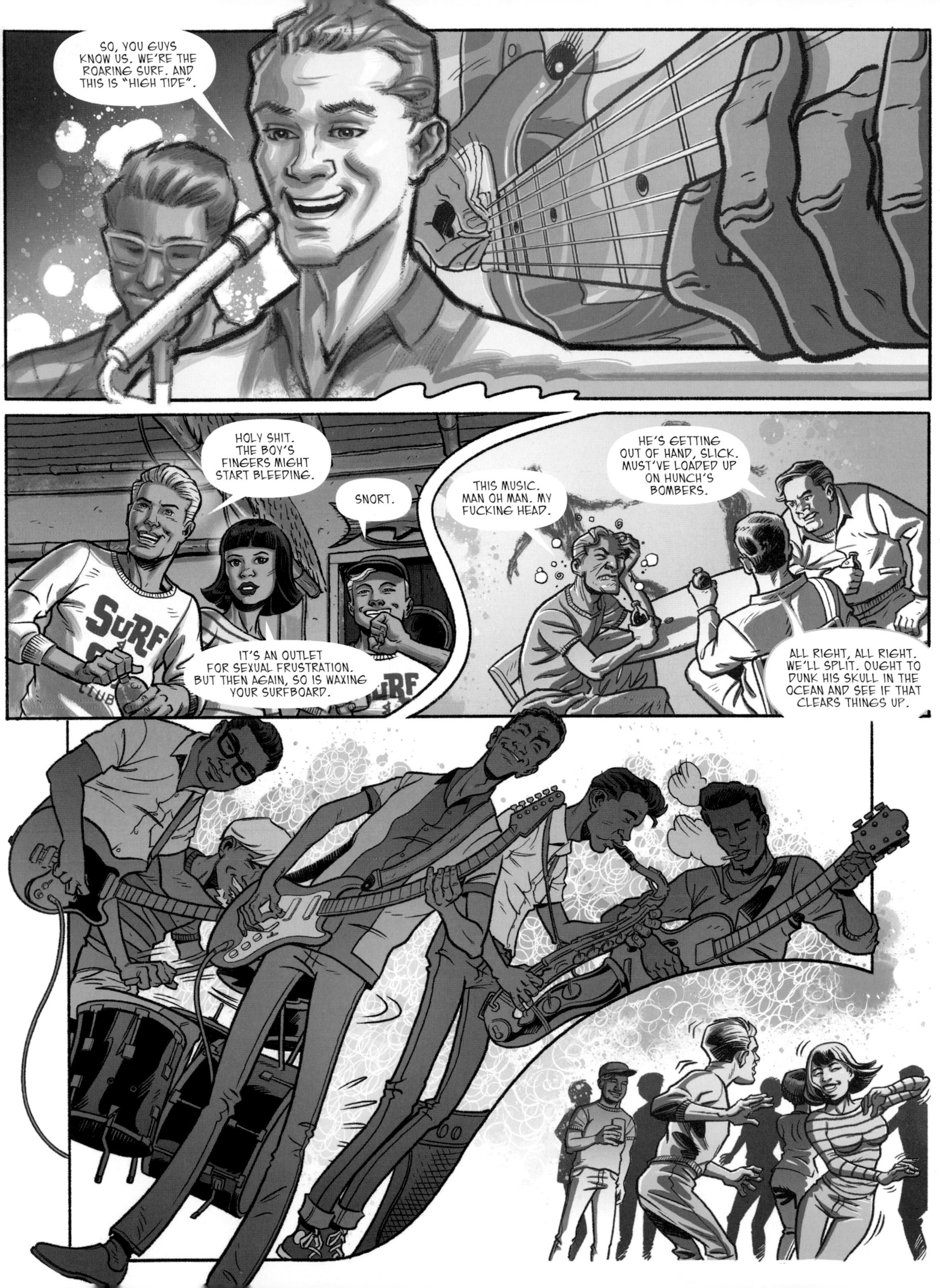
SO, YOU GUYS KNOW US. WE'RE THE ROARING SURF. AND THIS IS "HIGH TIDE".
HOLY SHIT. THE BOY'S FINGERS MIGHT START BLEEDING.
SNORT.
IT'S AN OUTLET FOR SEXUAL FRUSTRATION. BUT THEN AGAIN, SO IS WAXING YOUR SURFBOARD.
SURF CLUB
SURF
THIS MUSIC. MAN OH MAN. MY FUCKING HEAD.
HE'S GETTING OUT OF HAND, SLICK. MUST'VE LOADED UP ON HUNCH'S BOMBERS.
ALL RIGHT, ALL RIGHT. WE'LL SPLIT. OUGHT TO DUNK HIS SKULL IN THE OCEAN AND SEE IF THAT CLEARS THINGS UP.

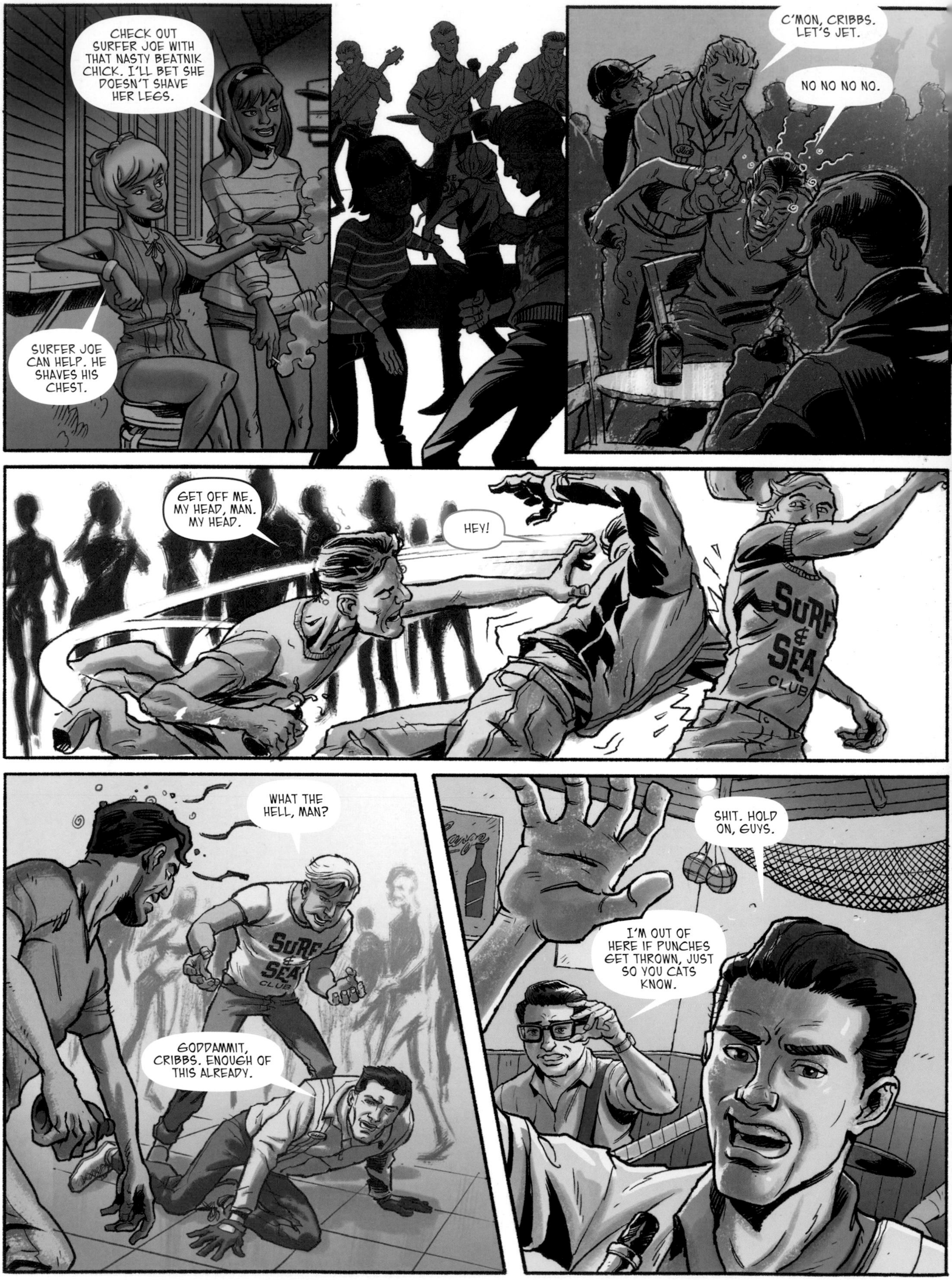
CHECK OUT SURFER JOE WITH THAT NASTY BEATNIK CHICK. I'LL BET SHE DOESN'T SHAVE HER LEGS.
SURFER JOE CAN HELP. HE SHAVES HIS CHEST.
C'MON, CRIBBS. LET'S JET.
NO NO NO NO.
GET OFF ME. MY HEAD, MAN. MY HEAD.
HEY!
WHAT THE HELL, MAN?
GODDAMMIT, CRIBBS. ENOUGH OF THIS ALREADY.
SHIT. HOLD ON, GUYS.
I'M OUT OF HERE IF PUNCHES GET THROWN, JUST SO YOU CATS KNOW.

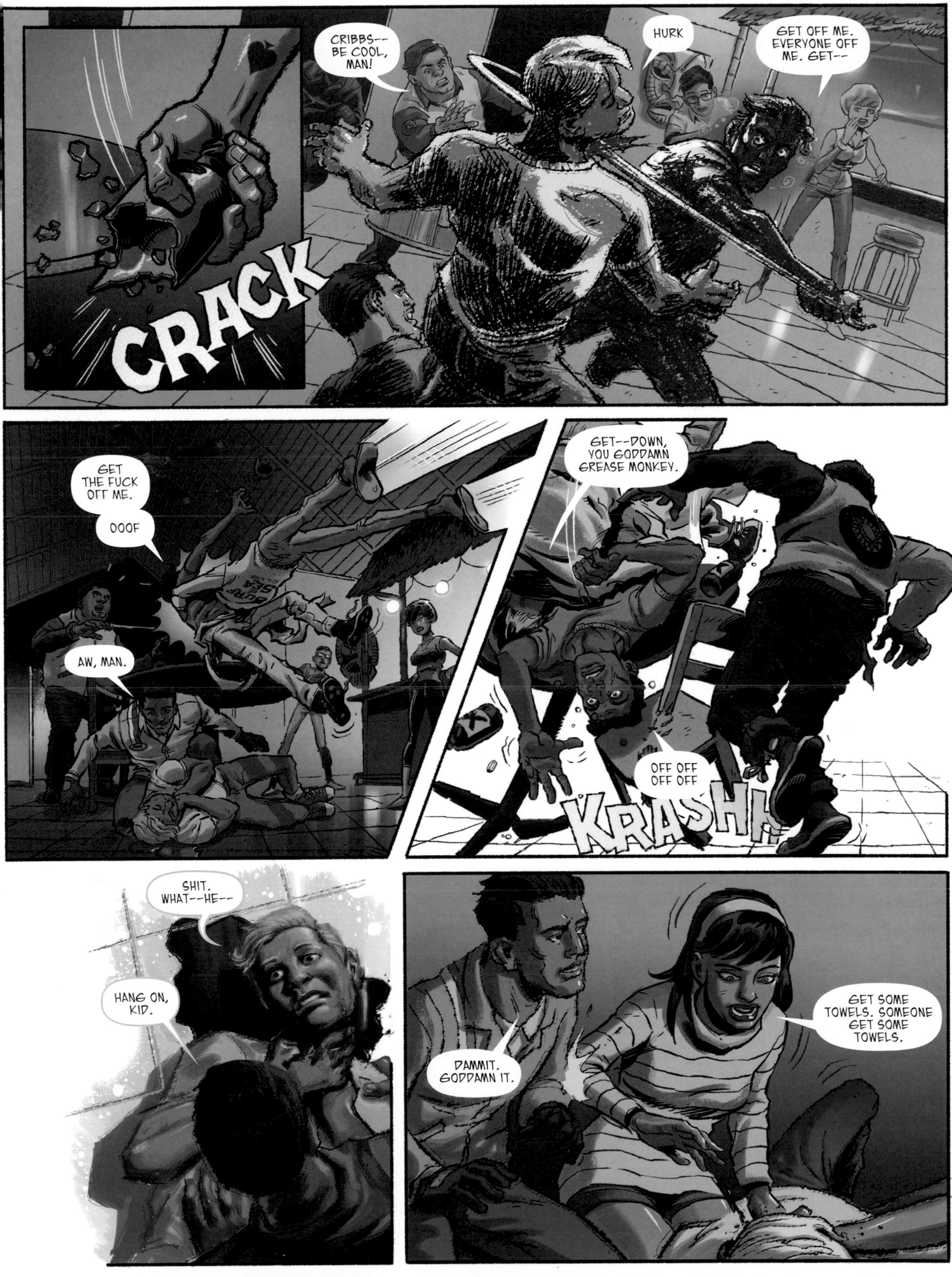
CRACK
CRIBBS-- BE COOL, MAN!
HURK
GET OFF ME. EVERYONE OFF ME. GET--
GET THE FUCK OFF ME.
OOOF
AW, MAN.
GET--DOWN, YOU GODDAMN GREASE MONKEY.
OFF OFF OFF OFF
KRASH
SHIT. WHAT--HE--
HANG ON, KID.
DAMMIT. GODDAMN IT.
GET SOME TOWELS. SOMEONE GET SOME TOWELS.

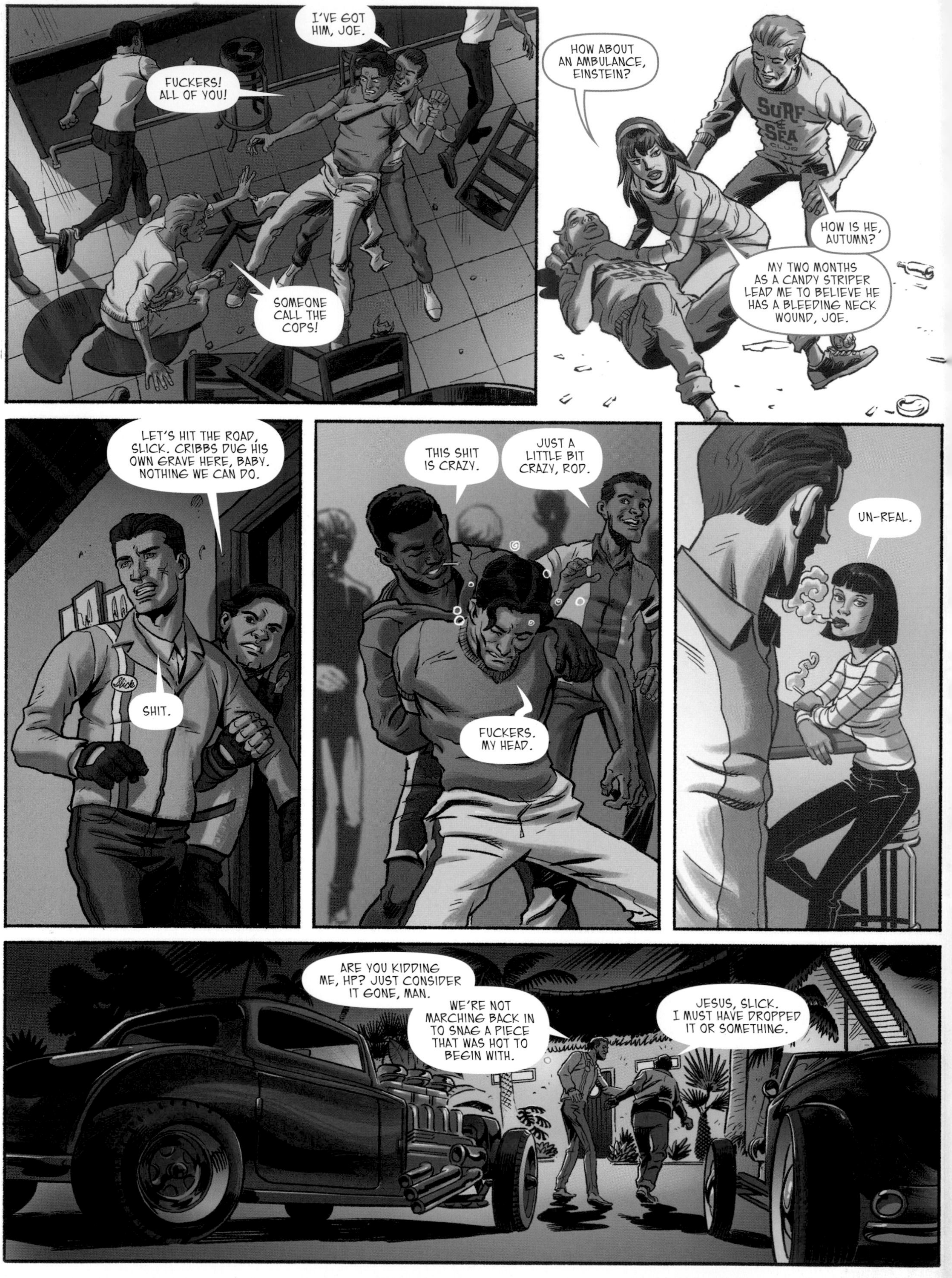
FUCKERS! ALL OF YOU!
I'VE GOT HIM, JOE.
SOMEONE CALL THE COPS!
HOW ABOUT AN AMBULANCE, EINSTEIN?
SURF & SEA CLUB
HOW IS HE, AUTUMN?
MY TWO MONTHS AS A CANDY STRIPER LEAD ME TO BELIEVE HE HAS A BLEEDING NECK WOUND, JOE.
LET'S HIT THE ROAD, SLICK. CRIBBS DUG HIS OWN GRAVE HERE, BABY. NOTHING WE CAN DO.
SHIT.
THIS SHIT IS CRAZY.
JUST A LITTLE BIT CRAZY, ROD.
FUCKERS. MY HEAD.
UN-REAL.
JESUS, SLICK. I MUST HAVE DROPPED IT OR SOMETHING.
ARE YOU KIDDING ME, HP? JUST CONSIDER IT GONE, MAN.
WE'RE NOT MARCHING BACK IN TO SNAG A PIECE THAT WAS HOT TO BEGIN WITH.

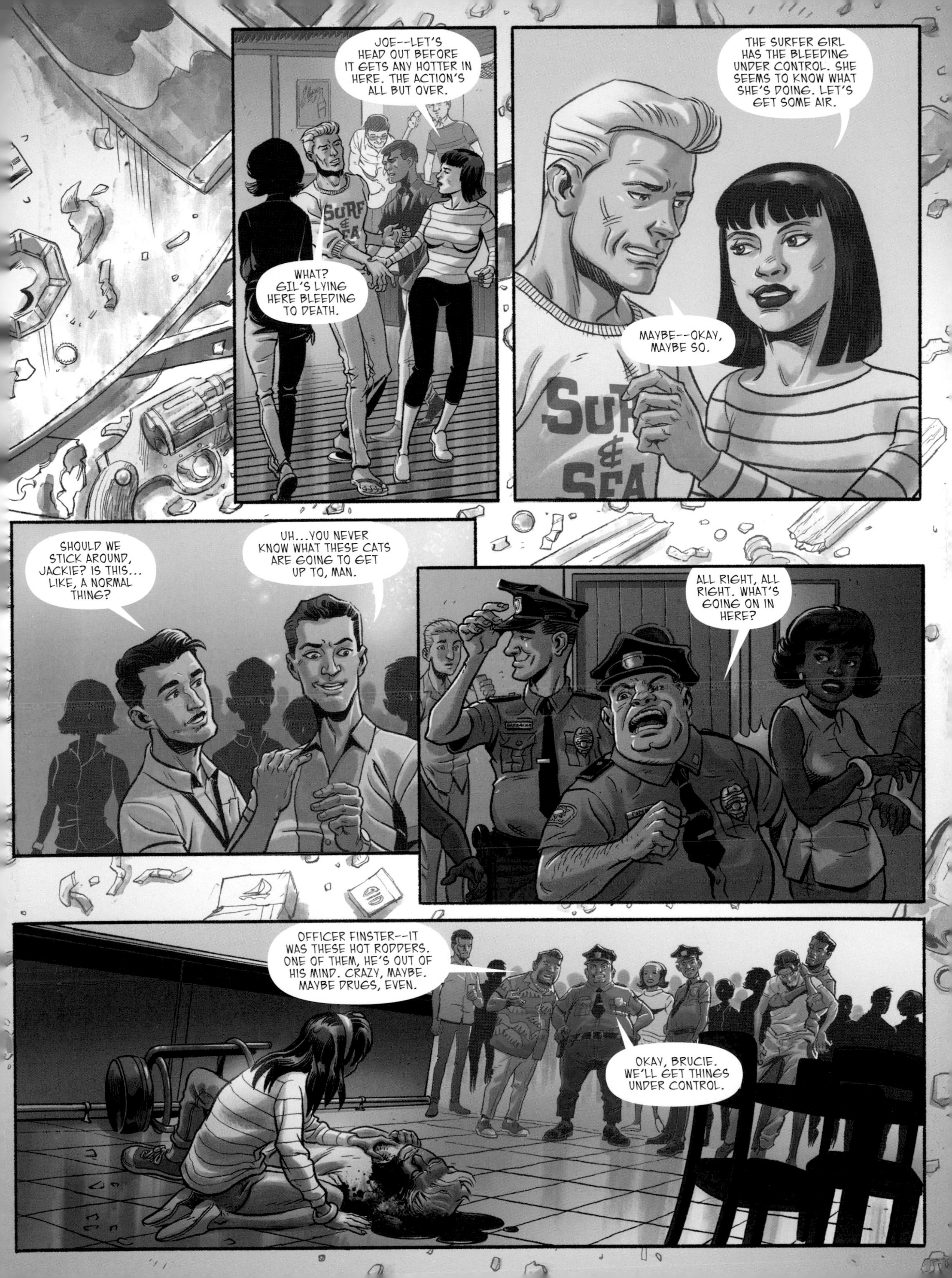
JOE--LET'S HEAD OUT BEFORE IT GETS ANY HOTTER IN HERE. THE ACTION'S ALL BUT OVER.
WHAT? GIL'S LYING HERE BLEEDING TO DEATH.
THE SURFER GIRL HAS THE BLEEDING UNDER CONTROL. SHE SEEMS TO KNOW WHAT SHE'S DOING. LET'S GET SOME AIR.
MAYBE--OKAY, MAYBE SO.
SHOULD WE STICK AROUND, JACKIE? IS THIS... LIKE, A NORMAL THING?
UH...YOU NEVER KNOW WHAT THESE CATS ARE GOING TO GET UP TO, MAN.
ALL RIGHT, ALL RIGHT. WHAT'S GOING ON IN HERE?
OFFICER FINSTER--IT WAS THESE HOT RODDERS. ONE OF THEM, HE'S OUT OF HIS MIND. CRAZY, MAYBE. MAYBE DRUGS, EVEN.
OKAY, BRUCIE. WE'LL GET THINGS UNDER CONTROL.

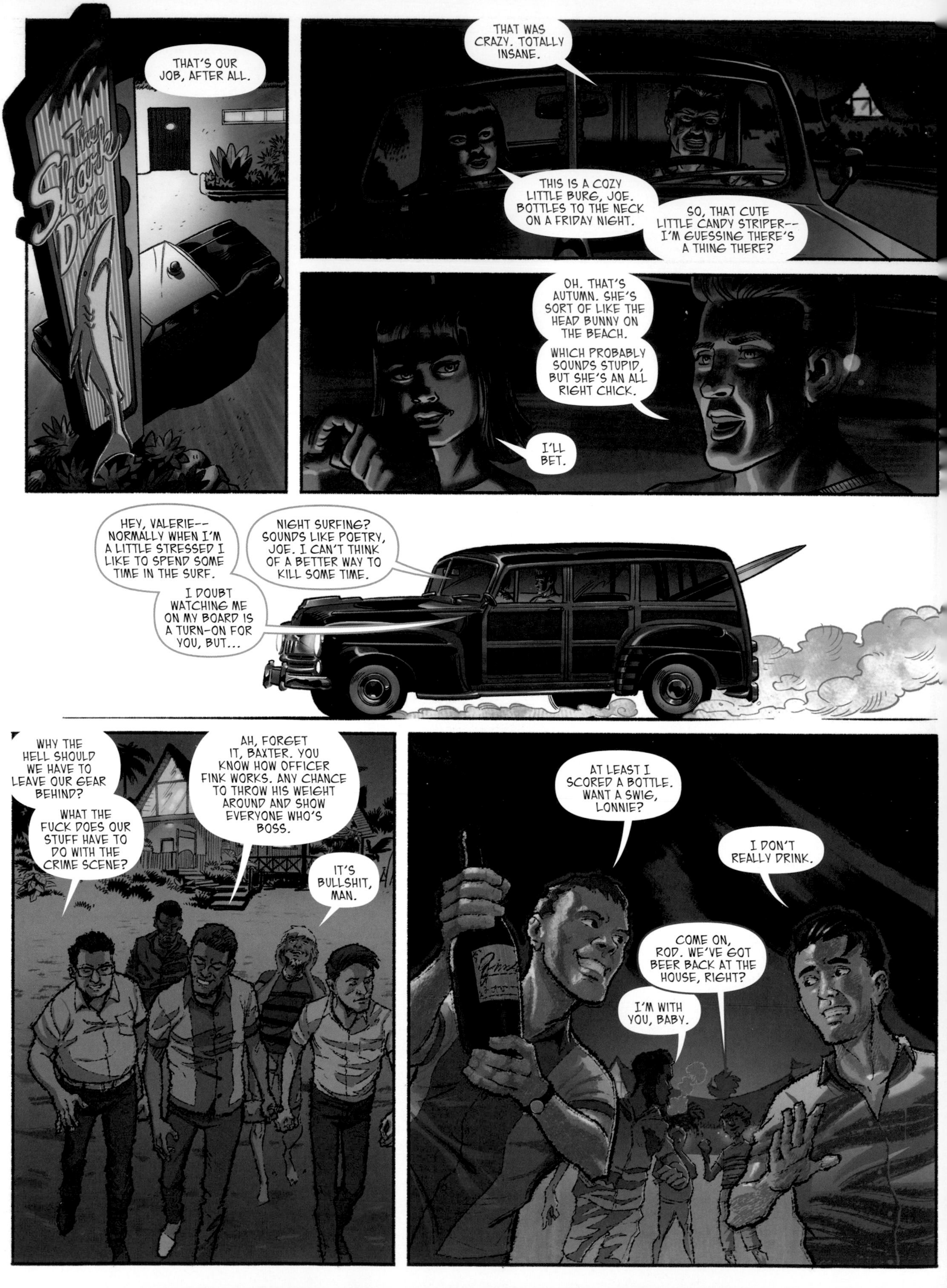
THAT'S OUR JOB, AFTER ALL.
The Shark Dive
THAT WAS CRAZY. TOTALLY INSANE.
THIS IS A COZY LITTLE BURG, JOE. BOTTLES TO THE NECK ON A FRIDAY NIGHT.
SO, THAT CUTE LITTLE CANDY STRIPER-- I'M GUESSING THERE'S A THING THERE?
OH. THAT'S AUTUMN. SHE'S SORT OF LIKE THE HEAD BUNNY ON THE BEACH.
WHICH PROBABLY SOUNDS STUPID, BUT SHE'S AN ALL RIGHT CHICK.
I'LL BET.
HEY, VALERIE-- NORMALLY WHEN I'M A LITTLE STRESSED I LIKE TO SPEND SOME TIME IN THE SURF.
I DOUBT WATCHING ME ON MY BOARD IS A TURN-ON FOR YOU, BUT...
NIGHT SURFING? SOUNDS LIKE POETRY, JOE. I CAN'T THINK OF A BETTER WAY TO KILL SOME TIME.
WHY THE HELL SHOULD WE HAVE TO LEAVE OUR GEAR BEHIND?
WHAT THE FUCK DOES OUR STUFF HAVE TO DO WITH THE CRIME SCENE?
AH, FORGET IT, BAXTER. YOU KNOW HOW OFFICER FINK WORKS. ANY CHANCE TO THROW HIS WEIGHT AROUND AND SHOW EVERYONE WHO'S BOSS.
IT'S BULLSHIT, MAN.
AT LEAST I SCORED A BOTTLE. WANT A SWIG, LONNIE?
I DON'T REALLY DRINK.
COME ON, ROD. WE'VE GOT BEER BACK AT THE HOUSE, RIGHT?
I'M WITH YOU, BABY.

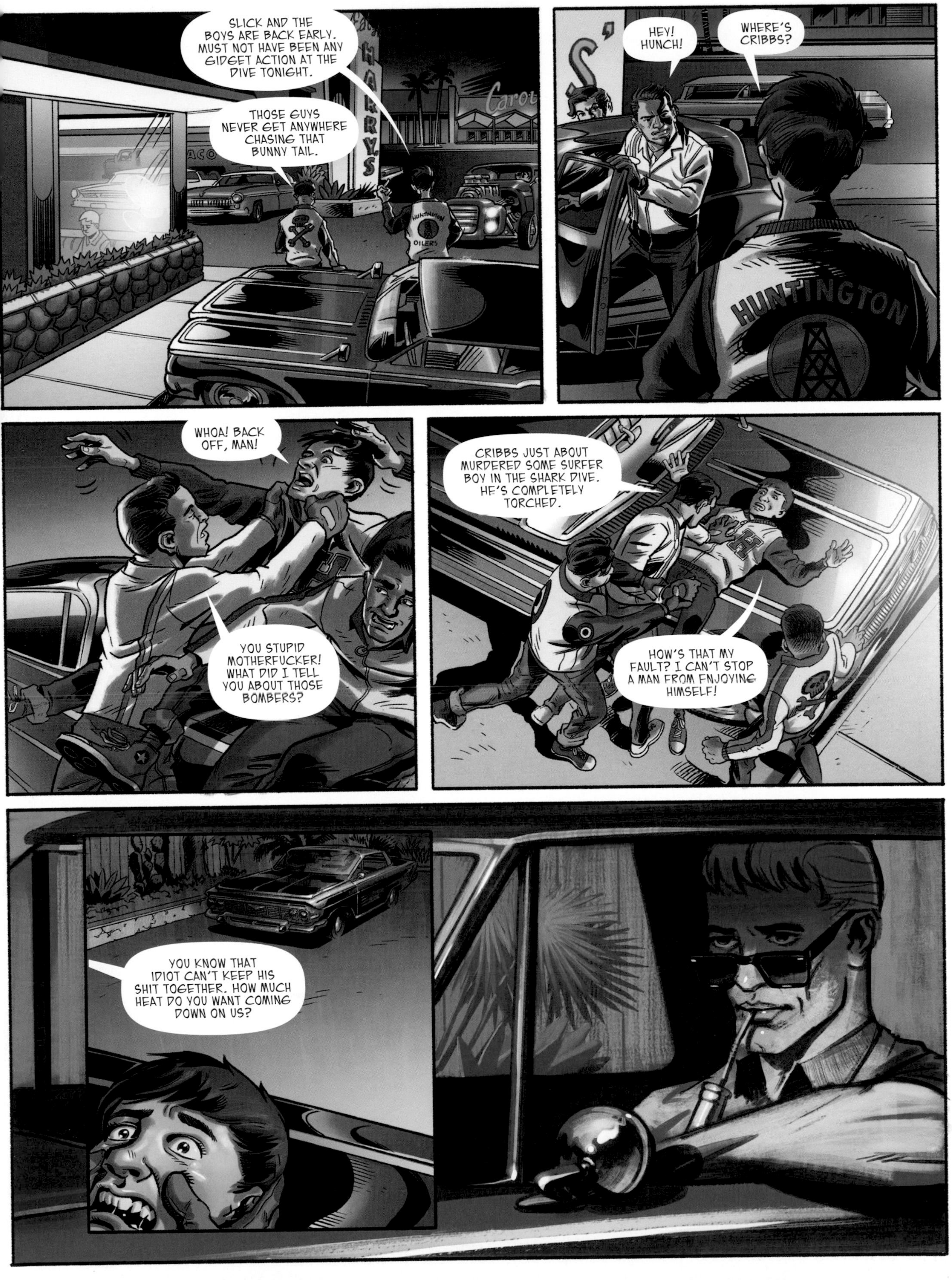
SLICK AND THE BOYS ARE BACK EARLY. MUST NOT HAVE BEEN ANY GIDGET ACTION AT THE DIVE TONIGHT.
THOSE GUYS NEVER GET ANYWHERE CHASING THAT BUNNY TAIL.
HARRYS
HUNTINGTON OILERS
HEY! HUNCH!
WHERE'S CRIBBS?
HUNTINGTON
WHOA! BACK OFF, MAN!
YOU STUPID MOTHERFUCKER! WHAT DID I TELL YOU ABOUT THOSE BOMBERS?
CRIBBS JUST ABOUT MURDERED SOME SURFER BOY IN THE SHARK DIVE. HE'S COMPLETELY TORCHED.
HOW'S THAT MY FAULT? I CAN'T STOP A MAN FROM ENJOYING HIMSELF!
YOU KNOW THAT IDIOT CAN'T KEEP HIS SHIT TOGETHER. HOW MUCH HEAT DO YOU WANT COMING DOWN ON US?

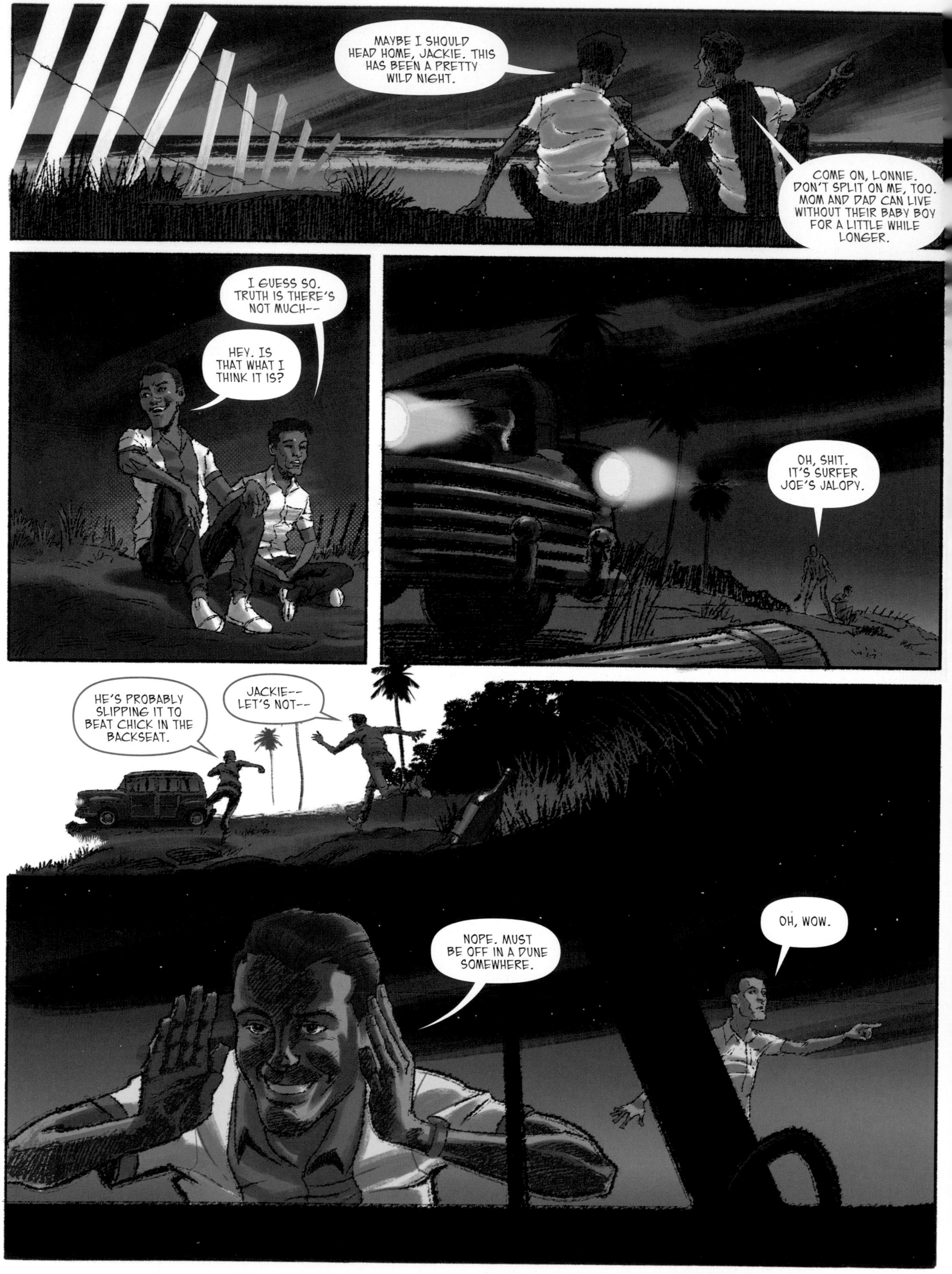
MAYBE I SHOULD HEAD HOME, JACKIE. THIS HAS BEEN A PRETTY WILD NIGHT.
COME ON, LONNIE. DON'T SPLIT ON ME, TOO. MOM AND DAD CAN LIVE WITHOUT THEIR BABY BOY FOR A LITTLE WHILE LONGER.
I GUESS SO. TRUTH IS THERE'S NOT MUCH--
HEY. IS THAT WHAT I THINK IT IS?
OH, SHIT. IT'S SURFER JOE'S JALOPY.
HE'S PROBABLY SLIPPING IT TO BEAT CHICK IN THE BACKSEAT.
JACKIE-- LET'S NOT--
NOPE. MUST BE OFF IN A DUNE SOMEWHERE.
OH, WOW.

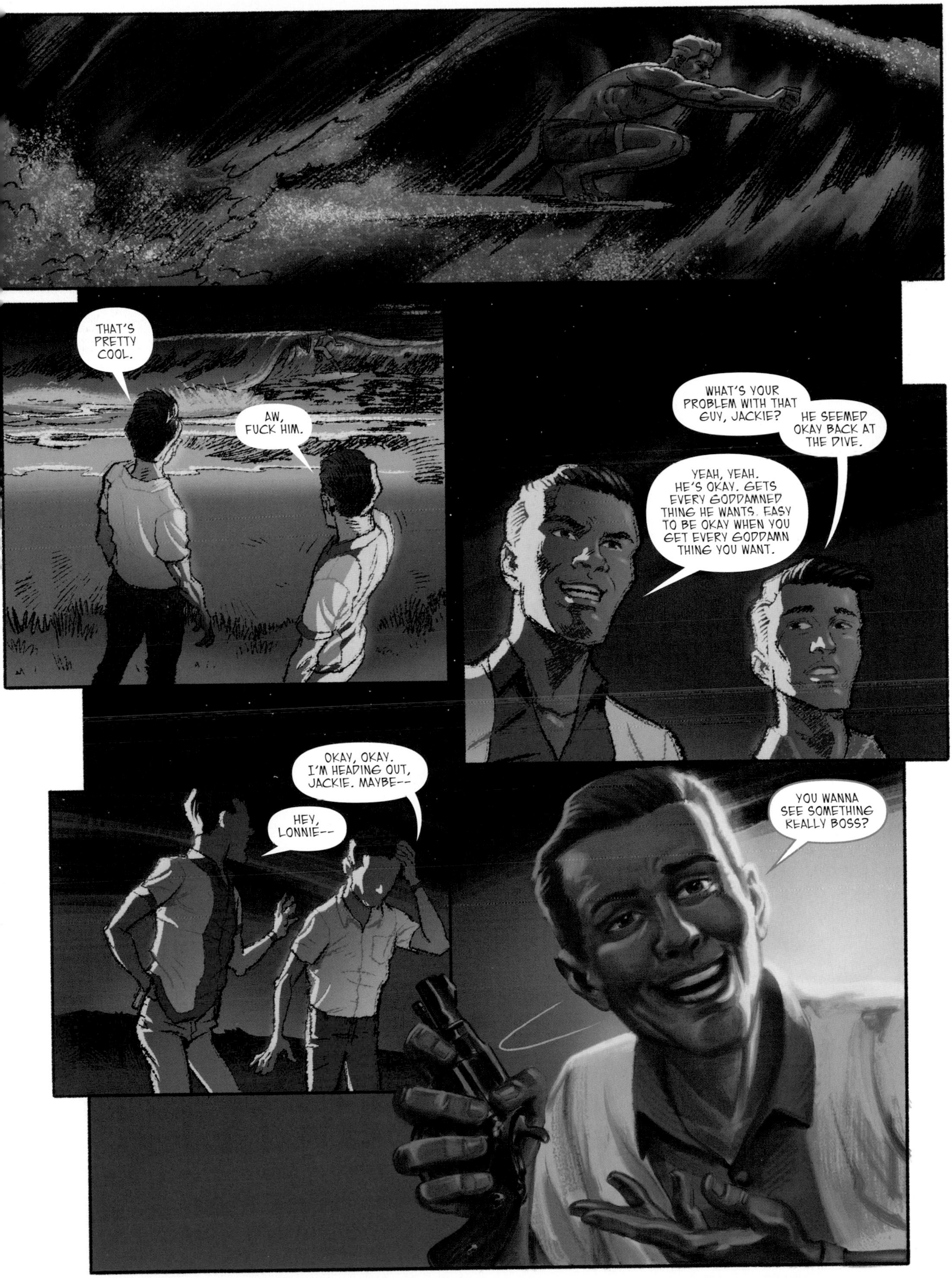

THAT'S PRETTY COOL.
AW, FUCK HIM.
WHAT'S YOUR PROBLEM WITH THAT GUY, JACKIE?
HE SEEMED OKAY BACK AT THE DIVE.
YEAH, YEAH. HE'S OKAY. GETS EVERY GODDAMNED THING HE WANTS. EASY TO BE OKAY WHEN YOU GET EVERY GODDAMN THING YOU WANT.
OKAY, OKAY. I'M HEADING OUT, JACKIE. MAYBE--
HEY, LONNIE--
YOU WANNA SEE SOMETHING REALLY BOSS?

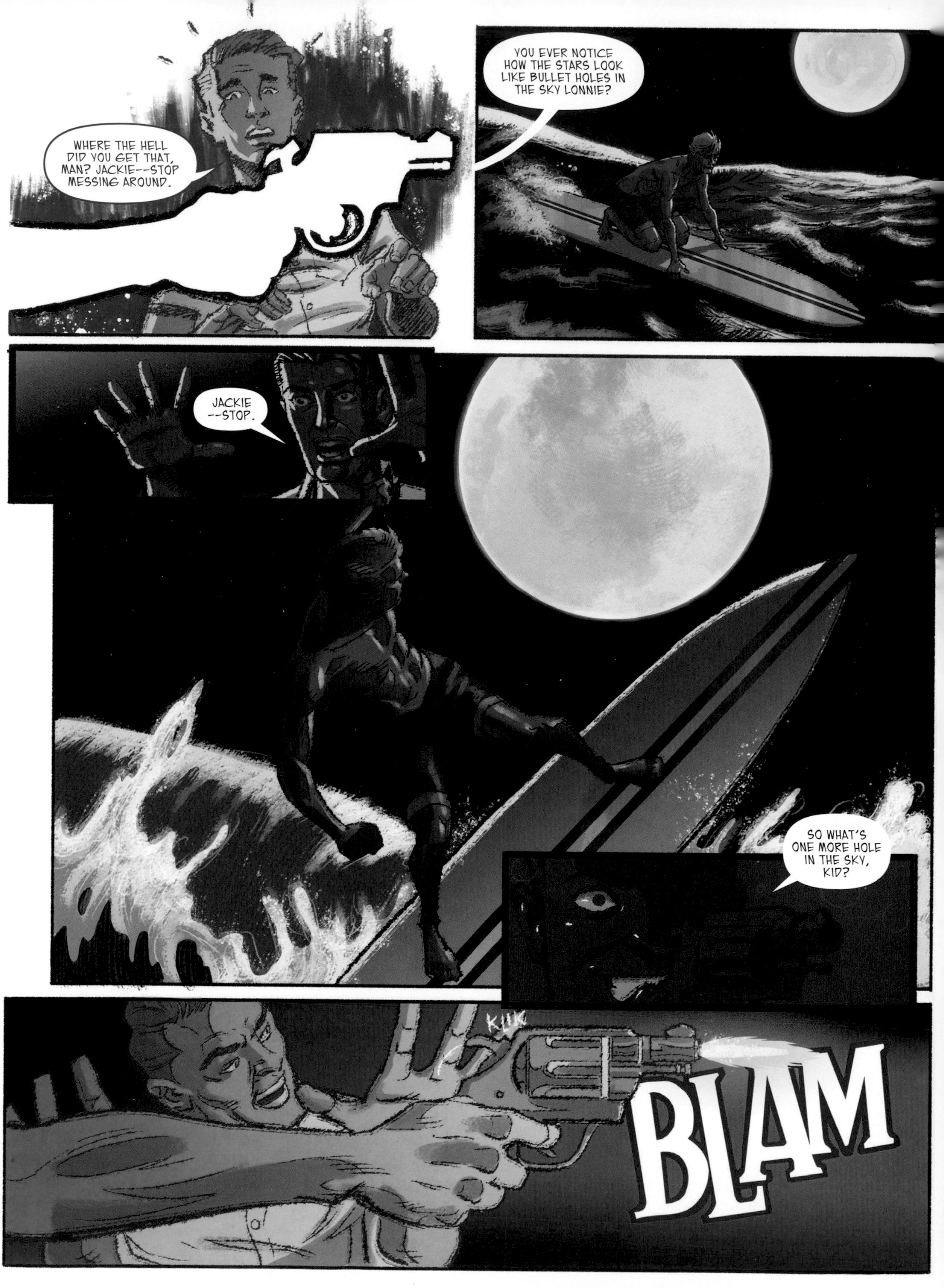
WHERE THE HELL DID YOU GET THAT, MAN? JACKIE--STOP MESSING AROUND.
YOU EVER NOTICE HOW THE STARS LOOK LIKE BULLET HOLES IN THE SKY LONNIE?
JACKIE --STOP.
SO WHAT'S ONE MORE HOLE IN THE SKY, KID?
KLIK
BLAM

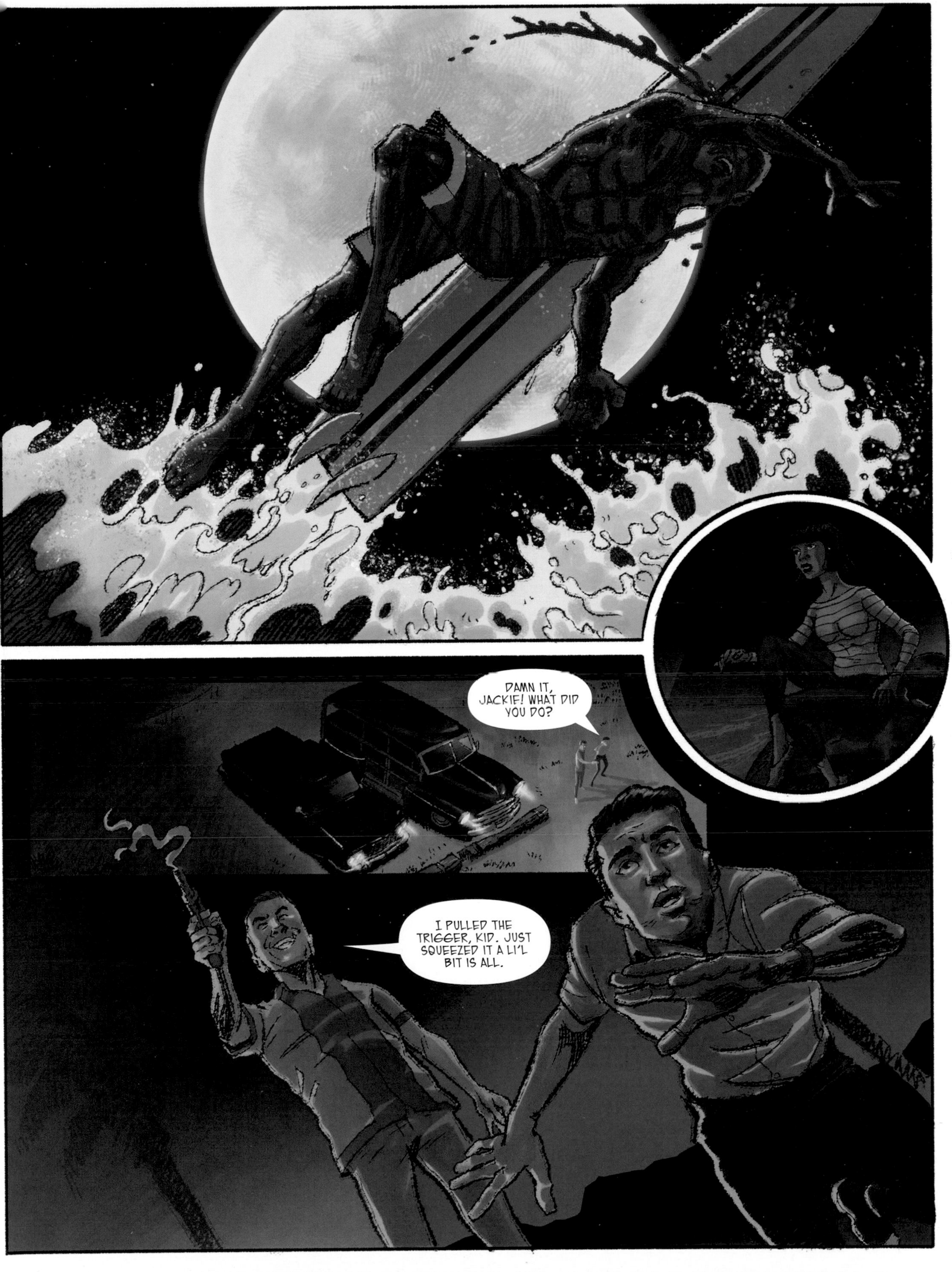
DAMN IT, JACKIE! WHAT DID YOU DO?
I PULLED THE TRIGGER, KID. JUST SQUEEZED IT A LI'L BIT IS ALL.

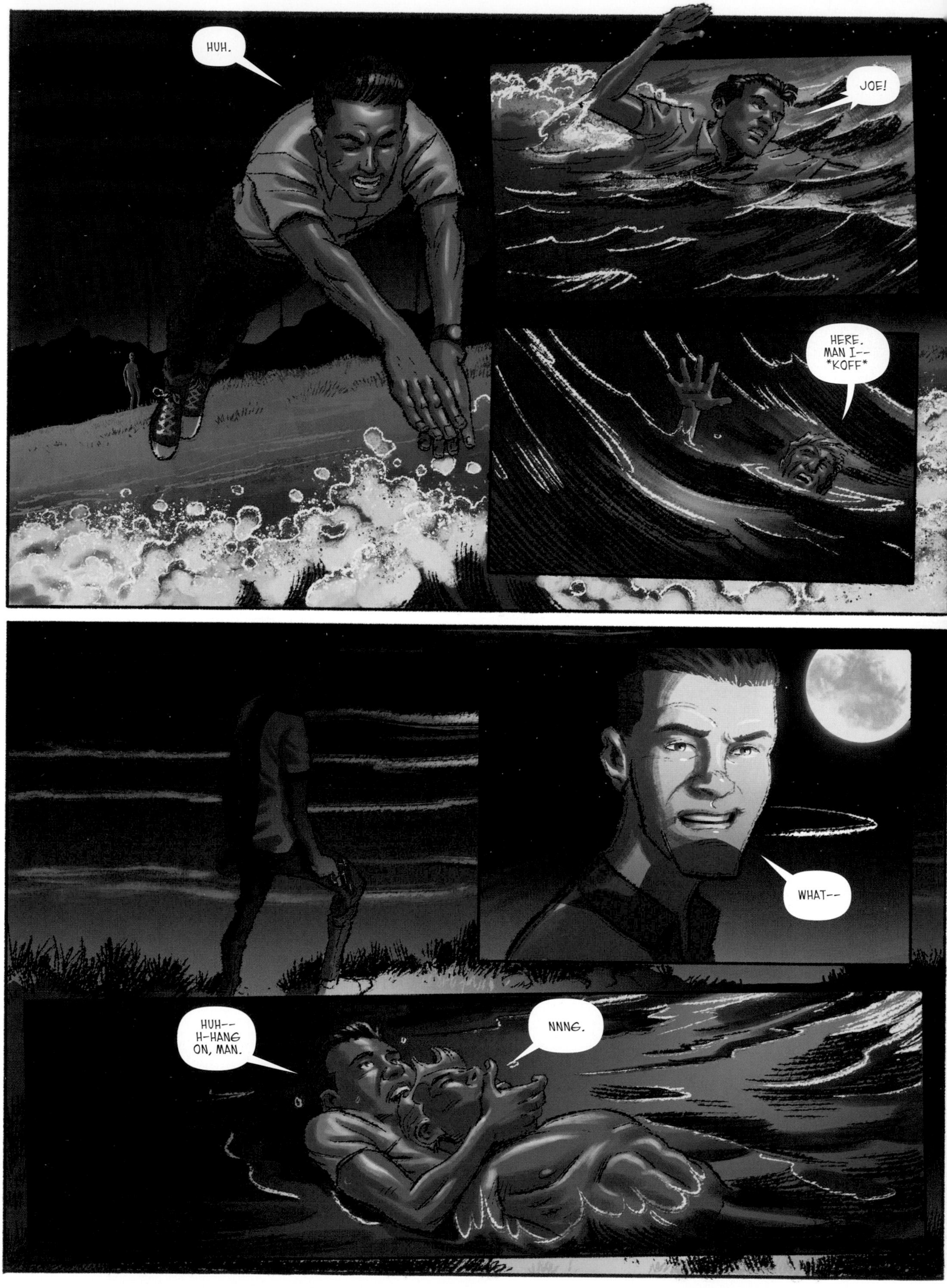
HUH.
JOE!
HERE. MAN I-- *KOFF*
WHAT--
HUH-- H-HANG ON, MAN.
NNNG.

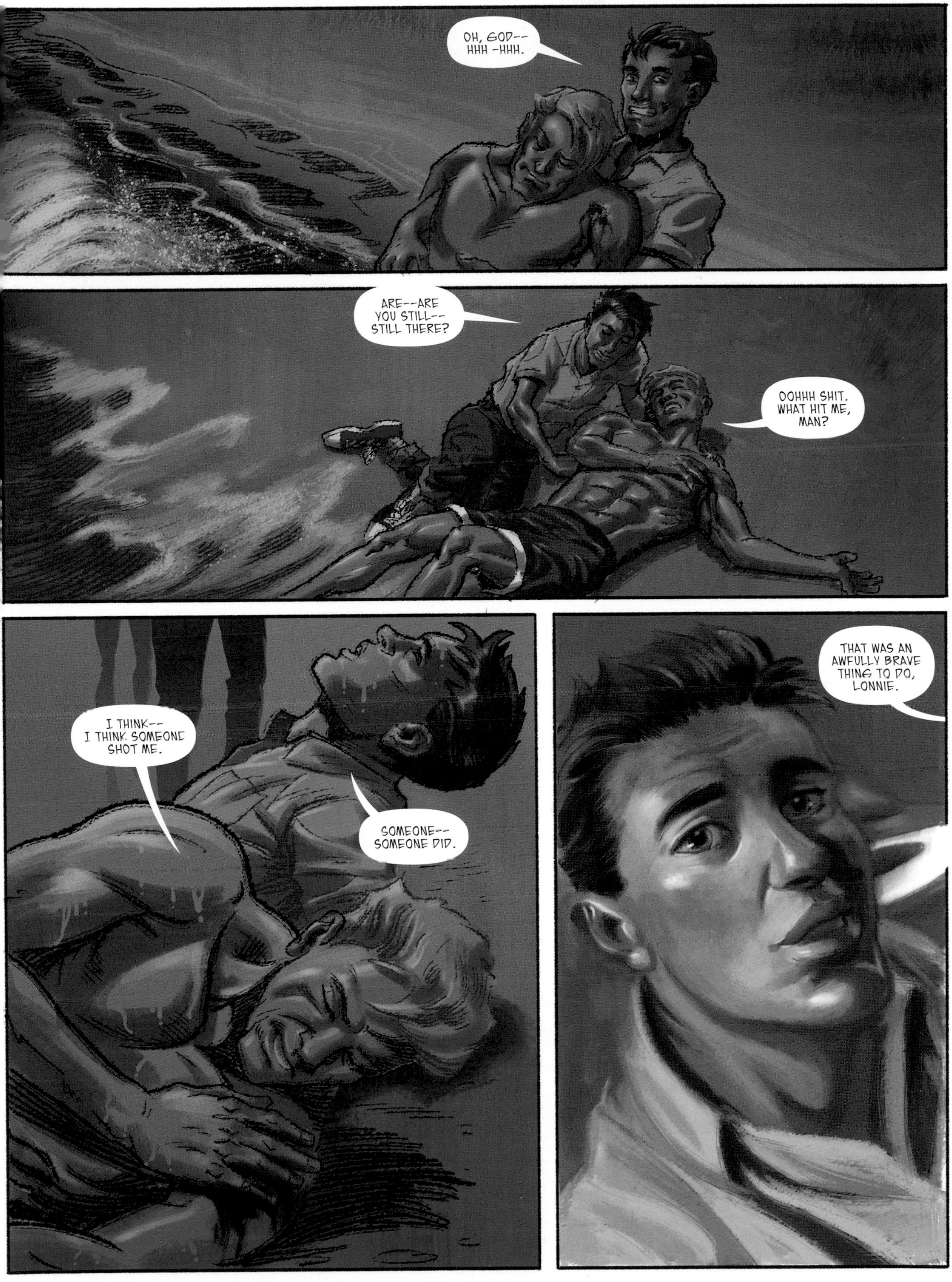
OH, GOD-- HHH -HHH.
ARE--ARE YOU STILL-- STILL THERE?
OOHHH SHIT. WHAT HIT ME, MAN?
I THINK-- I THINK SOMEONE SHOT ME.
SOMEONE-- SOMEONE DID.
THAT WAS AN AWFULLY BRAVE THING TO DO, LONNIE.

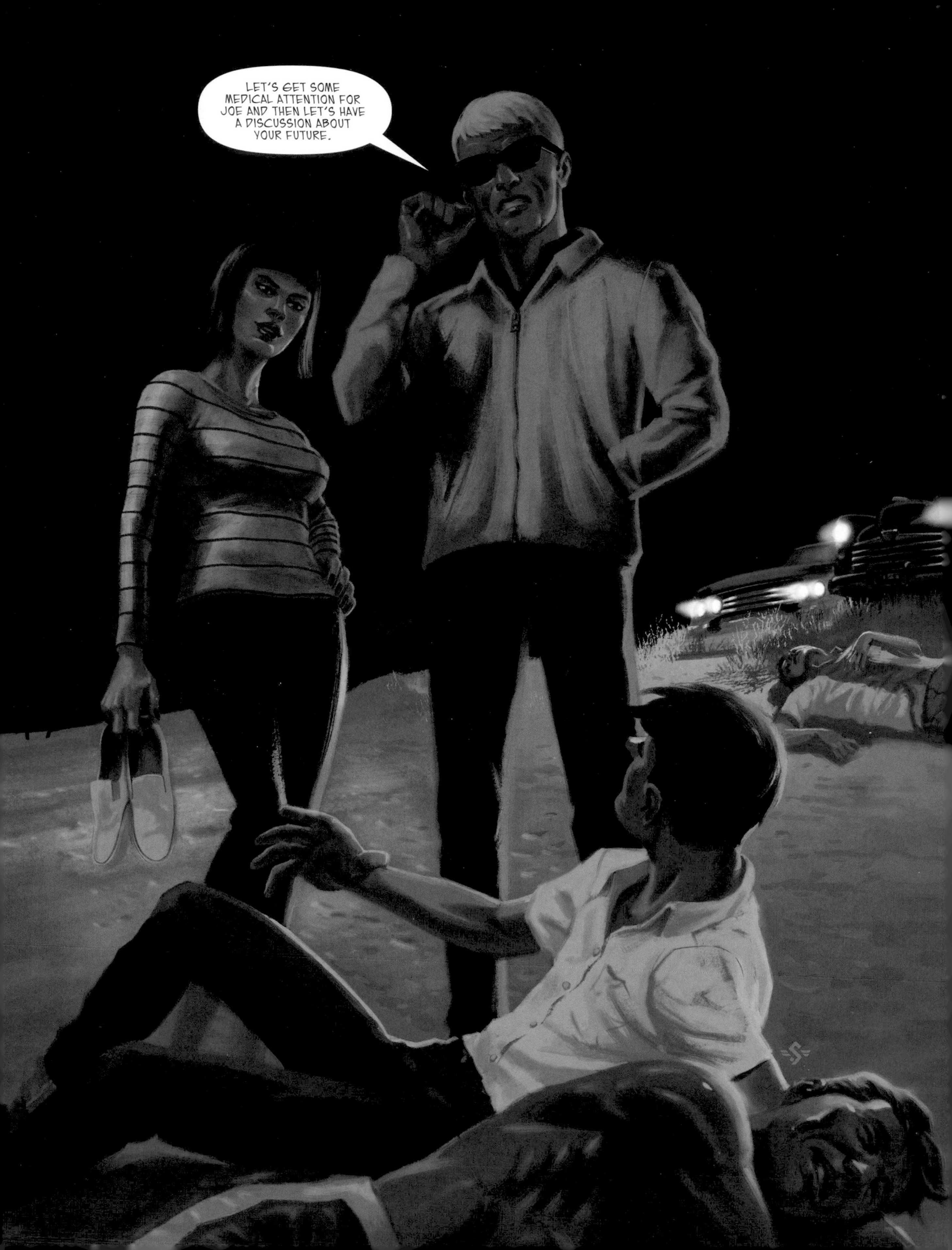
LET'S GET SOME MEDICAL ATTENTION FOR JOE AND THEN LET'S HAVE A DISCUSSION ABOUT YOUR FUTURE.

PART 2

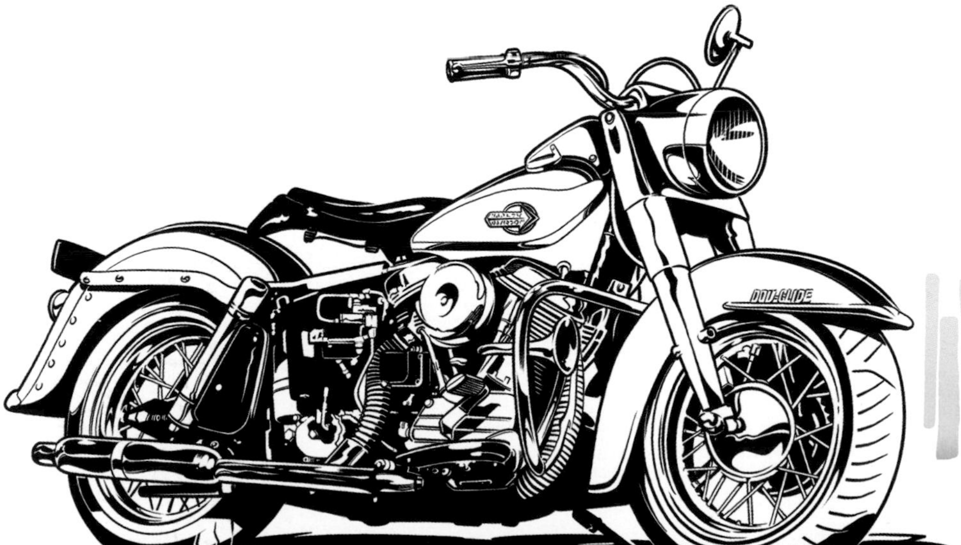
DUO-GLIDE

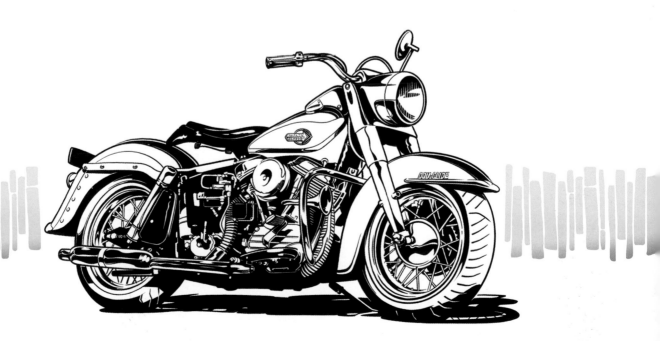

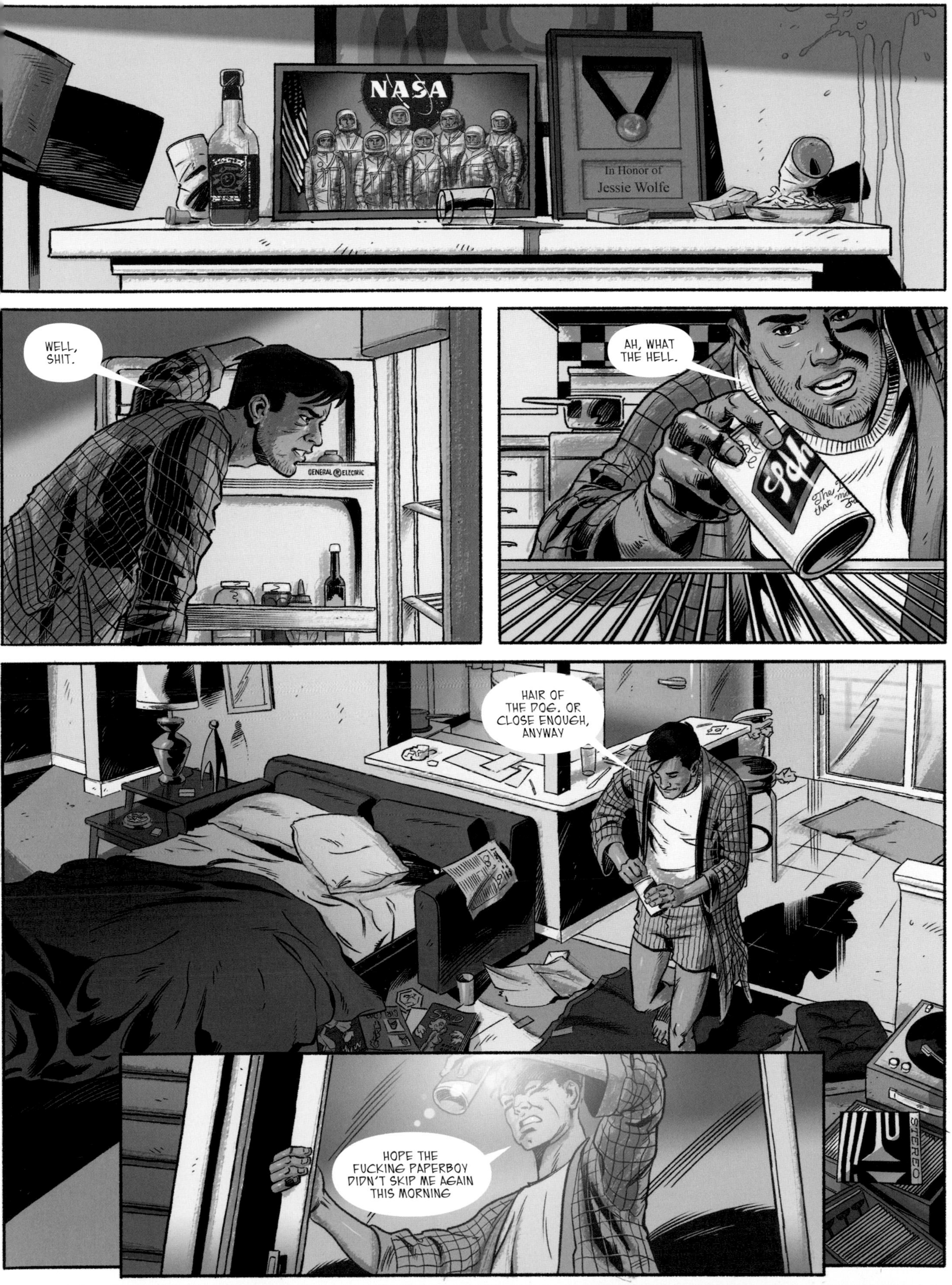
In Honor of
Jessie Wolfe
WELL, SHIT.
AH, WHAT THE HELL.
HAIR OF THE DOG. OR CLOSE ENOUGH, ANYWAY
HOPE THE FUCKING PAPERBOY DIDN'T SKIP ME AGAIN THIS MORNING

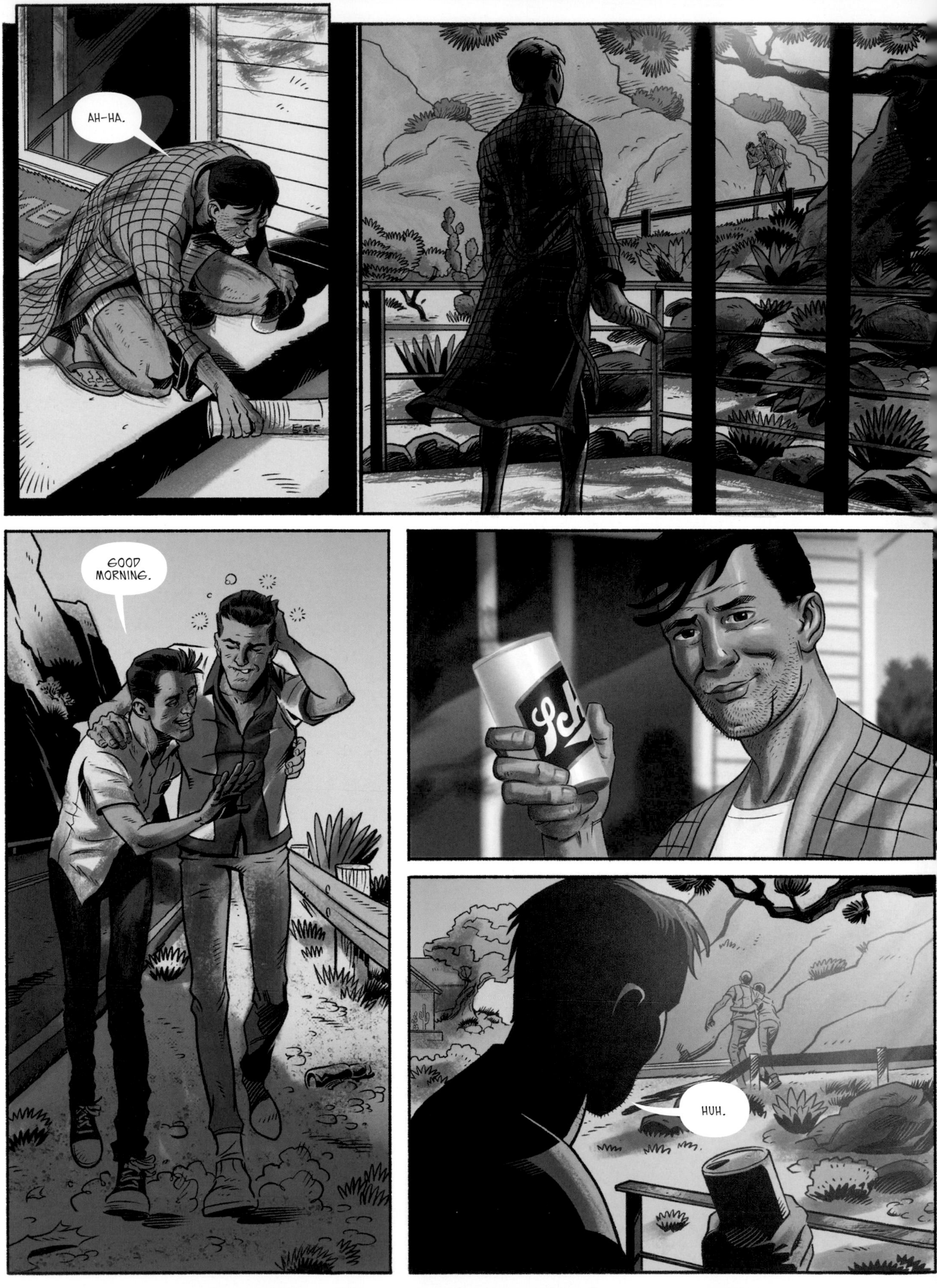
AH-HA.
GOOD MORNING.
HUH.

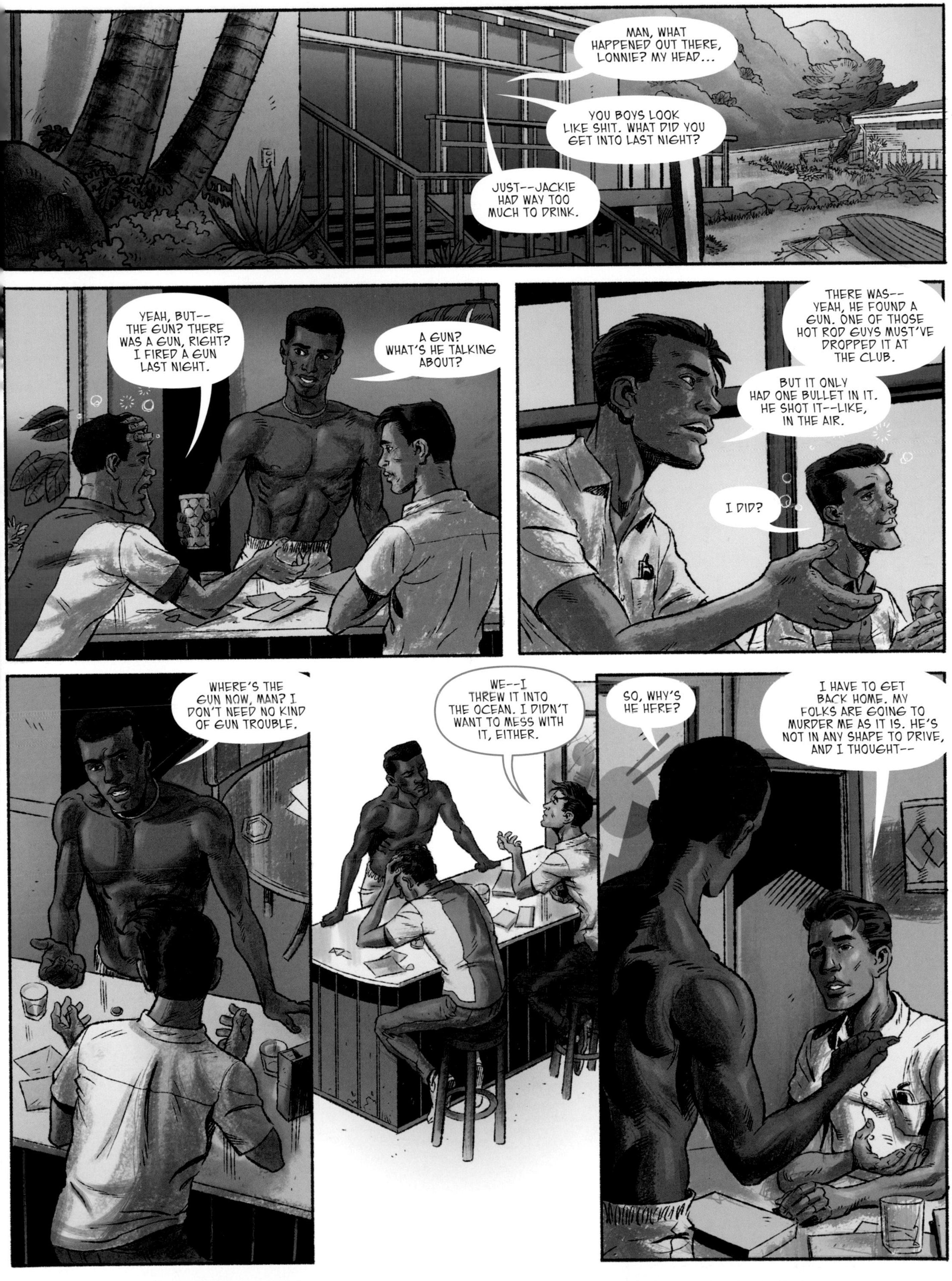
MAN, WHAT HAPPENED OUT THERE, LONNIE? MY HEAD...
YOU BOYS LOOK LIKE SHIT. WHAT DID YOU GET INTO LAST NIGHT?
JUST--JACKIE HAD WAY TOO MUCH TO DRINK.
YEAH, BUT-- THE GUN? THERE WAS A GUN, RIGHT? I FIRED A GUN LAST NIGHT.
A GUN? WHAT'S HE TALKING ABOUT?
THERE WAS-- YEAH, HE FOUND A GUN. ONE OF THOSE HOT ROD GUYS MUST'VE DROPPED IT AT THE CLUB.
BUT IT ONLY HAD ONE BULLET IN IT. HE SHOT IT--LIKE, IN THE AIR.
I DID?
WHERE'S THE GUN NOW, MAN? I DON'T NEED NO KIND OF GUN TROUBLE.
WE--I THREW IT INTO THE OCEAN. I DIDN'T WANT TO MESS WITH IT, EITHER.
SO, WHY'S HE HERE?
I HAVE TO GET BACK HOME. MY FOLKS ARE GOING TO MURDER ME AS IT IS. HE'S NOT IN ANY SHAPE TO DRIVE, AND I THOUGHT--

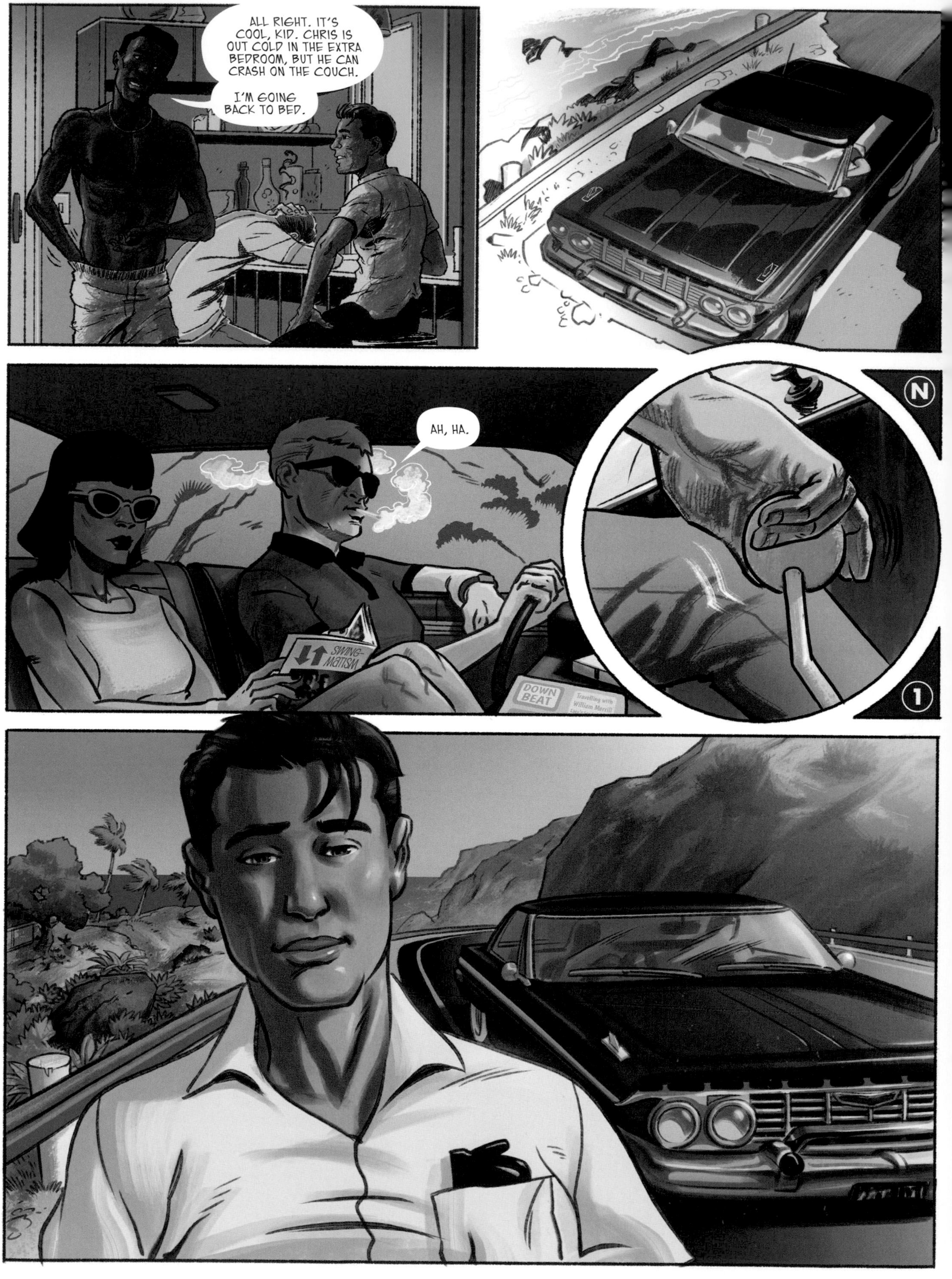
ALL RIGHT. IT'S COOL, KID. CHRIS IS OUT COLD IN THE EXTRA BEDROOM, BUT HE CAN CRASH ON THE COUCH.
I'M GOING BACK TO BED.
AH, HA.
N
1
DOWN BEAT
Travelling with William Merrill

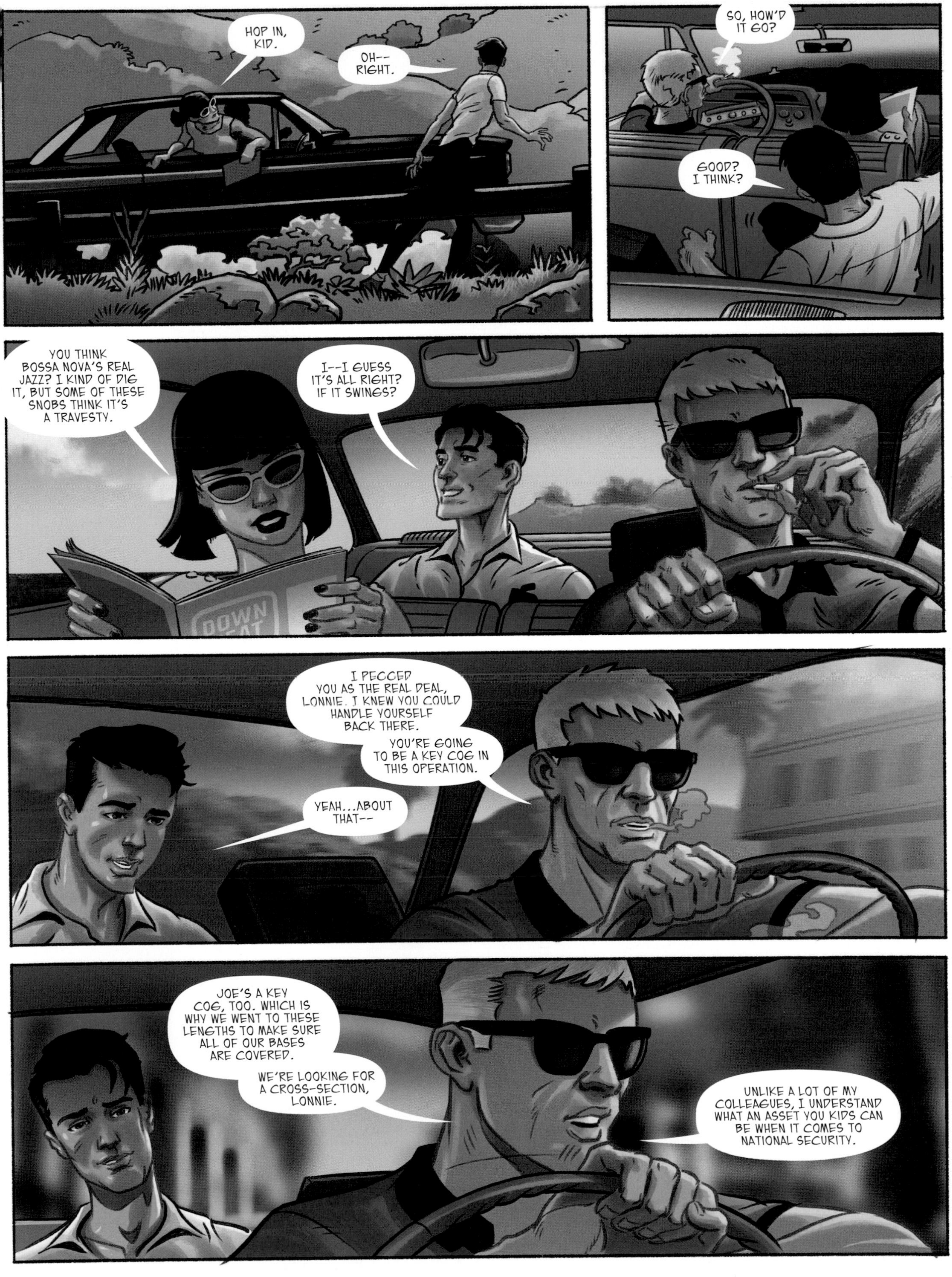

HOP IN, KID.
OH-- RIGHT.
SO, HOW'D IT GO?
GOOD? I THINK?
YOU THINK BOSSA NOVA'S REAL JAZZ? I KIND OF DIG IT, BUT SOME OF THESE SNOBS THINK IT'S A TRAVESTY.
I--I GUESS IT'S ALL RIGHT? IF IT SWINGS?
DOWN BEAT
I PEGGED YOU AS THE REAL DEAL, LONNIE. I KNEW YOU COULD HANDLE YOURSELF BACK THERE.
YOU'RE GOING TO BE A KEY COG IN THIS OPERATION.
YEAH...ABOUT THAT--
JOE'S A KEY COG, TOO. WHICH IS WHY WE WENT TO THESE LENGTHS TO MAKE SURE ALL OF OUR BASES ARE COVERED.
WE'RE LOOKING FOR A CROSS-SECTION, LONNIE.
UNLIKE A LOT OF MY COLLEAGUES, I UNDERSTAND WHAT AN ASSET YOU KIDS CAN BE WHEN IT COMES TO NATIONAL SECURITY.

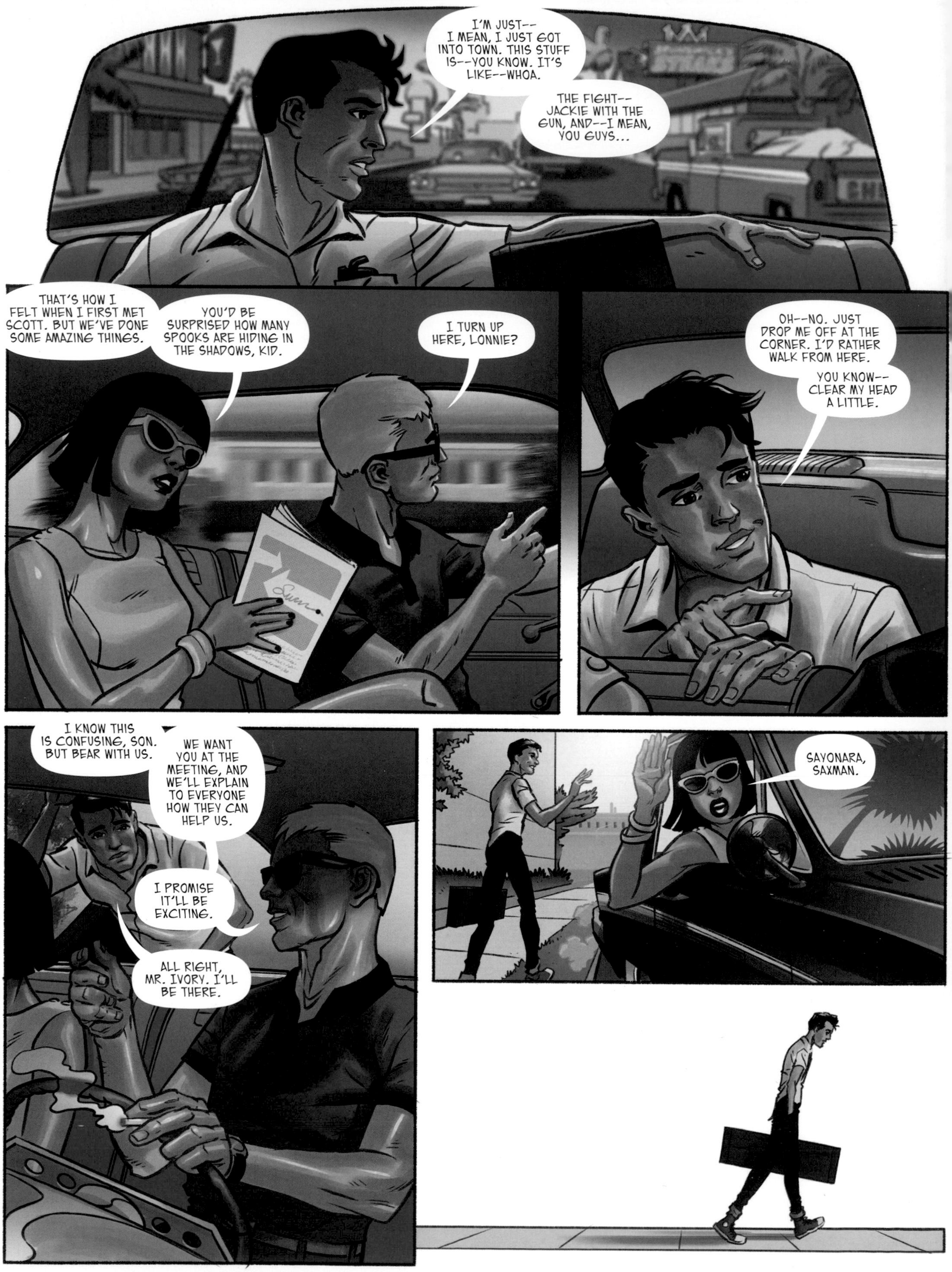
I'M JUST-- I MEAN, I JUST GOT INTO TOWN. THIS STUFF IS--YOU KNOW. IT'S LIKE--WHOA.
THE FIGHT-- JACKIE WITH THE GUN, AND--I MEAN, YOU GUYS...
THAT'S HOW I FELT WHEN I FIRST MET SCOTT. BUT WE'VE DONE SOME AMAZING THINGS.
YOU'D BE SURPRISED HOW MANY SPOOKS ARE HIDING IN THE SHADOWS, KID.
I TURN UP HERE, LONNIE?
OH--NO. JUST DROP ME OFF AT THE CORNER. I'D RATHER WALK FROM HERE.
YOU KNOW-- CLEAR MY HEAD A LITTLE.
I KNOW THIS IS CONFUSING, SON. BUT BEAR WITH US.
WE WANT YOU AT THE MEETING, AND WE'LL EXPLAIN TO EVERYONE HOW THEY CAN HELP US.
I PROMISE IT'LL BE EXCITING.
ALL RIGHT, MR. IVORY. I'LL BE THERE.
SAYONARA, SAXMAN.

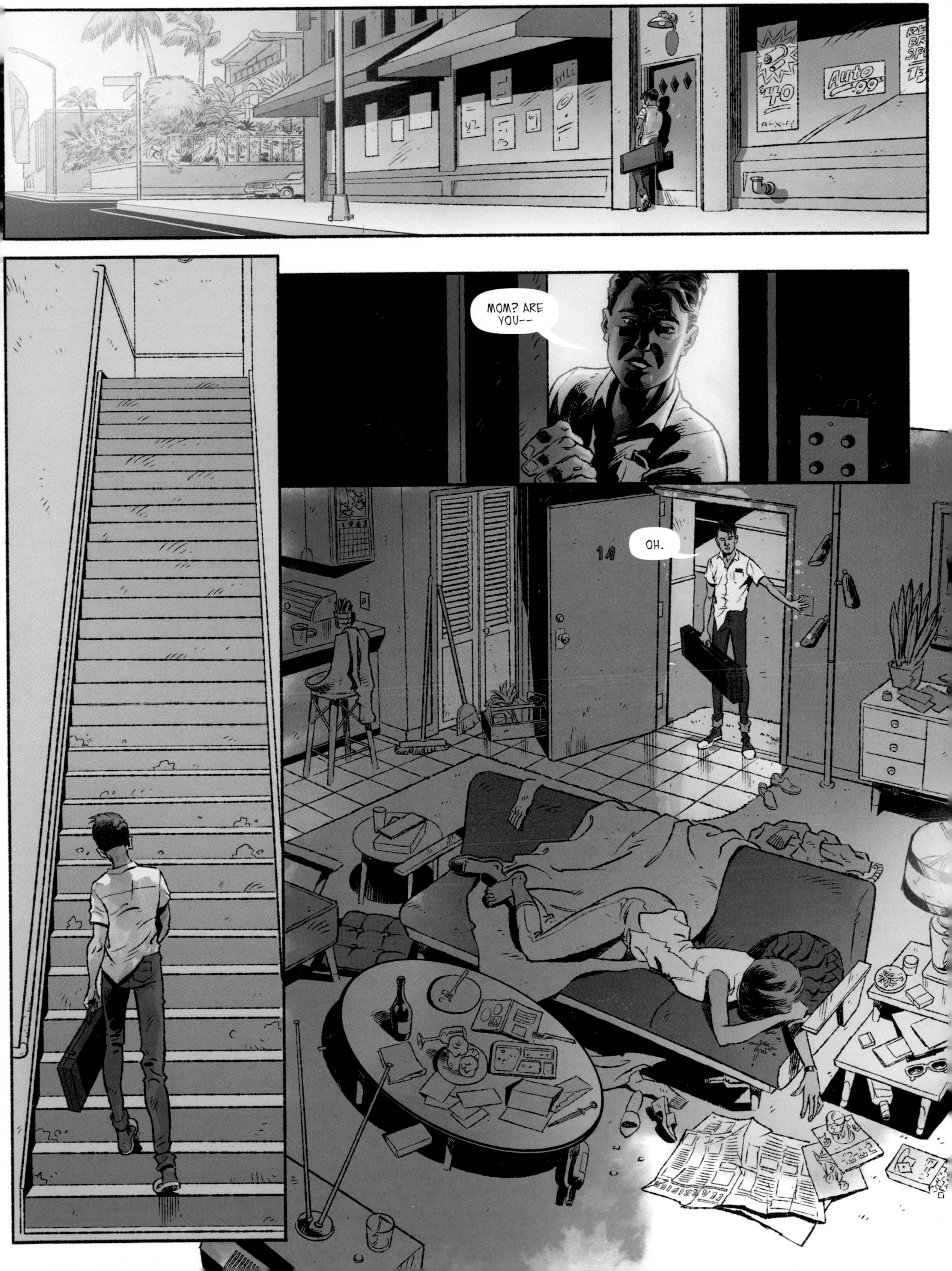
MOM? ARE YOU--
OH.

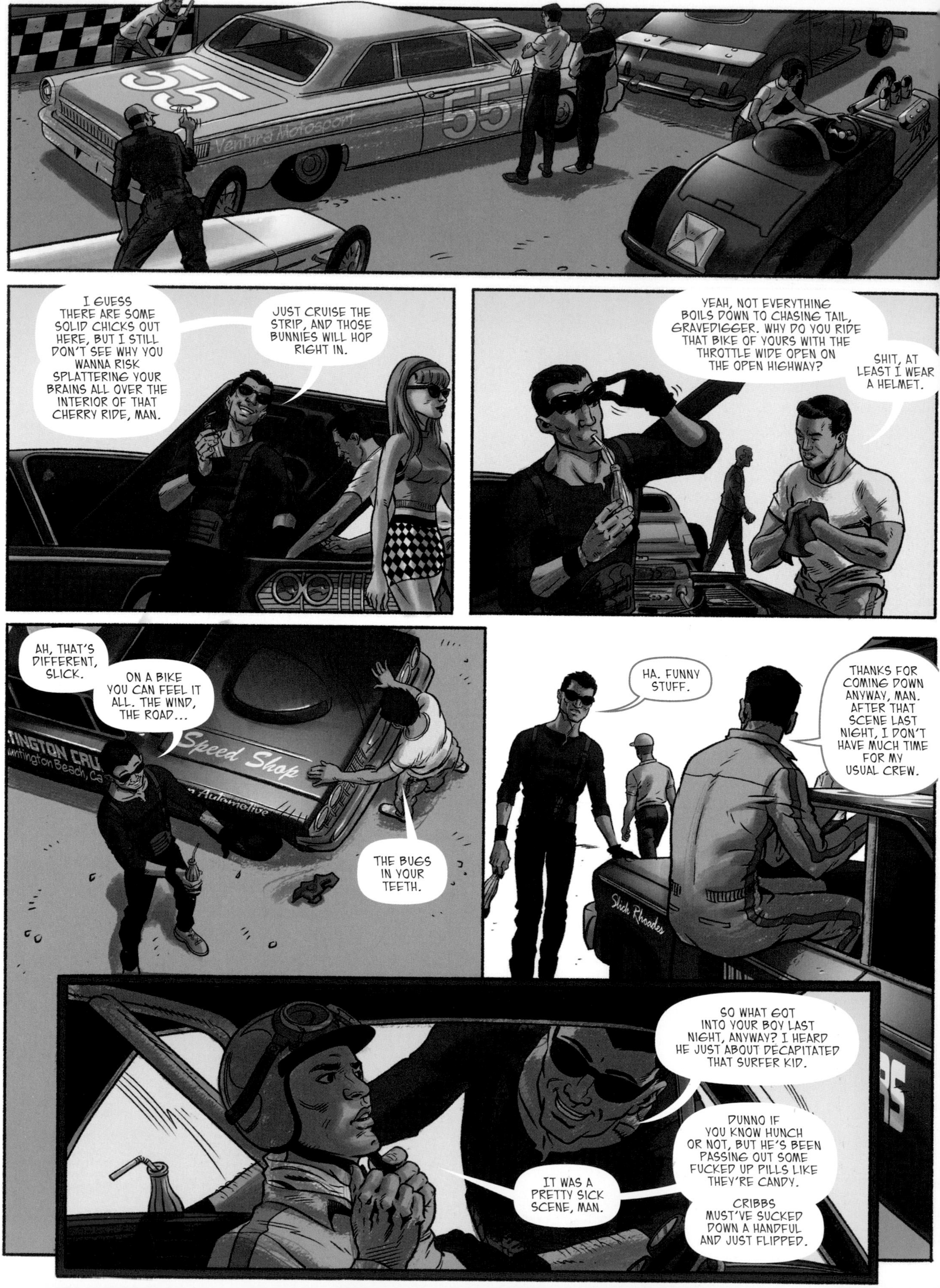
55
Ventura Motosport
55
I GUESS THERE ARE SOME SOLID CHICKS OUT HERE, BUT I STILL DON'T SEE WHY YOU WANNA RISK SPLATTERING YOUR BRAINS ALL OVER THE INTERIOR OF THAT CHERRY RIDE, MAN.
JUST CRUISE THE STRIP, AND THOSE BUNNIES WILL HOP RIGHT IN.
YEAH, NOT EVERYTHING BOILS DOWN TO CHASING TAIL, GRAVEDIGGER. WHY DO YOU RIDE THAT BIKE OF YOURS WITH THE THROTTLE WIDE OPEN ON THE OPEN HIGHWAY?
SHIT, AT LEAST I WEAR A HELMET.
AH, THAT'S DIFFERENT, SLICK.
ON A BIKE YOU CAN FEEL IT ALL. THE WIND, THE ROAD...
Speed Shop
THE BUGS IN YOUR TEETH.
HA. FUNNY STUFF.
THANKS FOR COMING DOWN ANYWAY, MAN. AFTER THAT SCENE LAST NIGHT, I DON'T HAVE MUCH TIME FOR MY USUAL CREW.
Slick Rhoades
SO WHAT GOT INTO YOUR BOY LAST NIGHT, ANYWAY? I HEARD HE JUST ABOUT DECAPITATED THAT SURFER KID.
IT WAS A PRETTY SICK SCENE, MAN.
DUNNO IF YOU KNOW HUNCH OR NOT, BUT HE'S BEEN PASSING OUT SOME FUCKED UP PILLS LIKE THEY'RE CANDY.
CRIBBS MUST'VE SUCKED DOWN A HANDFUL AND JUST FLIPPED.

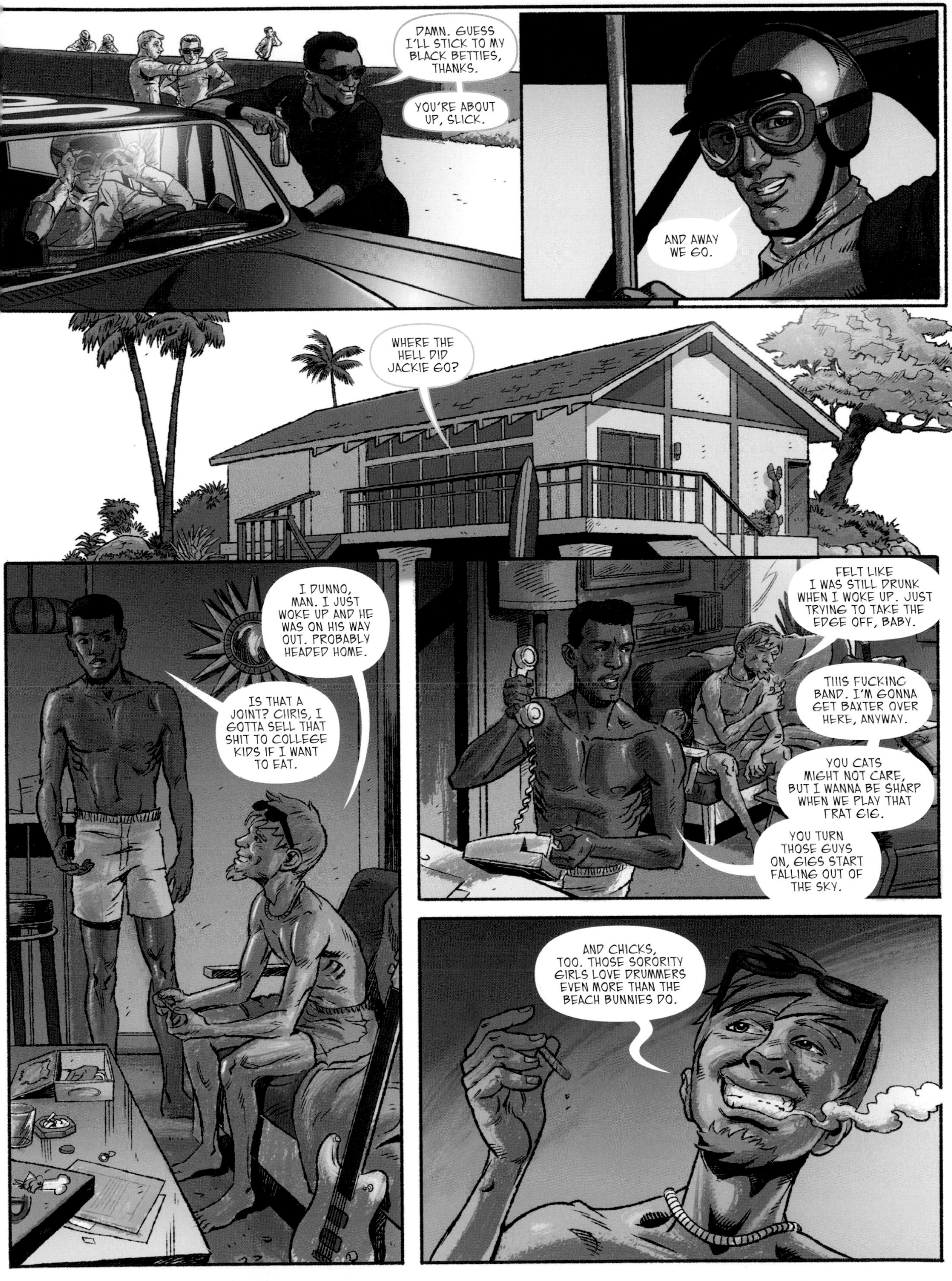
DAMN. GUESS I'LL STICK TO MY BLACK BETTIES, THANKS.
YOU'RE ABOUT UP, SLICK.
AND AWAY WE GO.
WHERE THE HELL DID JACKIE GO?
I DUNNO, MAN. I JUST WOKE UP AND HE WAS ON HIS WAY OUT. PROBABLY HEADED HOME.
IS THAT A JOINT? CHRIS, I GOTTA SELL THAT SHIT TO COLLEGE KIDS IF I WANT TO EAT.
FELT LIKE I WAS STILL DRUNK WHEN I WOKE UP. JUST TRYING TO TAKE THE EDGE OFF, BABY.
THIS FUCKING BAND. I'M GONNA GET BAXTER OVER HERE, ANYWAY.
YOU CATS MIGHT NOT CARE, BUT I WANNA BE SHARP WHEN WE PLAY THAT FRAT GIG.
YOU TURN THOSE GUYS ON, GIGS START FALLING OUT OF THE SKY.
AND CHICKS, TOO. THOSE SORORITY GIRLS LOVE DRUMMERS EVEN MORE THAN THE BEACH BUNNIES DO.

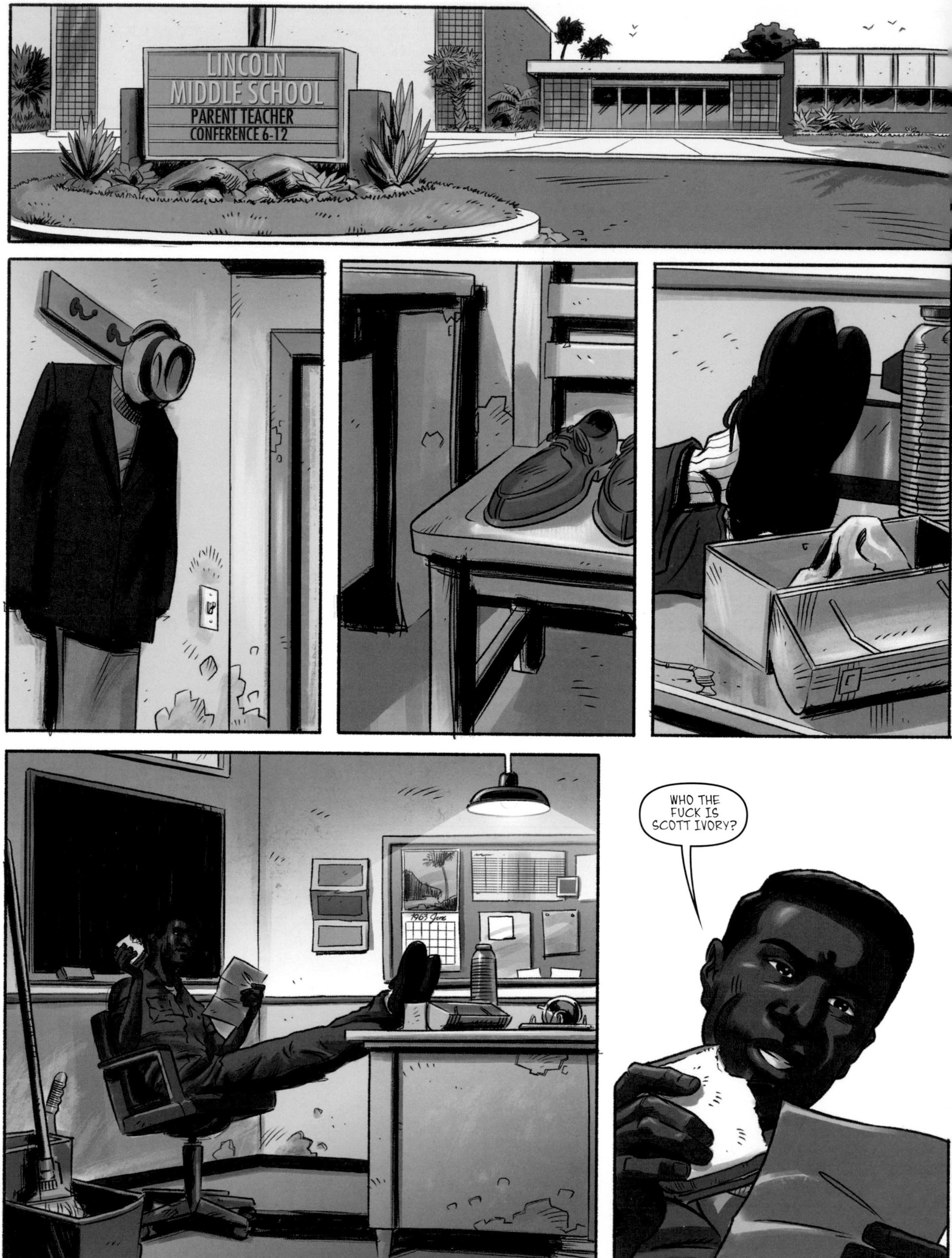

LINCOLN MIDDLE SCHOOL
PARENT TEACHER CONFERENCE 6-12
1963 June
WHO THE FUCK IS SCOTT IVORY?

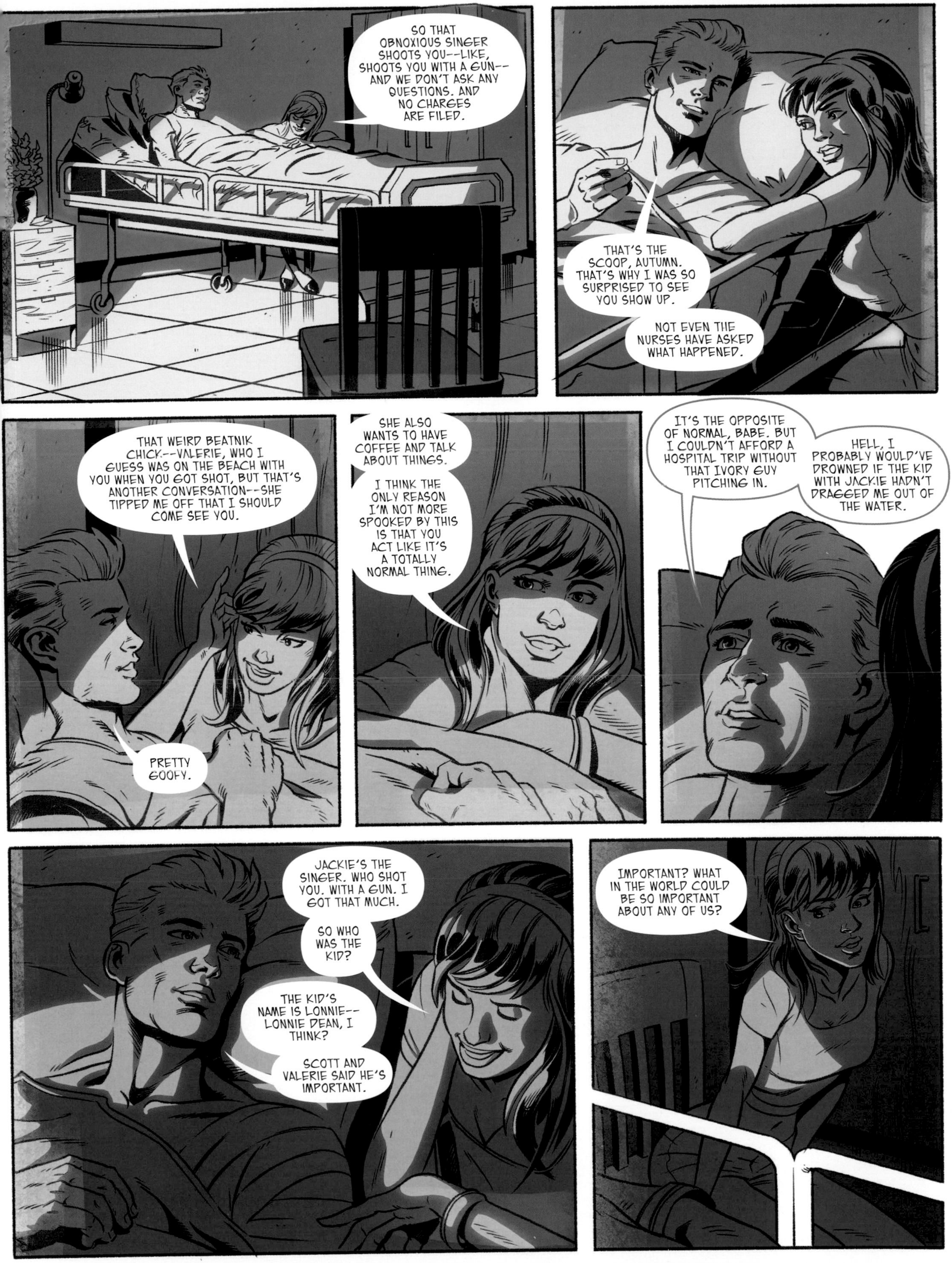
SO THAT OBNOXIOUS SINGER SHOOTS YOU--LIKE, SHOOTS YOU WITH A GUN--AND WE DON'T ASK ANY QUESTIONS. AND NO CHARGES ARE FILED.
THAT'S THE SCOOP, AUTUMN. THAT'S WHY I WAS SO SURPRISED TO SEE YOU SHOW UP.
NOT EVEN THE NURSES HAVE ASKED WHAT HAPPENED.
THAT WEIRD BEATNIK CHICK--VALERIE, WHO I GUESS WAS ON THE BEACH WITH YOU WHEN YOU GOT SHOT, BUT THAT'S ANOTHER CONVERSATION--SHE TIPPED ME OFF THAT I SHOULD COME SEE YOU.
PRETTY GOOFY.
SHE ALSO WANTS TO HAVE COFFEE AND TALK ABOUT THINGS.
I THINK THE ONLY REASON I'M NOT MORE SPOOKED BY THIS IS THAT YOU ACT LIKE IT'S A TOTALLY NORMAL THING.
IT'S THE OPPOSITE OF NORMAL, BABE. BUT I COULDN'T AFFORD A HOSPITAL TRIP WITHOUT THAT IVORY GUY PITCHING IN.
HELL, I PROBABLY WOULD'VE DROWNED IF THE KID WITH JACKIE HADN'T DRAGGED ME OUT OF THE WATER.
JACKIE'S THE SINGER. WHO SHOT YOU. WITH A GUN. I GOT THAT MUCH.
SO WHO WAS THE KID?
THE KID'S NAME IS LONNIE--LONNIE DEAN, I THINK?
SCOTT AND VALERIE SAID HE'S IMPORTANT.
IMPORTANT? WHAT IN THE WORLD COULD BE SO IMPORTANT ABOUT ANY OF US?

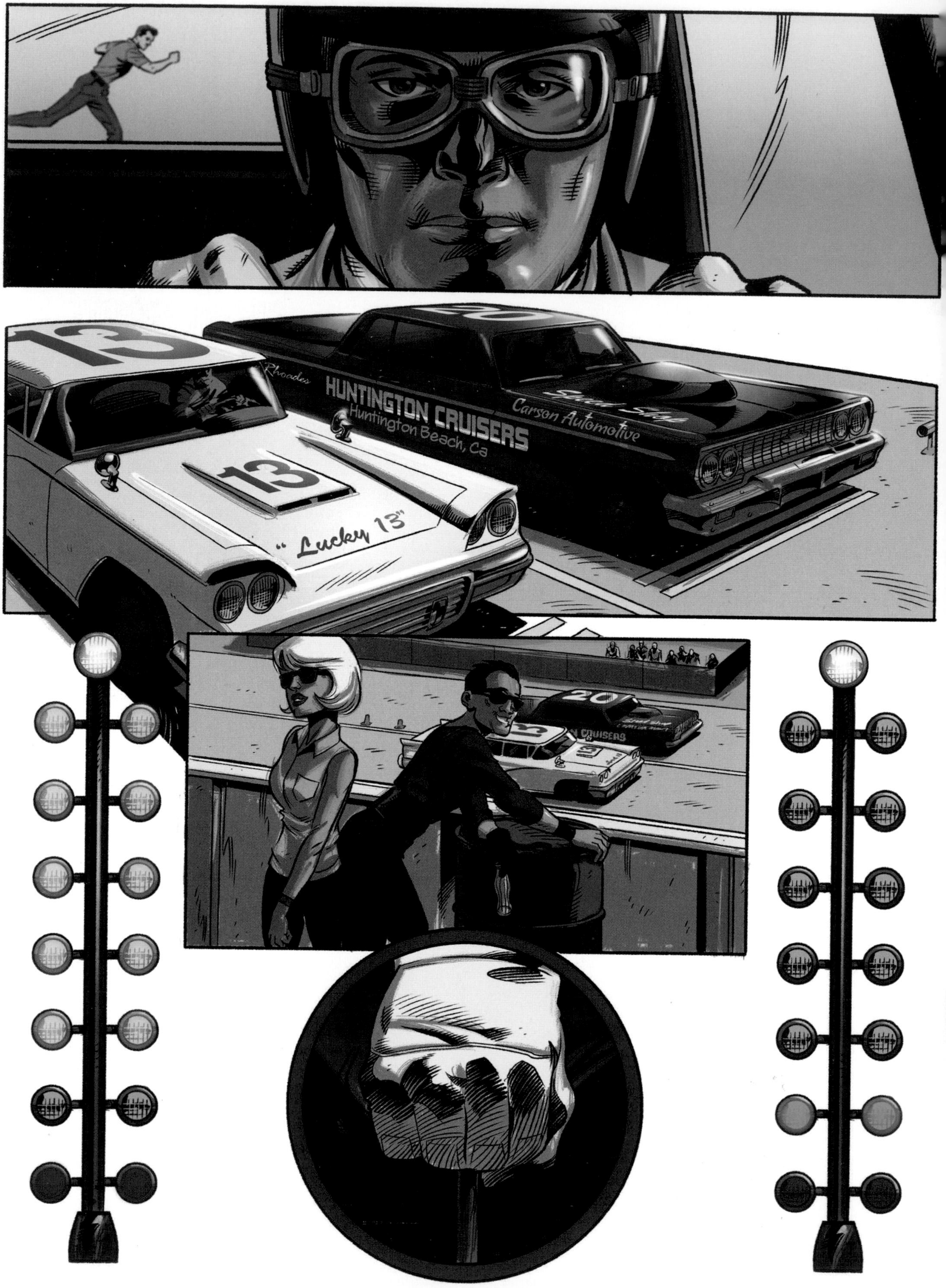

13
20
Rhoades
HUNTINGTON CRUISERS
Huntington Beach, Ca
Speed Shop
Carson Automotive
13
"Lucky 13"
20
13
13
N CRUISERS

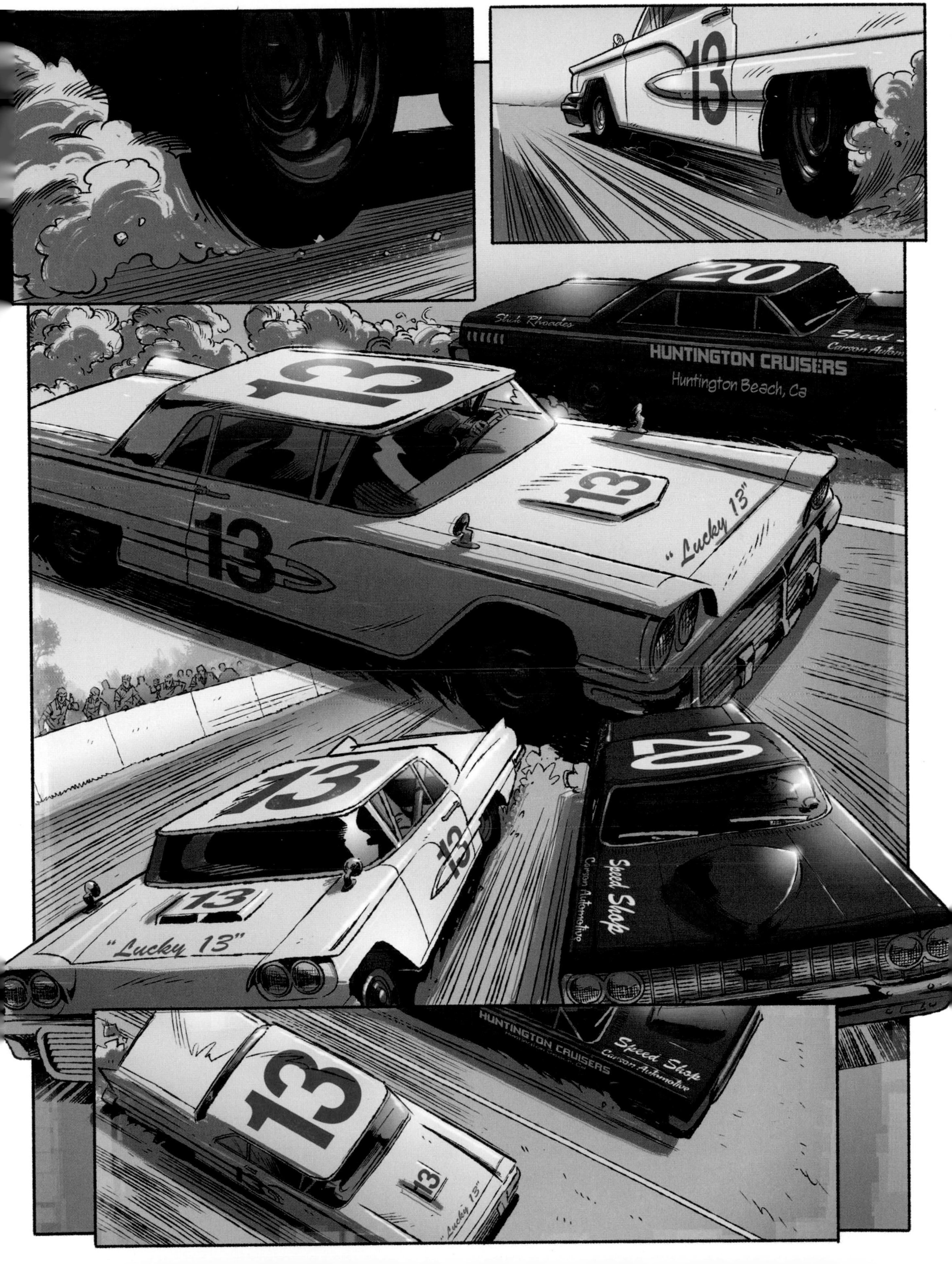

13
20
HUNTINGTON CRUISERS
Huntington Beach, Ca
13
13
13
"Lucky 13"
13
20
13
13
"Lucky 13"
Speed Shop
Carson Automotive
HUNTINGTON CRUISERS
Speed Shop
Carson Automotive
13
13
"Lucky 13"

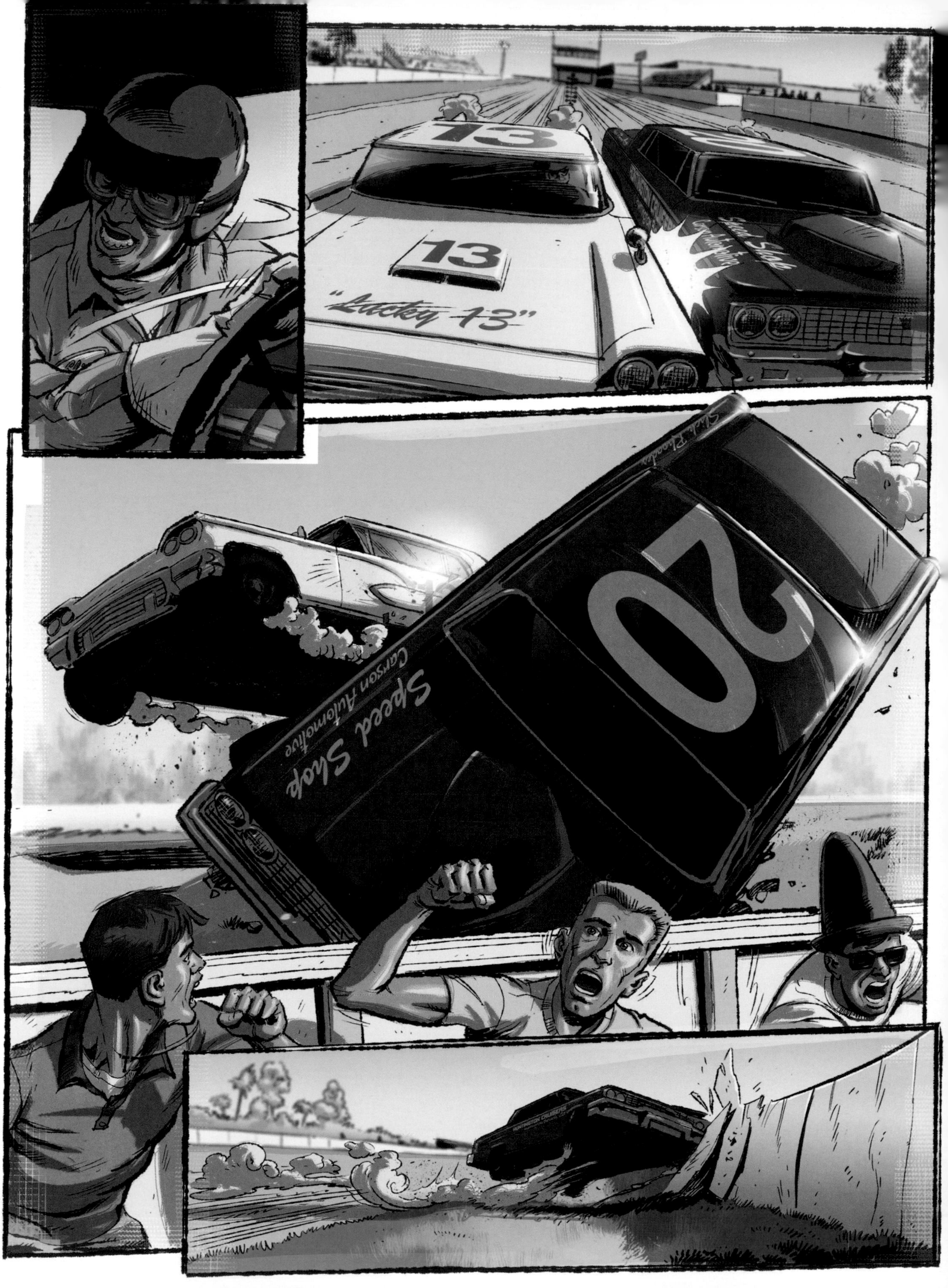

13
13
"Lucky 13"
20
Speed Shop
Carson Automotive

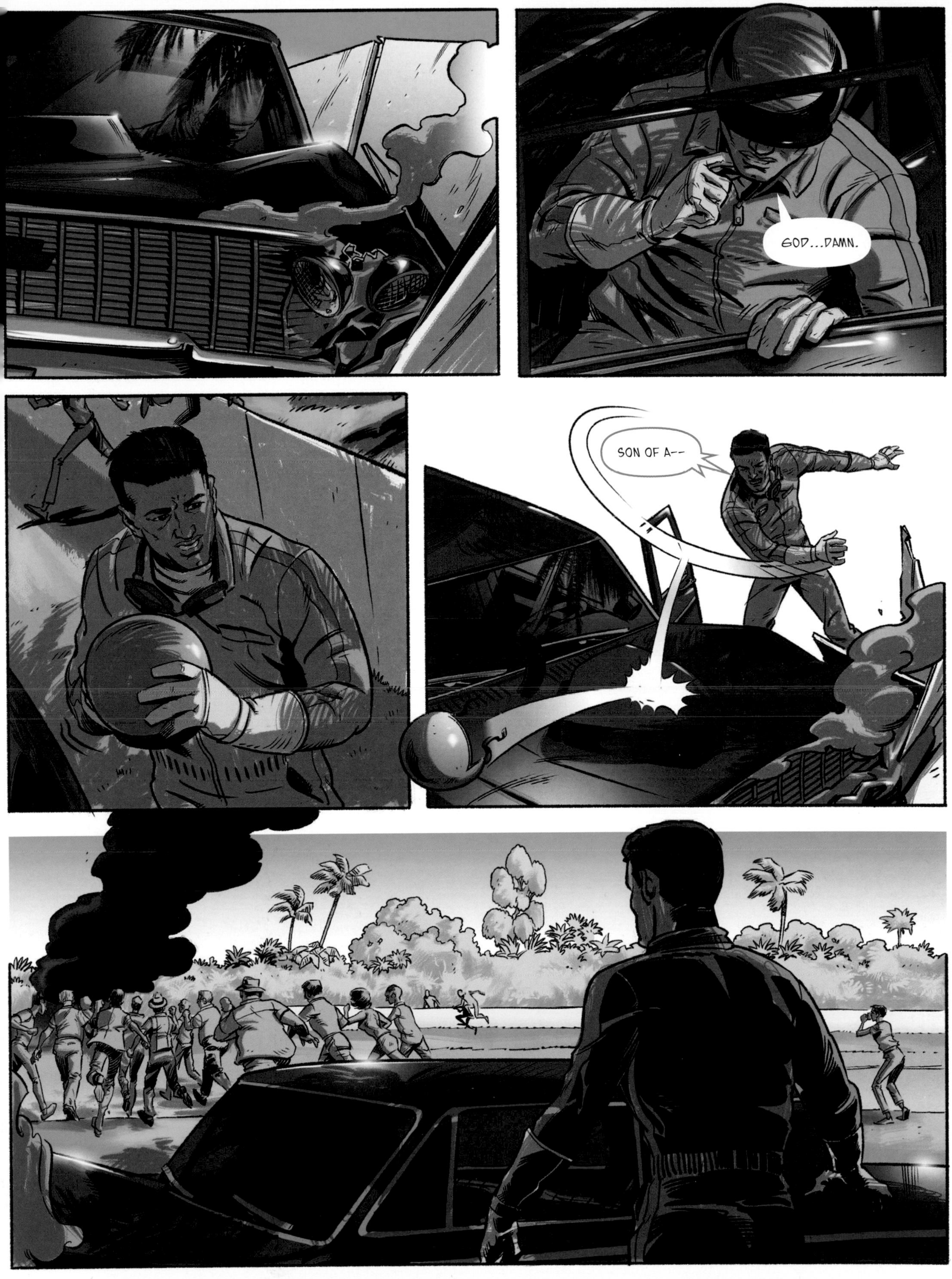
GOD...DAMN.
SON OF A--

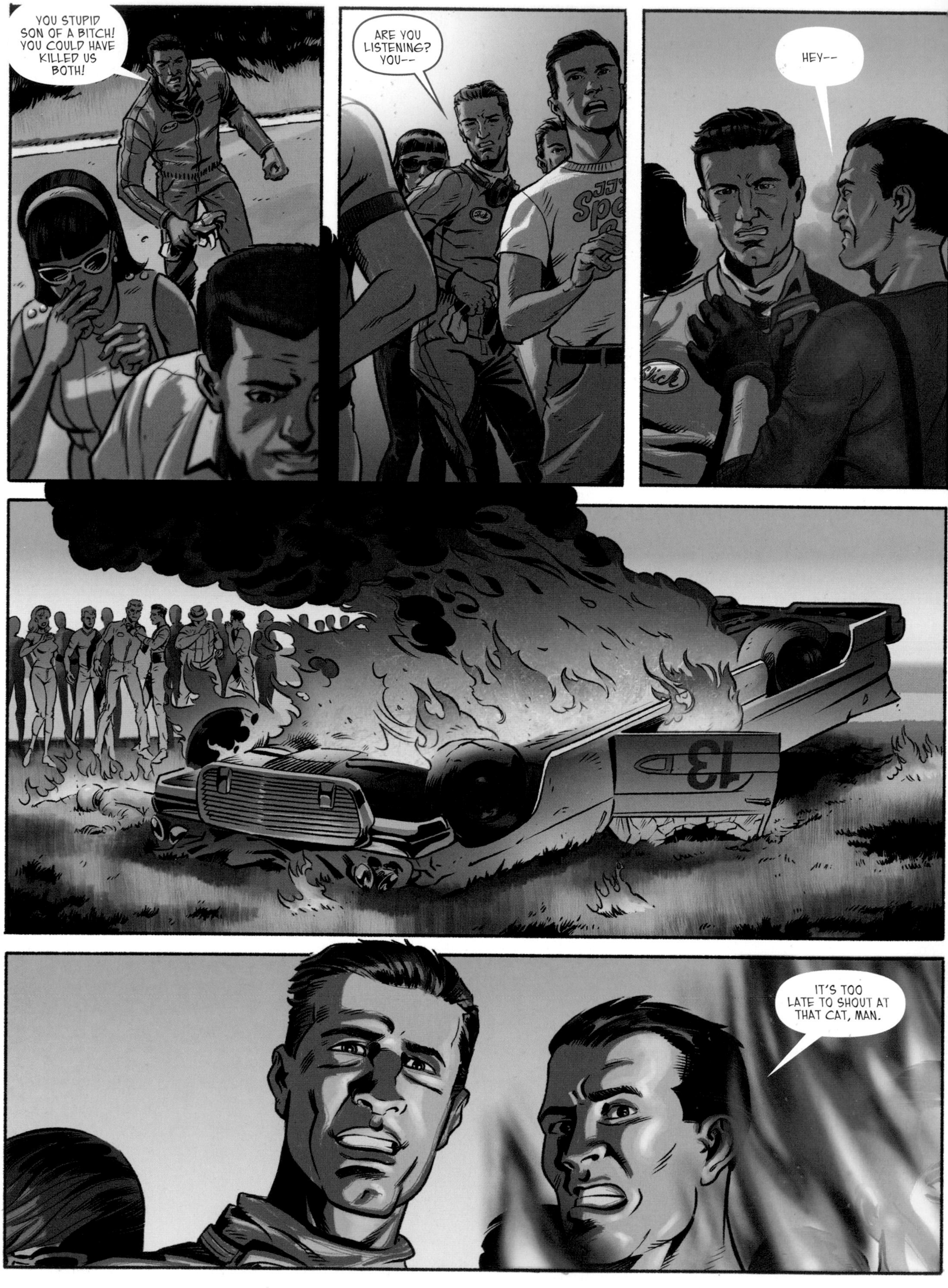
YOU STUPID SON OF A BITCH! YOU COULD HAVE KILLED US BOTH!
ARE YOU LISTENING? YOU--
HEY--
13
IT'S TOO LATE TO SHOUT AT THAT CAT, MAN.

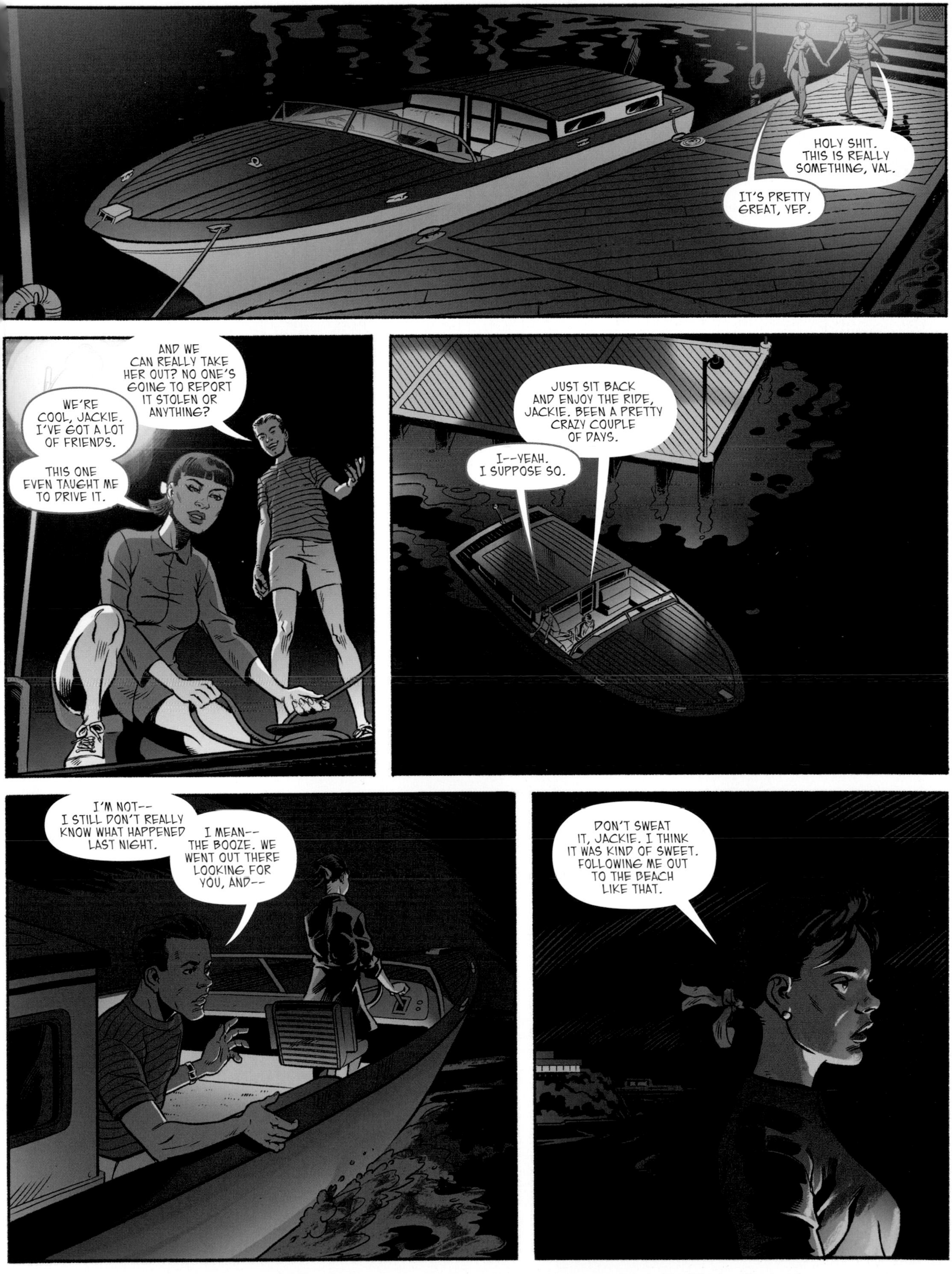
HOLY SHIT. THIS IS REALLY SOMETHING, VAL.
IT'S PRETTY GREAT, YEP.
AND WE CAN REALLY TAKE HER OUT? NO ONE'S GOING TO REPORT IT STOLEN OR ANYTHING?
WE'RE COOL, JACKIE. I'VE GOT A LOT OF FRIENDS.
THIS ONE EVEN TAUGHT ME TO DRIVE IT.
JUST SIT BACK AND ENJOY THE RIDE, JACKIE. BEEN A PRETTY CRAZY COUPLE OF DAYS.
I--YEAH. I SUPPOSE SO.
I'M NOT-- I STILL DON'T REALLY KNOW WHAT HAPPENED LAST NIGHT.
I MEAN-- THE BOOZE. WE WENT OUT THERE LOOKING FOR YOU, AND--
DON'T SWEAT IT, JACKIE. I THINK IT WAS KIND OF SWEET. FOLLOWING ME OUT TO THE BEACH LIKE THAT.

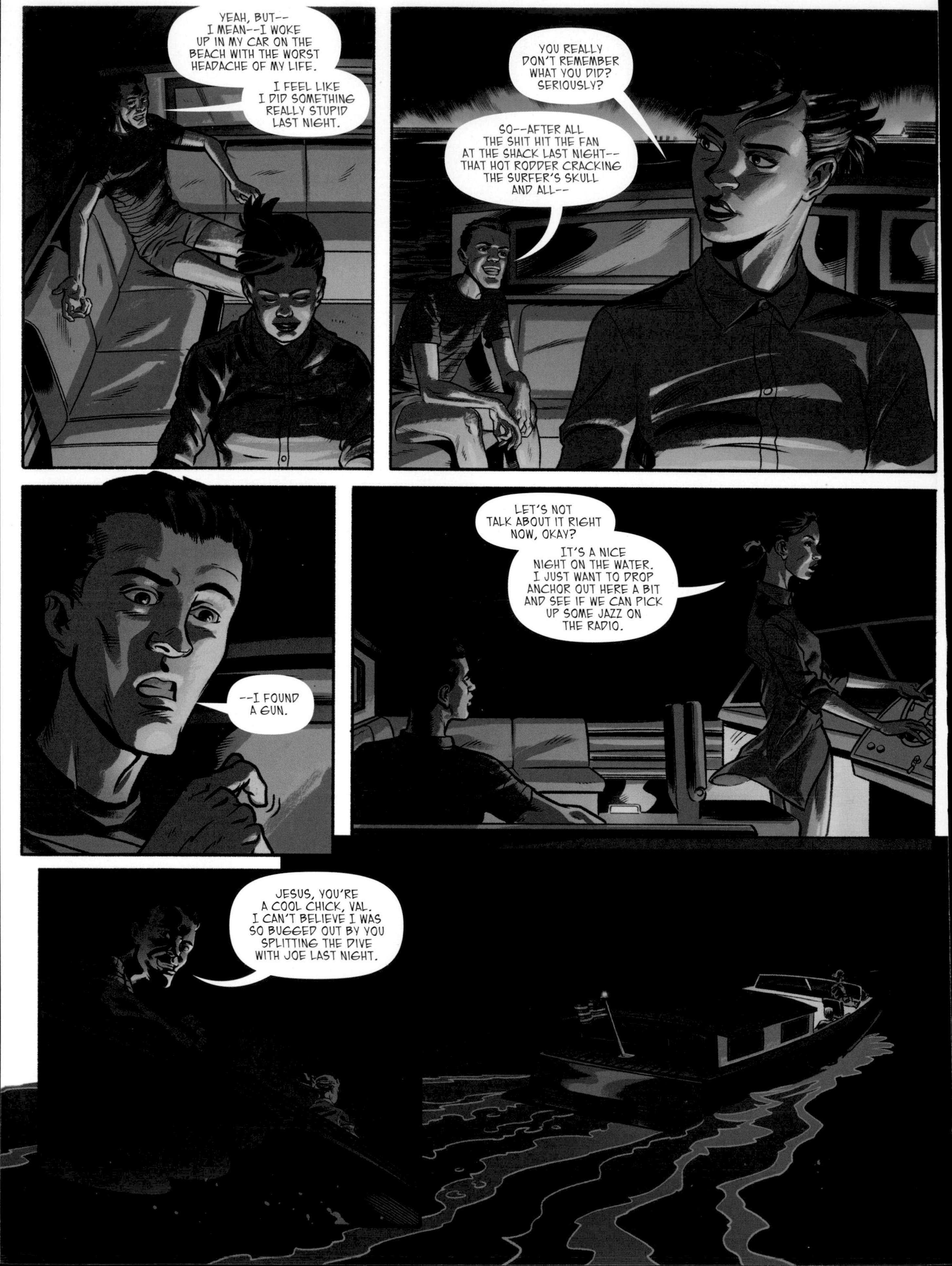
YEAH, BUT-- I MEAN--I WOKE UP IN MY CAR ON THE BEACH WITH THE WORST HEADACHE OF MY LIFE.
I FEEL LIKE I DID SOMETHING REALLY STUPID LAST NIGHT.
YOU REALLY DON'T REMEMBER WHAT YOU DID? SERIOUSLY?
SO--AFTER ALL THE SHIT HIT THE FAN AT THE SHACK LAST NIGHT--THAT HOT RODDER CRACKING THE SURFER'S SKULL AND ALL--
--I FOUND A GUN.
LET'S NOT TALK ABOUT IT RIGHT NOW, OKAY?
IT'S A NICE NIGHT ON THE WATER. I JUST WANT TO DROP ANCHOR OUT HERE A BIT AND SEE IF WE CAN PICK UP SOME JAZZ ON THE RADIO.
JESUS, YOU'RE A COOL CHICK, VAL. I CAN'T BELIEVE I WAS SO BUGGED OUT BY YOU SPLITTING THE DIVE WITH JOE LAST NIGHT.

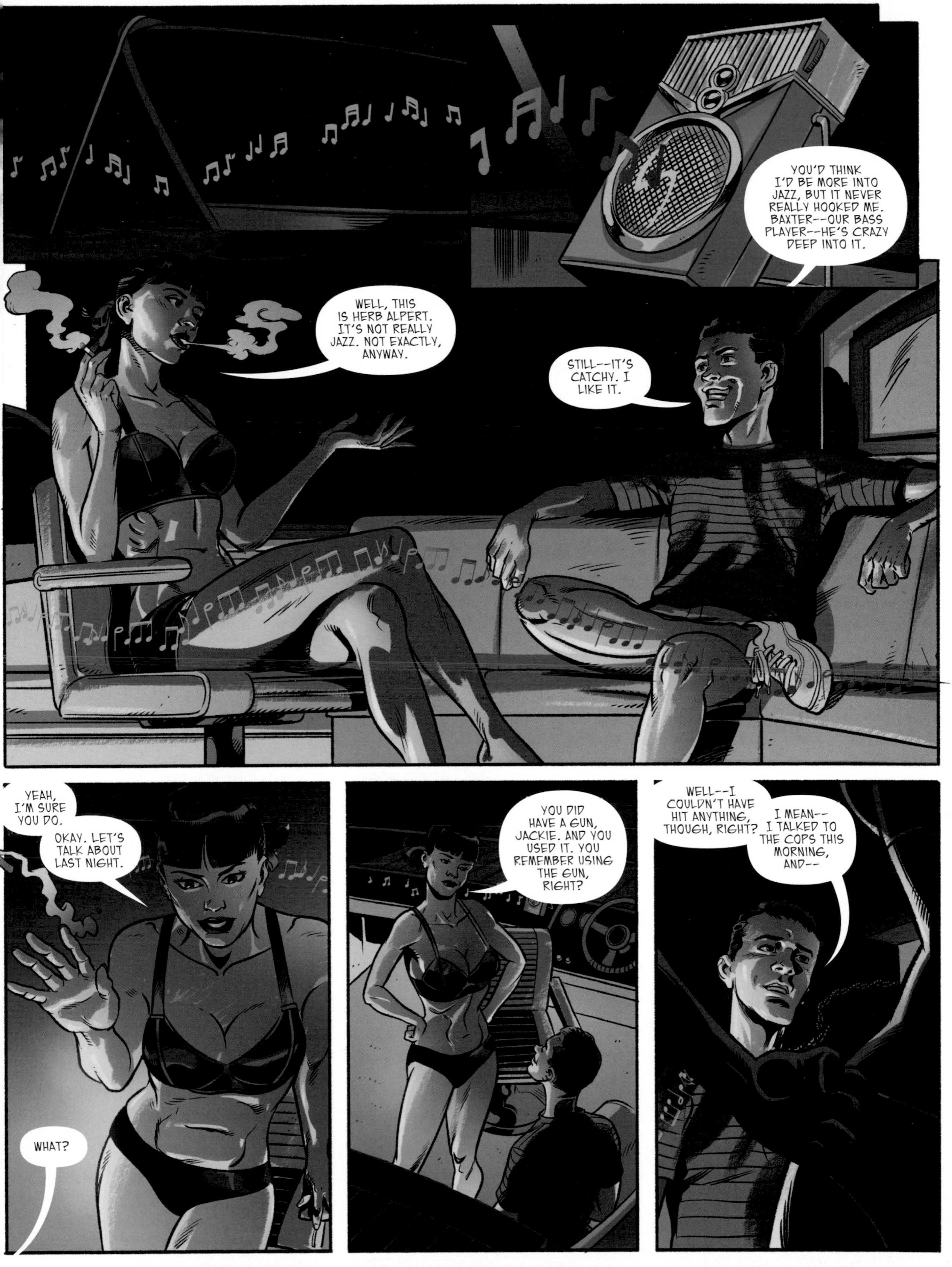
YOU'D THINK I'D BE MORE INTO JAZZ, BUT IT NEVER REALLY HOOKED ME. BAXTER--OUR BASS PLAYER--HE'S CRAZY DEEP INTO IT.
WELL, THIS IS HERB ALPERT. IT'S NOT REALLY JAZZ. NOT EXACTLY, ANYWAY.
STILL--IT'S CATCHY. I LIKE IT.
YEAH, I'M SURE YOU DO.
OKAY. LET'S TALK ABOUT LAST NIGHT.
WHAT?
YOU DID HAVE A GUN, JACKIE. AND YOU USED IT. YOU REMEMBER USING THE GUN, RIGHT?
WELL--I COULDN'T HAVE HIT ANYTHING, THOUGH, RIGHT?
I MEAN-- I TALKED TO THE COPS THIS MORNING, AND--

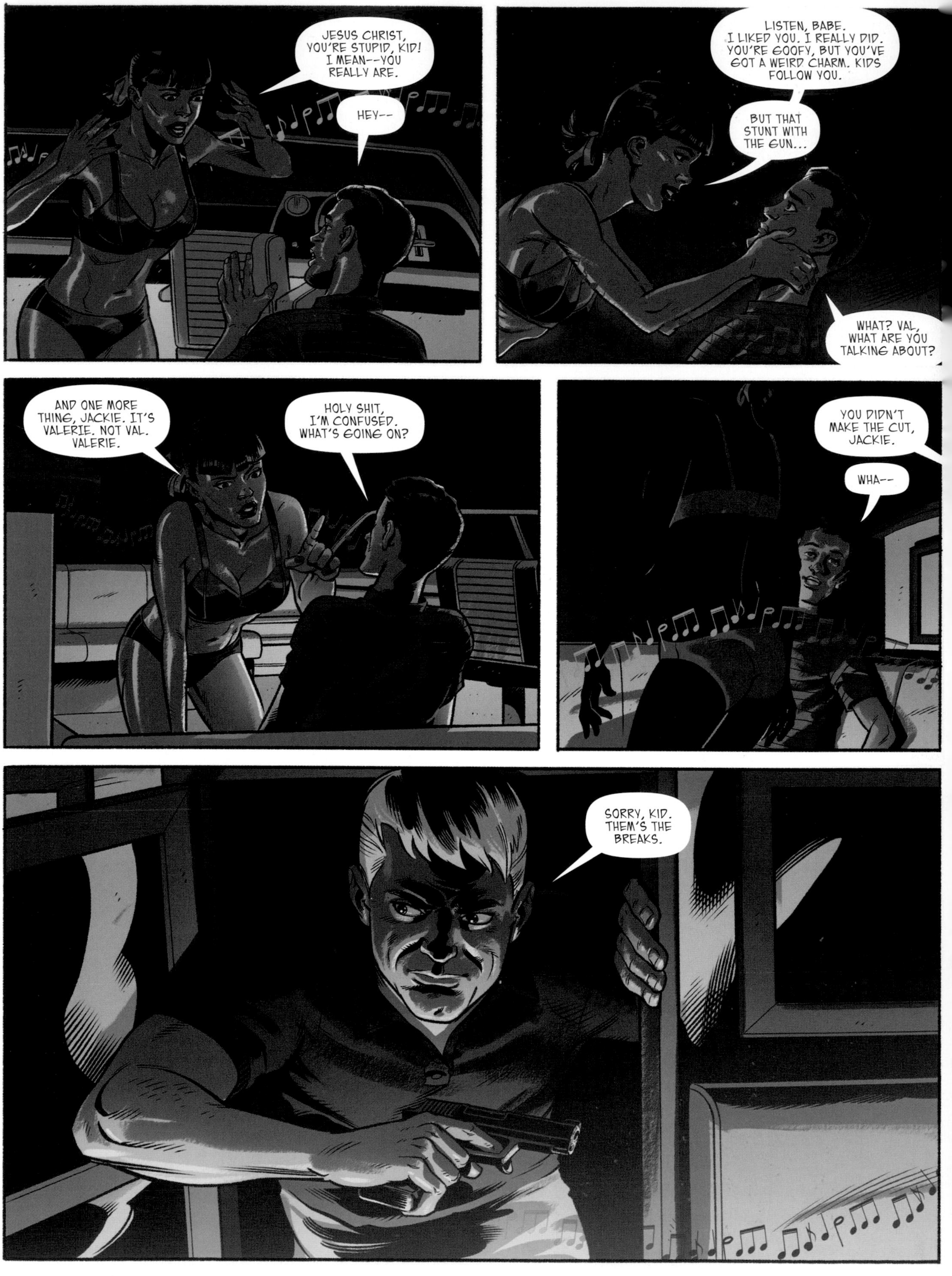
JESUS CHRIST, YOU'RE STUPID, KID! I MEAN--YOU REALLY ARE.
HEY--
LISTEN, BABE. I LIKED YOU. I REALLY DID. YOU'RE GOOFY, BUT YOU'VE GOT A WEIRD CHARM. KIDS FOLLOW YOU.
BUT THAT STUNT WITH THE GUN...
WHAT? VAL, WHAT ARE YOU TALKING ABOUT?
AND ONE MORE THING, JACKIE. IT'S VALERIE. NOT VAL. VALERIE.
HOLY SHIT, I'M CONFUSED. WHAT'S GOING ON?
YOU DIDN'T MAKE THE CUT, JACKIE.
WHA--
SORRY, KID. THEM'S THE BREAKS.

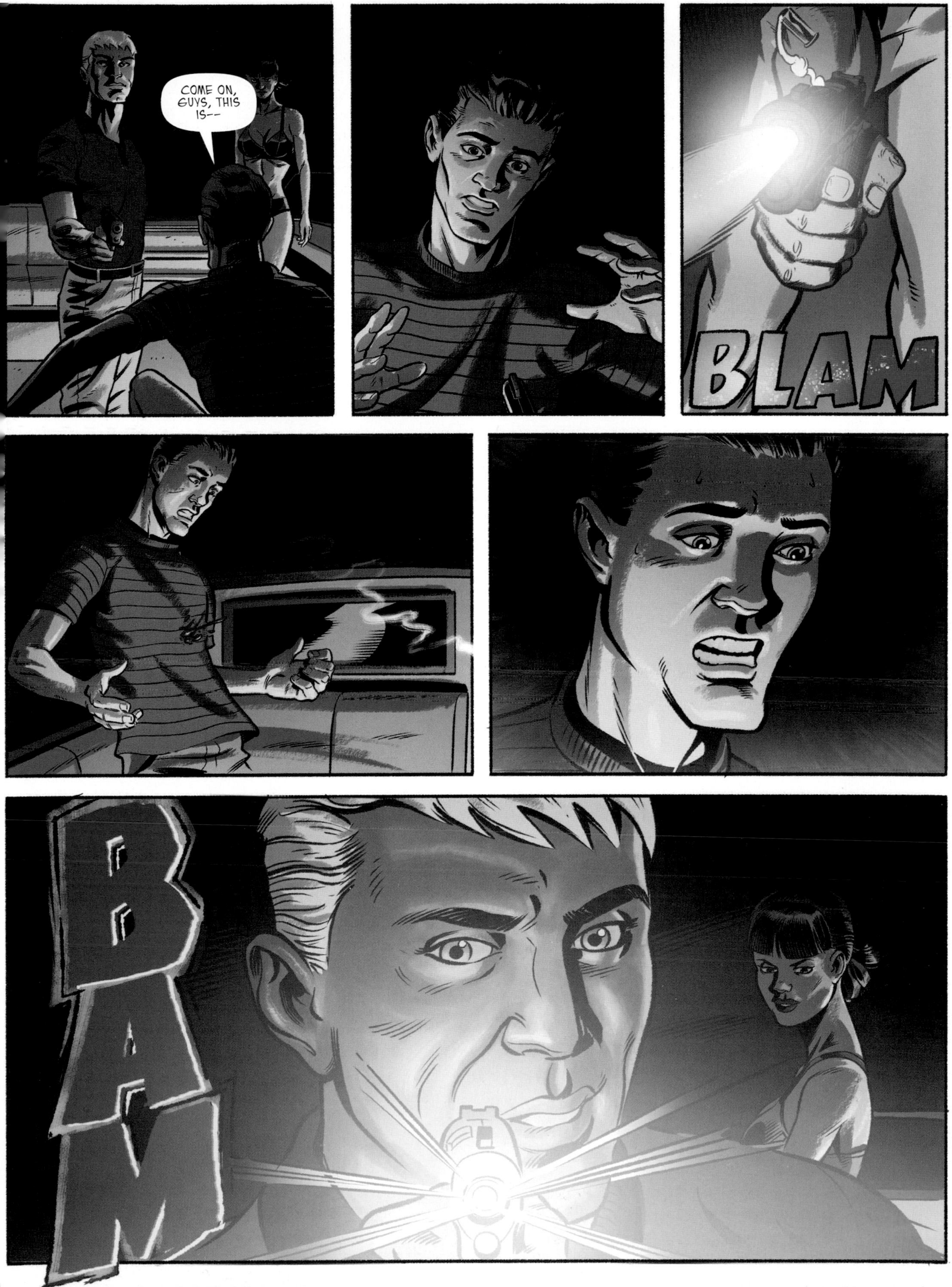
COME ON, GUYS, THIS IS--
BLAM
BAM

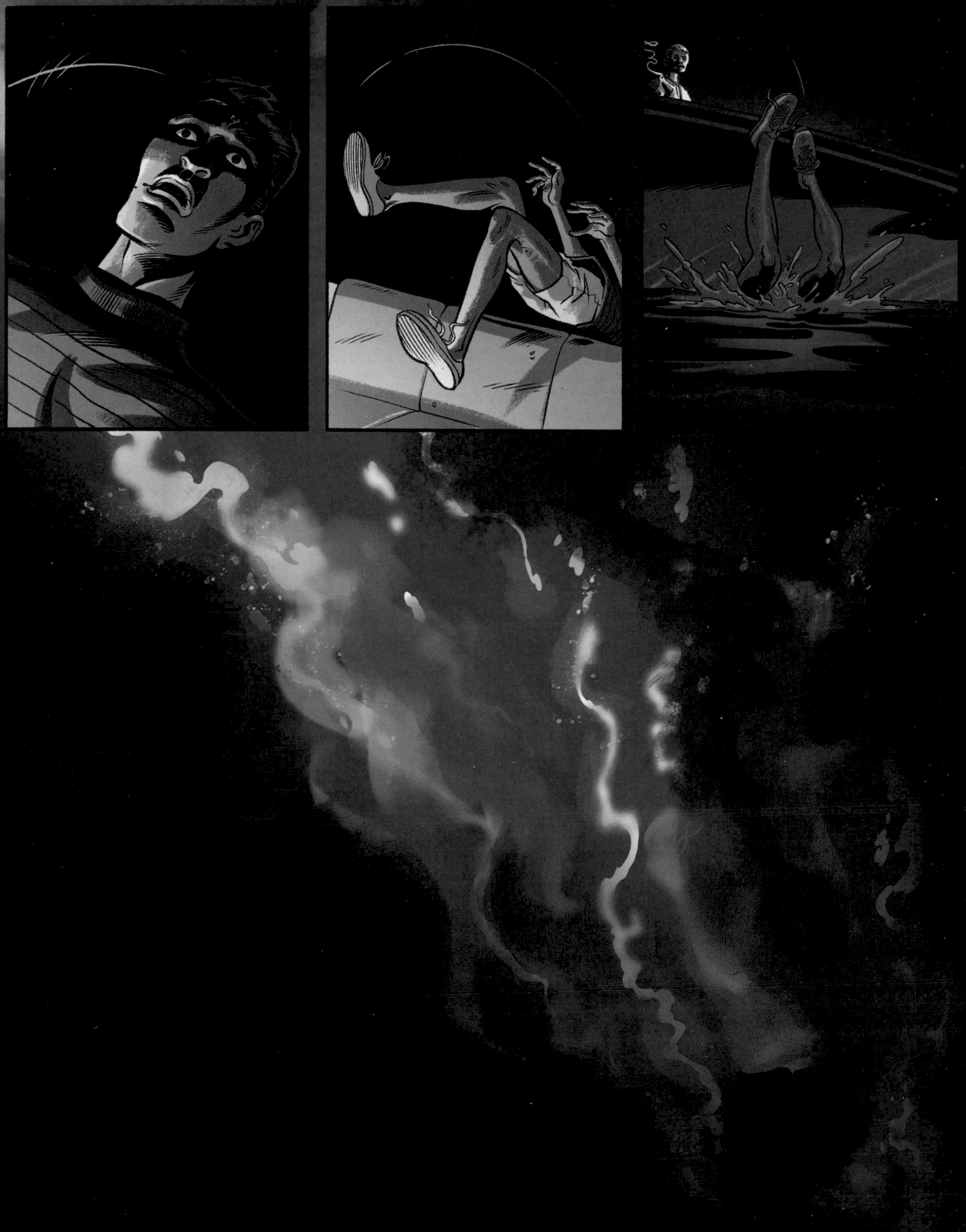

PART 3

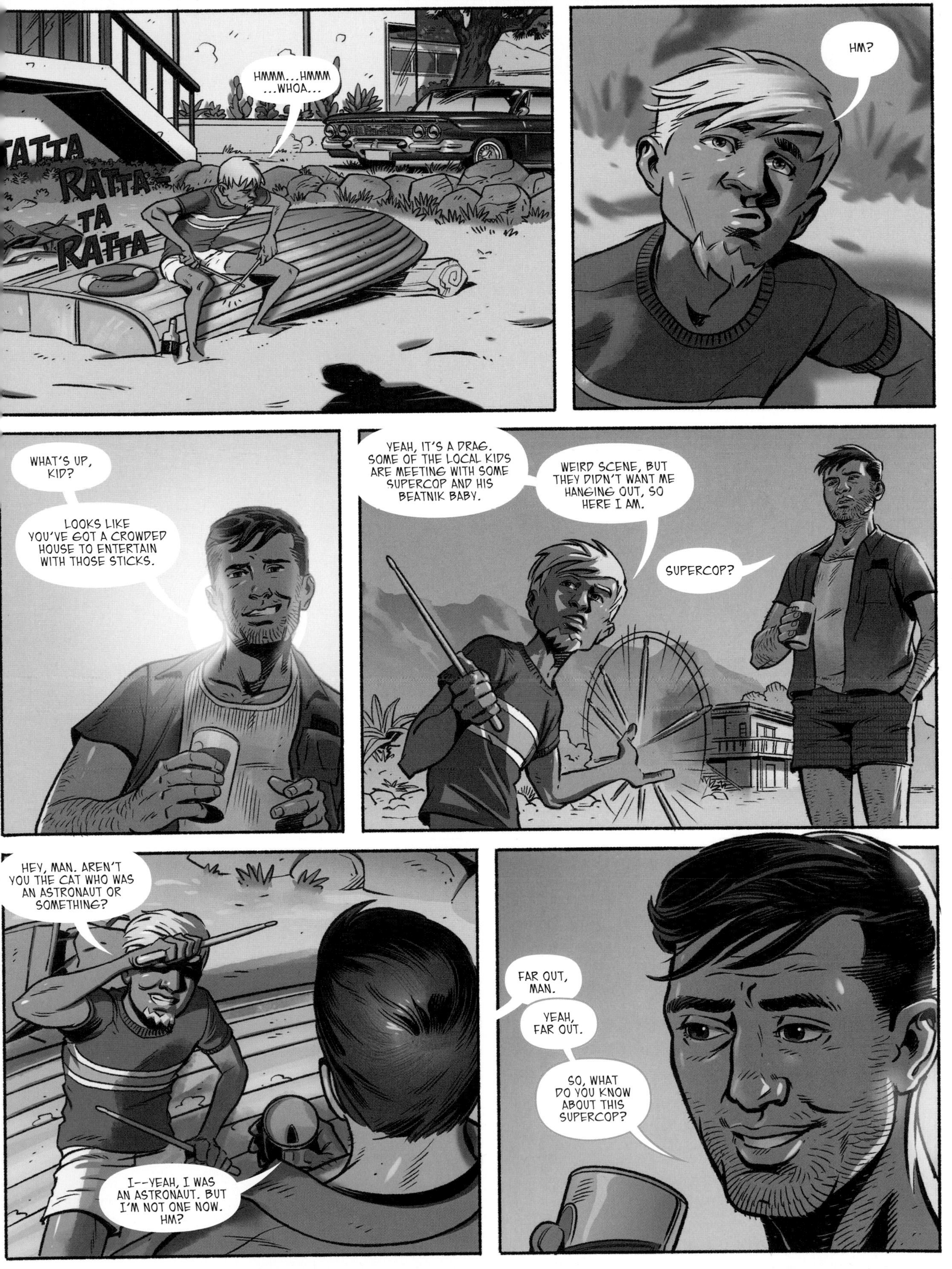
TATTA RATTA TA RATTA
HMMM...HMMM ...WHOA...
HM?
WHAT'S UP, KID?
LOOKS LIKE YOU'VE GOT A CROWDED HOUSE TO ENTERTAIN WITH THOSE STICKS.
YEAH, IT'S A DRAG. SOME OF THE LOCAL KIDS ARE MEETING WITH SOME SUPERCOP AND HIS BEATNIK BABY.
WEIRD SCENE, BUT THEY DIDN'T WANT ME HANGING OUT, SO HERE I AM.
SUPERCOP?
HEY, MAN. AREN'T YOU THE CAT WHO WAS AN ASTRONAUT OR SOMETHING?
I--YEAH, I WAS AN ASTRONAUT. BUT I'M NOT ONE NOW. HM?
FAR OUT, MAN.
YEAH, FAR OUT.
SO, WHAT DO YOU KNOW ABOUT THIS SUPERCOP?

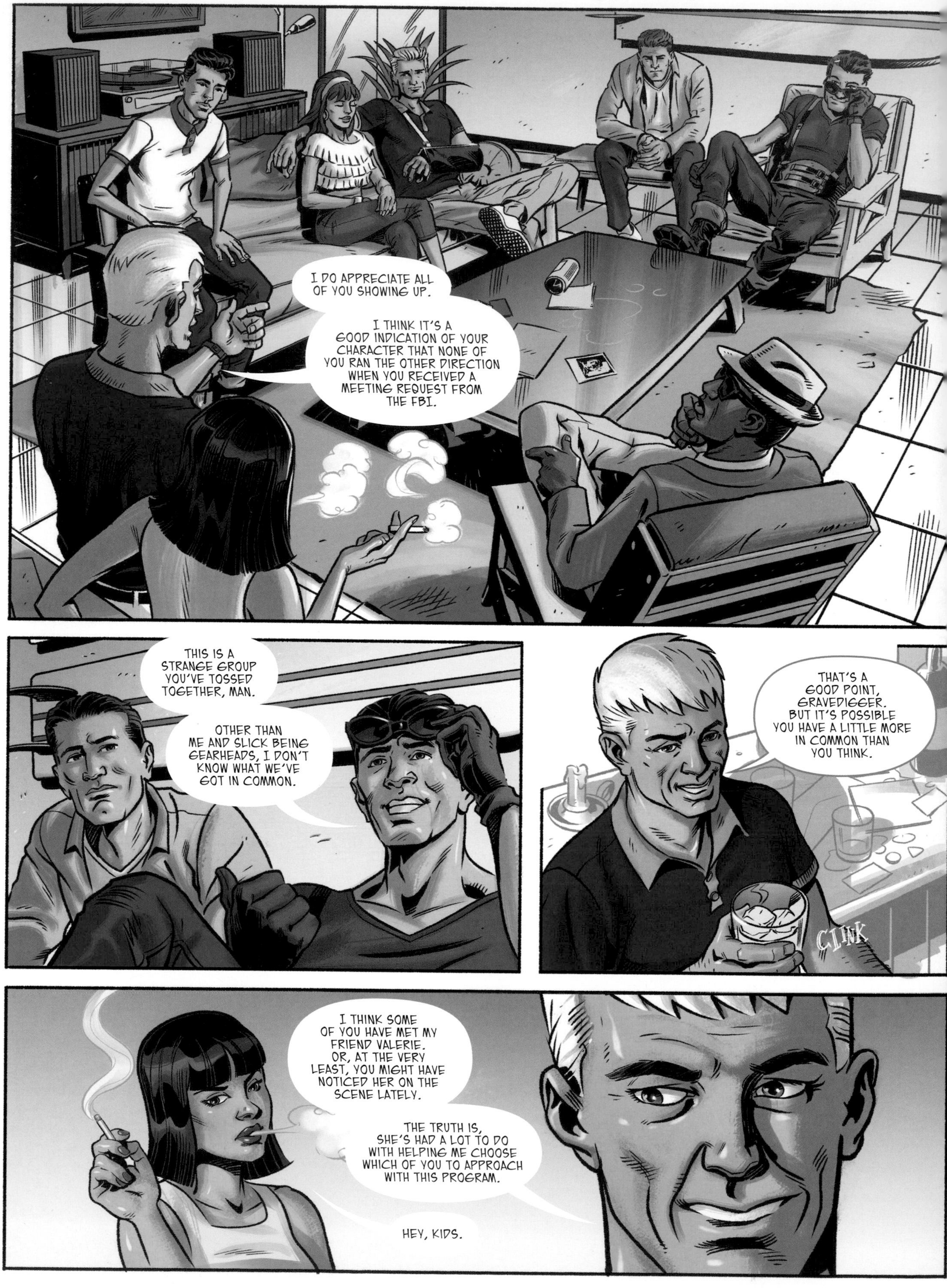
I DO APPRECIATE ALL OF YOU SHOWING UP.
I THINK IT'S A GOOD INDICATION OF YOUR CHARACTER THAT NONE OF YOU RAN THE OTHER DIRECTION WHEN YOU RECEIVED A MEETING REQUEST FROM THE FBI.
THIS IS A STRANGE GROUP YOU'VE TOSSED TOGETHER, MAN.
OTHER THAN ME AND SLICK BEING GEARHEADS, I DON'T KNOW WHAT WE'VE GOT IN COMMON.
THAT'S A GOOD POINT, GRAVEDIGGER. BUT IT'S POSSIBLE YOU HAVE A LITTLE MORE IN COMMON THAN YOU THINK.
CLINK
I THINK SOME OF YOU HAVE MET MY FRIEND VALERIE. OR, AT THE VERY LEAST, YOU MIGHT HAVE NOTICED HER ON THE SCENE LATELY.
THE TRUTH IS, SHE'S HAD A LOT TO DO WITH HELPING ME CHOOSE WHICH OF YOU TO APPROACH WITH THIS PROGRAM.
HEY, KIDS.

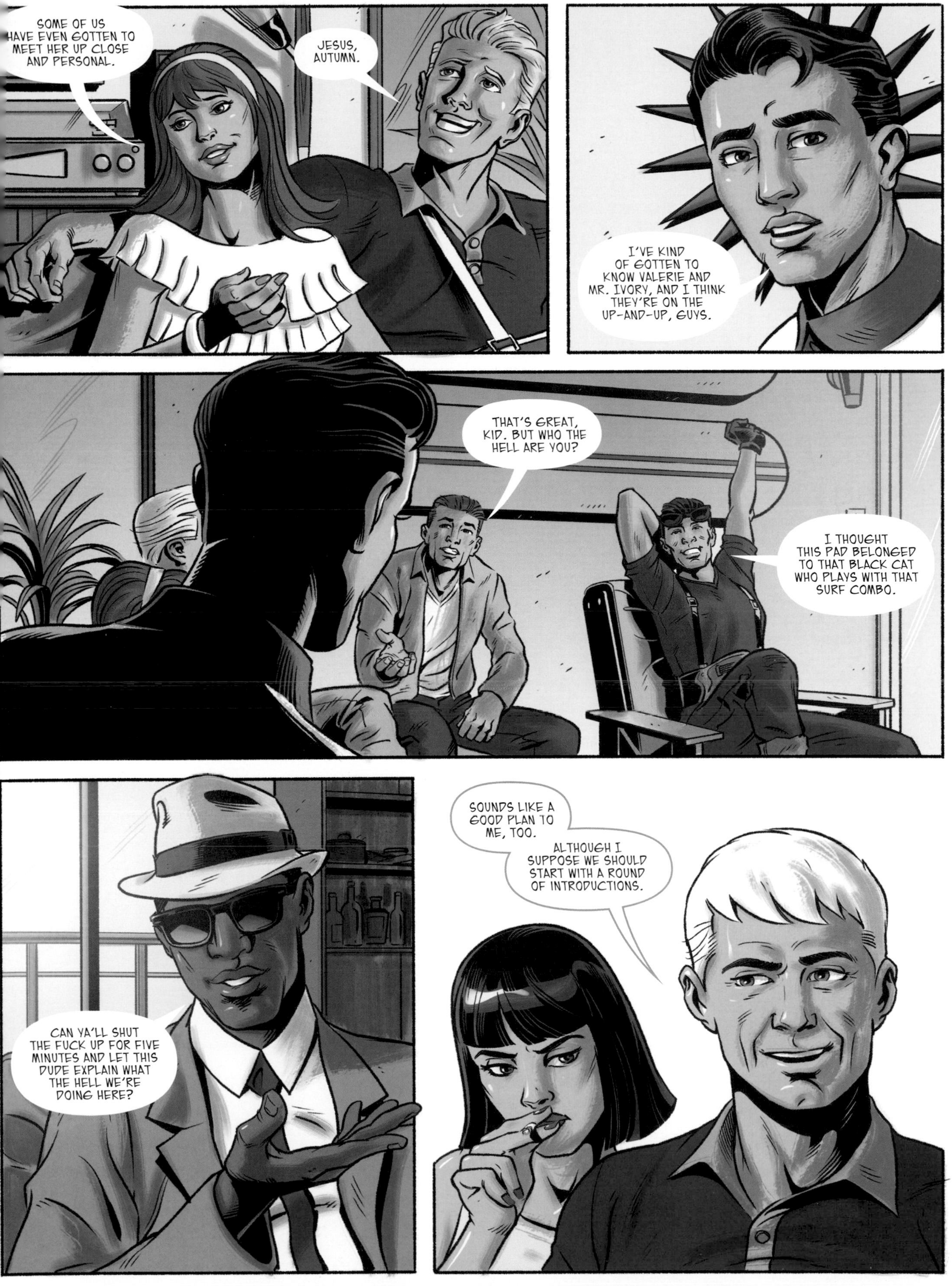
SOME OF US HAVE EVEN GOTTEN TO MEET HER UP CLOSE AND PERSONAL.
JESUS, AUTUMN.
I'VE KIND OF GOTTEN TO KNOW VALERIE AND MR. IVORY, AND I THINK THEY'RE ON THE UP-AND-UP, GUYS.
THAT'S GREAT, KID. BUT WHO THE HELL ARE YOU?
I THOUGHT THIS PAD BELONGED TO THAT BLACK CAT WHO PLAYS WITH THAT SURF COMBO.
CAN YA'LL SHUT THE FUCK UP FOR FIVE MINUTES AND LET THIS DUDE EXPLAIN WHAT THE HELL WE'RE DOING HERE?
SOUNDS LIKE A GOOD PLAN TO ME, TOO.
ALTHOUGH I SUPPOSE WE SHOULD START WITH A ROUND OF INTRODUCTIONS.

ALL OF YOU PROBABLY KNOW JOE CONRAD AND AUTUMN BLAZE. JOE AND AUTUMN RUN WITH THE SURFING CROWD. LITERALLY A CHAMPION SURFER AND A BEAUTY QUEEN.

MISS COPPERSUN LOTION, 1961. I WON A YEAR'S WORTH OF SUNTAN LOTION AND THE MAYOR'S HAND ON MY ASS DURING THE CROWNING CEREMONY.

SLICK RHODES--PRESIDENT OF ONE OF THE LOCAL CAR CLUBS AND ONE HELL OF A DRIVER. GRAVEDIGGER IS PRESIDENT OF THE MOONDAWGS, A GROUP OF BIKERS MOST OF YOU HAVE PROBABLY RUN INTO HERE AND--

LEADER, NOT PRESIDENT. PRESIDENTS ARE ELECTED. NO ELECTIONS IN THE MOONDAWGS. LEADER FOR LIFE, DAD.

AND SNAPS HERE IS THE LEADER OF THE SPADES, A LOCAL NEGRO CLUB, NOTORIOUS FOR THEIR--

--STYLE. YOU CAN SAY IT, POPS. WE'VE GOT STYLE.

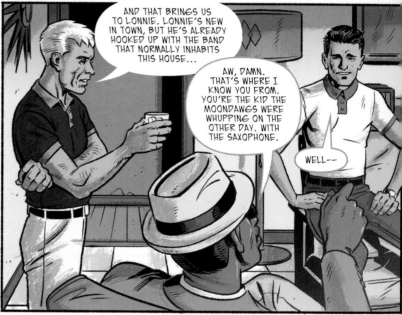

AND THAT BRINGS US TO LONNIE. LONNIE'S NEW IN TOWN, BUT HE'S ALREADY HOOKED UP WITH THE BAND THAT NORMALLY INHABITS THIS HOUSE...

AW, DAMN. THAT'S WHERE I KNOW YOU FROM. YOU'RE THE KID THE MOONDAWGS WERE WHUPPING ON THE OTHER DAY. WITH THE SAXOPHONE.

WELL--

OH, SHIT. WAS THAT YOU? MAN, I'M SORRY ABOUT THAT, KID. THOSE ASSHOLES GET OUT OF HAND WHEN I'M NOT AROUND TO KEEP THEM IN LINE.

YEAH. IT'S FINE. REALLY.

OKAY, SO WE KNOW EACH OTHER. BUT WHO ARE YOU, EXACTLY? I MEAN, YOU TOLD US ALL YOU'RE WITH THE FBI, AND THAT NONE OF US IS IN ANY KIND OF TROUBLE. SO-- WHAT'S THE STORY?

I AM WITH THE FBI. AND I MADE THAT CLEAR UP FRONT TO LET YOU KNOW YOU COULD TRUST ME. I'M NOT HIDING ANYTHING FROM ANY OF YOU.

AS FOR THE STORY...

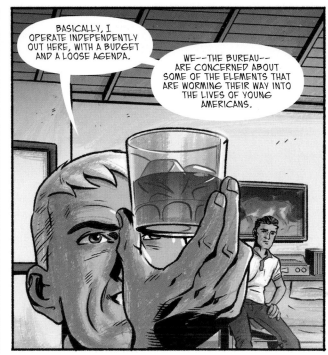

BASICALLY, I OPERATE INDEPENDENTLY OUT HERE, WITH A BUDGET AND A LOOSE AGENDA.

WE--THE BUREAU-- ARE CONCERNED ABOUT SOME OF THE ELEMENTS THAT ARE WORMING THEIR WAY INTO THE LIVES OF YOUNG AMERICANS.

YOUNG AMERICANS SUCH AS YOURSELVES.

"ELEMENTS"? WHAT KIND OF ELEMENTS? I FEEL LIKE THERE ARE SOME QUESTIONABLE ELEMENTS SITTING RIGHT HERE, MAN.

FOREIGN POLITICAL AGENTS LOOKING TO TAKE ADVANTAGE OF AN EXPLODING YOUTH CONSUMER CULTURE, CRIME CARTELS WORKING TO HOOK KIDS ON ANY NUMBER OF DANGEROUS, ADDICTIVE NARCOTICS, WITH THE MONEY BEING FUNNELED RIGHT BACK INTO ANY NUMBER OF CRIMINAL ENTERPRISES...

I'VE BEEN TASKED WITH ORGANIZING WHAT WE CALL COUNTER INTELLIGENCE PROGRAMS-- COINTELPRO FOR SHORT-- DESIGNED TO ROOT OUT THESE...

ELEMENTS.

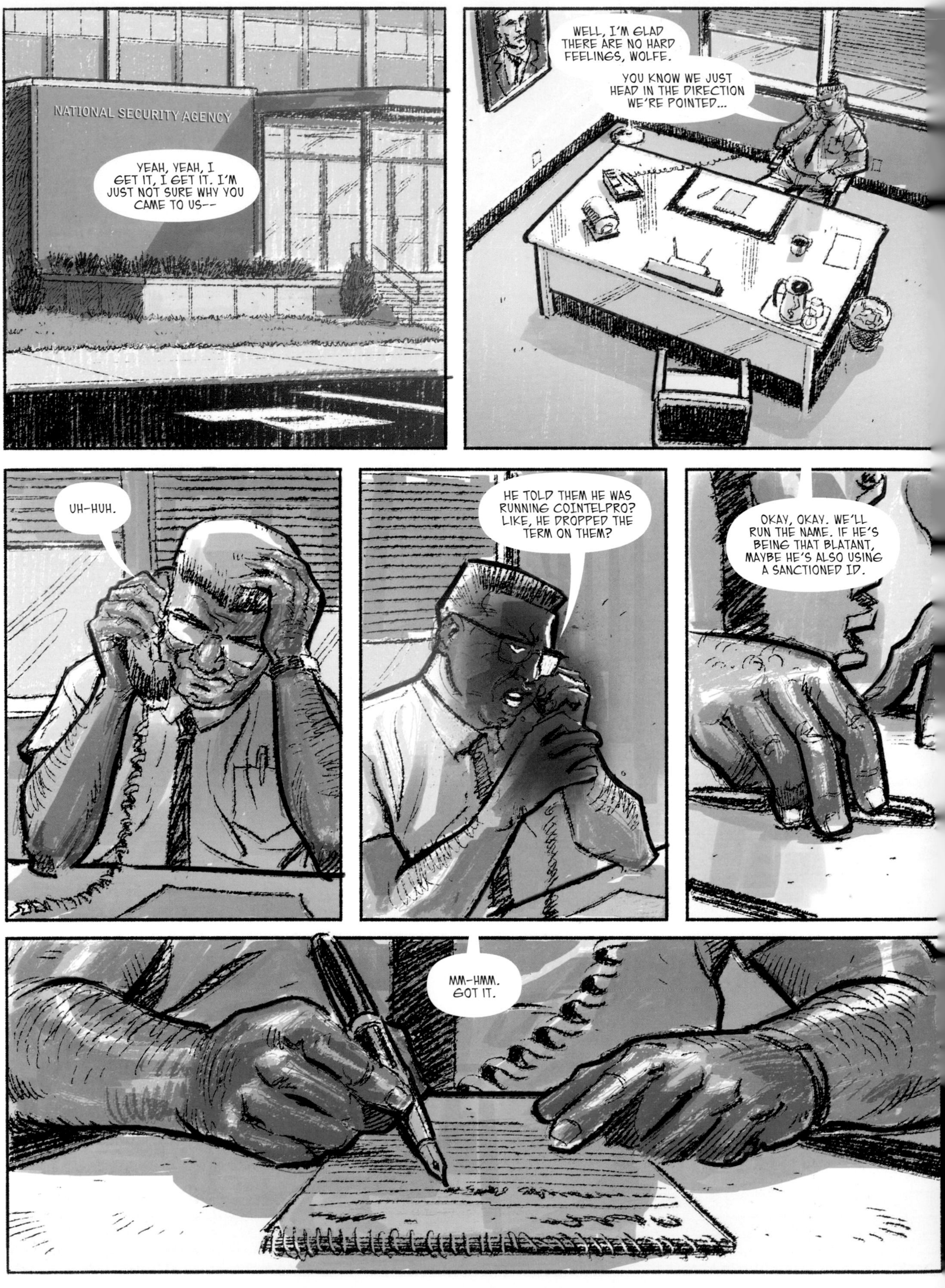
NATIONAL SECURITY AGENCY
YEAH, YEAH, I GET IT, I GET IT. I'M JUST NOT SURE WHY YOU CAME TO US--
WELL, I'M GLAD THERE ARE NO HARD FEELINGS, WOLFE.
YOU KNOW WE JUST HEAD IN THE DIRECTION WE'RE POINTED...
UH-HUH.
HE TOLD THEM HE WAS RUNNING COINTELPRO? LIKE, HE DROPPED THE TERM ON THEM?
OKAY, OKAY. WE'LL RUN THE NAME. IF HE'S BEING THAT BLATANT, MAYBE HE'S ALSO USING A SANCTIONED ID.
MM-HMM. GOT IT.

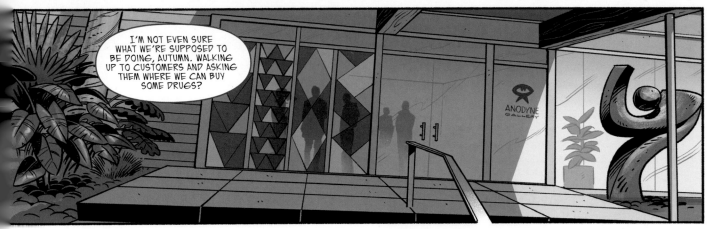

I'M NOT EVEN SURE WHAT WE'RE SUPPOSED TO BE DOING, AUTUMN. WALKING UP TO CUSTOMERS AND ASKING THEM WHERE WE CAN BUY SOME DRUGS?

PATRONS, JOE. NOT CUSTOMERS. AND QUIT FRETTING. JUST KEEP YOUR EAR TO THE GROUND AND LISTEN FOR ANYTHING, LIKE, ODD.

AND ENJOY THE SHOW, DARLING. I THINK ONE OF THESE MASTERPIECES WOULD LOOK SIMPLY SMASHING HANGING NEXT TO YOUR SURFBOARD.

I THINK SOME OF THESE MASTERPIECES WOULD LOOK SMASHING IF WE WERE SMASHED.

HA! MAYBE WE CAN SAMPLE SOME OF THE MERCHANDISE IF WE DISCOVER...THE STUFF.

I WONDER HOW SNAPS AND THE KID ARE DOING. SEEMS LIKE BOTH OF THEM MIGHT, YOU KNOW-- STAND OUT A LITTLE IN HERE.

OH, WOULD THEY? DON'T LOOK NOW, SURFER JOE, BUT WE'RE THE ONLY ONES HERE WITH TANLINES.

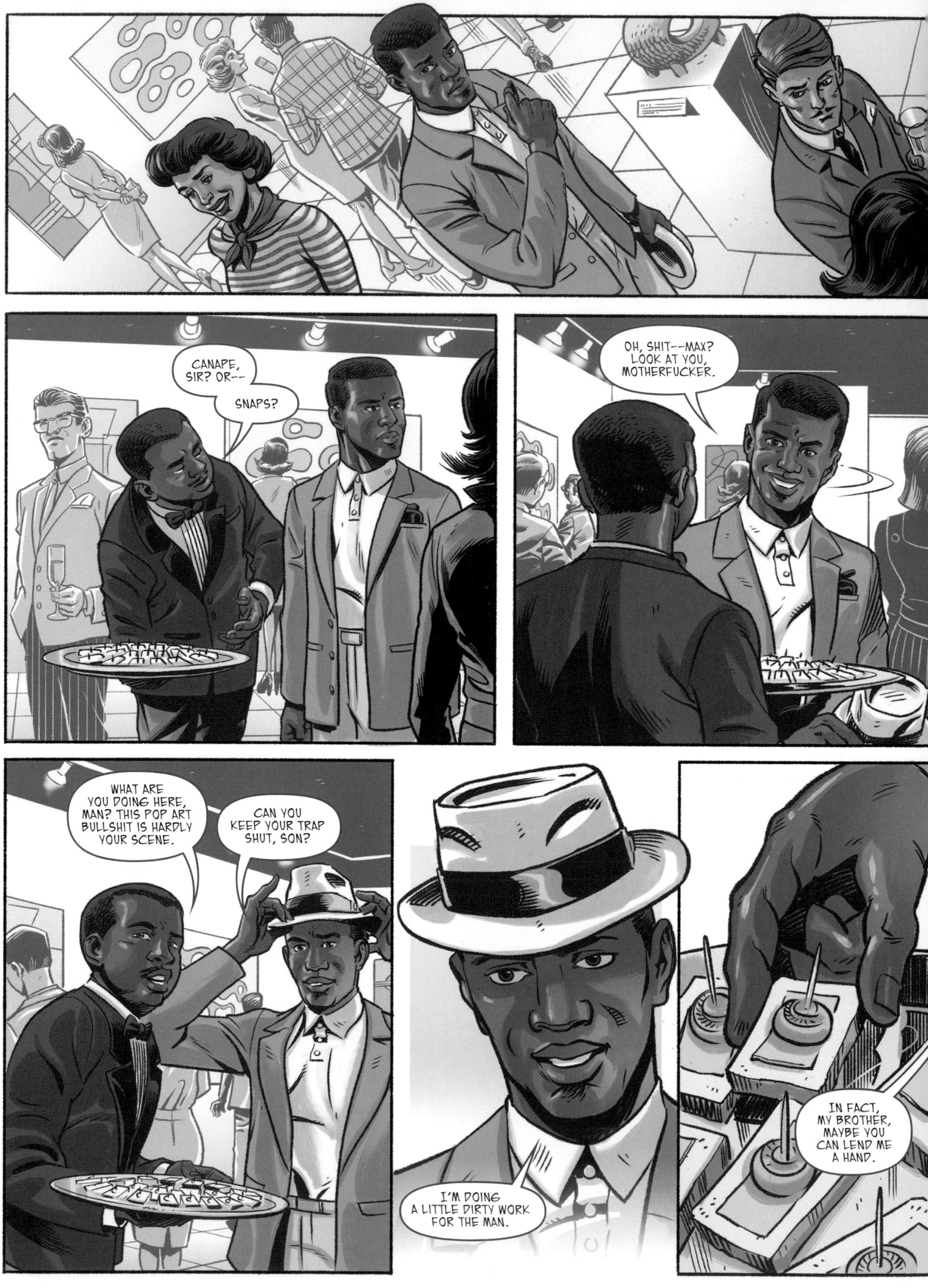
CANAPE, SIR? OR--
SNAPS?
OH, SHIT--MAX? LOOK AT YOU, MOTHERFUCKER.
WHAT ARE YOU DOING HERE, MAN? THIS POP ART BULLSHIT IS HARDLY YOUR SCENE.
CAN YOU KEEP YOUR TRAP SHUT, SON?
I'M DOING A LITTLE DIRTY WORK FOR THE MAN.
IN FACT, MY BROTHER, MAYBE YOU CAN LEND ME A HAND.

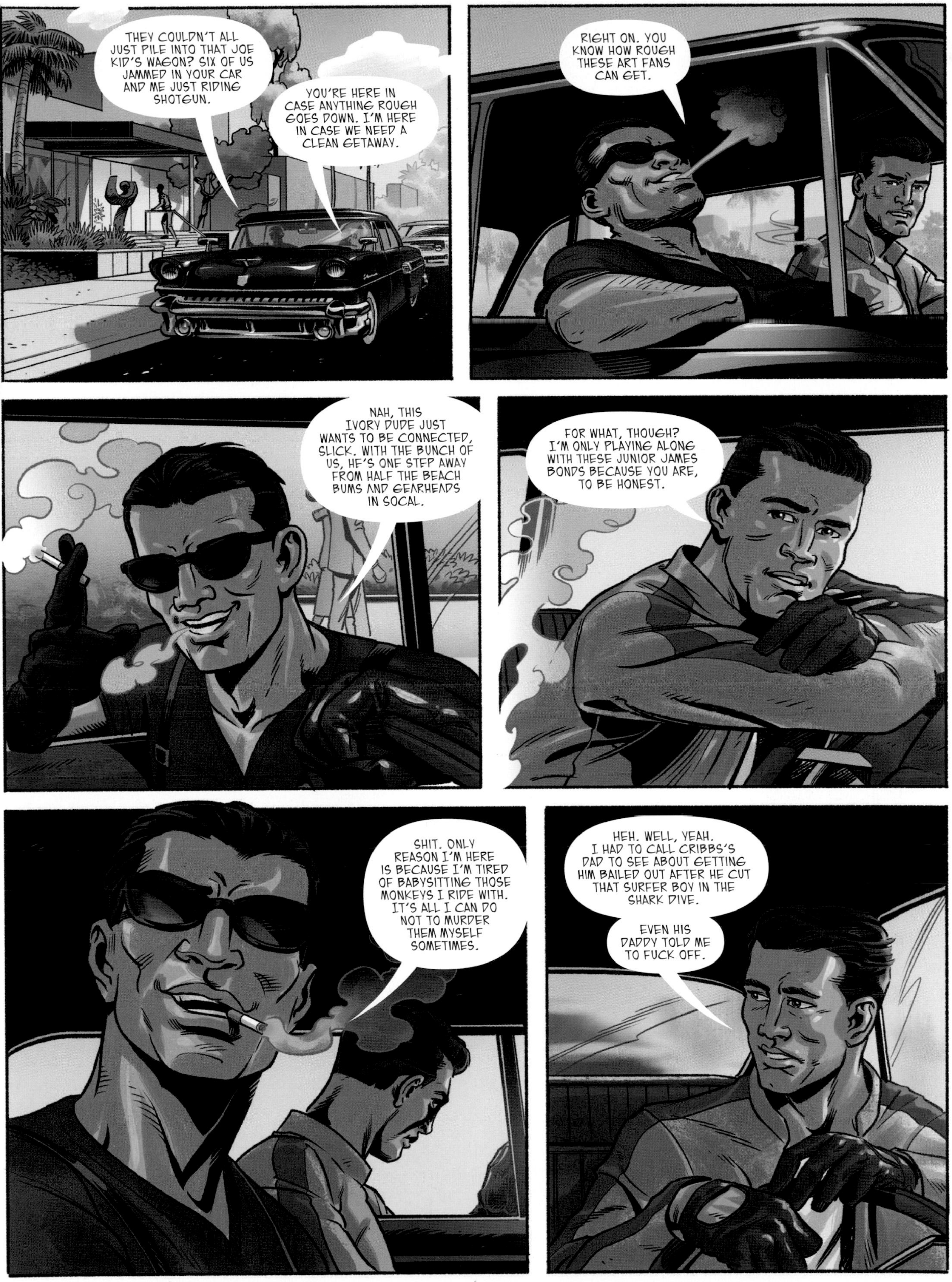
THEY COULDN'T ALL JUST PILE INTO THAT JOE KID'S WAGON? SIX OF US JAMMED IN YOUR CAR AND ME JUST RIDING SHOTGUN.
YOU'RE HERE IN CASE ANYTHING ROUGH GOES DOWN. I'M HERE IN CASE WE NEED A CLEAN GETAWAY.
RIGHT ON. YOU KNOW HOW ROUGH THESE ART FANS CAN GET.
NAH, THIS IVORY DUDE JUST WANTS TO BE CONNECTED, SLICK. WITH THE BUNCH OF US, HE'S ONE STEP AWAY FROM HALF THE BEACH BUMS AND GEARHEADS IN SOCAL.
FOR WHAT, THOUGH? I'M ONLY PLAYING ALONG WITH THESE JUNIOR JAMES BONDS BECAUSE YOU ARE, TO BE HONEST.
SHIT. ONLY REASON I'M HERE IS BECAUSE I'M TIRED OF BABYSITTING THOSE MONKEYS I RIDE WITH. IT'S ALL I CAN DO NOT TO MURDER THEM MYSELF SOMETIMES.
HEH. WELL, YEAH. I HAD TO CALL CRIBBS'S DAD TO SEE ABOUT GETTING HIM BAILED OUT AFTER HE CUT THAT SURFER BOY IN THE SHARK DIVE.
EVEN HIS DADDY TOLD ME TO FUCK OFF.

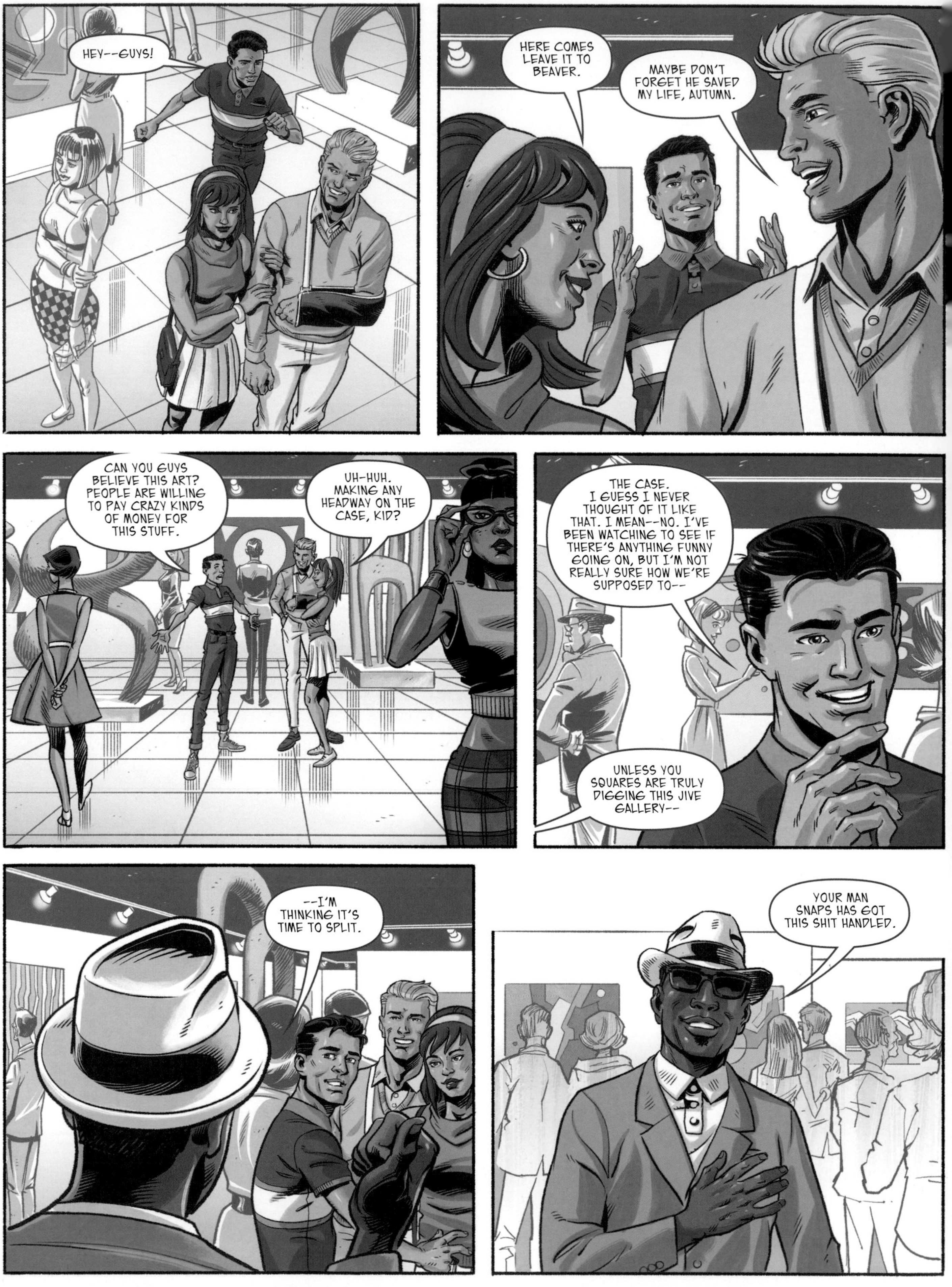
HEY--GUYS!
HERE COMES LEAVE IT TO BEAVER.
MAYBE DON'T FORGET HE SAVED MY LIFE, AUTUMN.
CAN YOU GUYS BELIEVE THIS ART? PEOPLE ARE WILLING TO PAY CRAZY KINDS OF MONEY FOR THIS STUFF.
UH-HUH. MAKING ANY HEADWAY ON THE CASE, KID?
THE CASE. I GUESS I NEVER THOUGHT OF IT LIKE THAT. I MEAN--NO. I'VE BEEN WATCHING TO SEE IF THERE'S ANYTHING FUNNY GOING ON, BUT I'M NOT REALLY SURE HOW WE'RE SUPPOSED TO--
UNLESS YOU SQUARES ARE TRULY DIGGING THIS JIVE GALLERY--
--I'M THINKING IT'S TIME TO SPLIT.
YOUR MAN SNAPS HAS GOT THIS SHIT HANDLED.

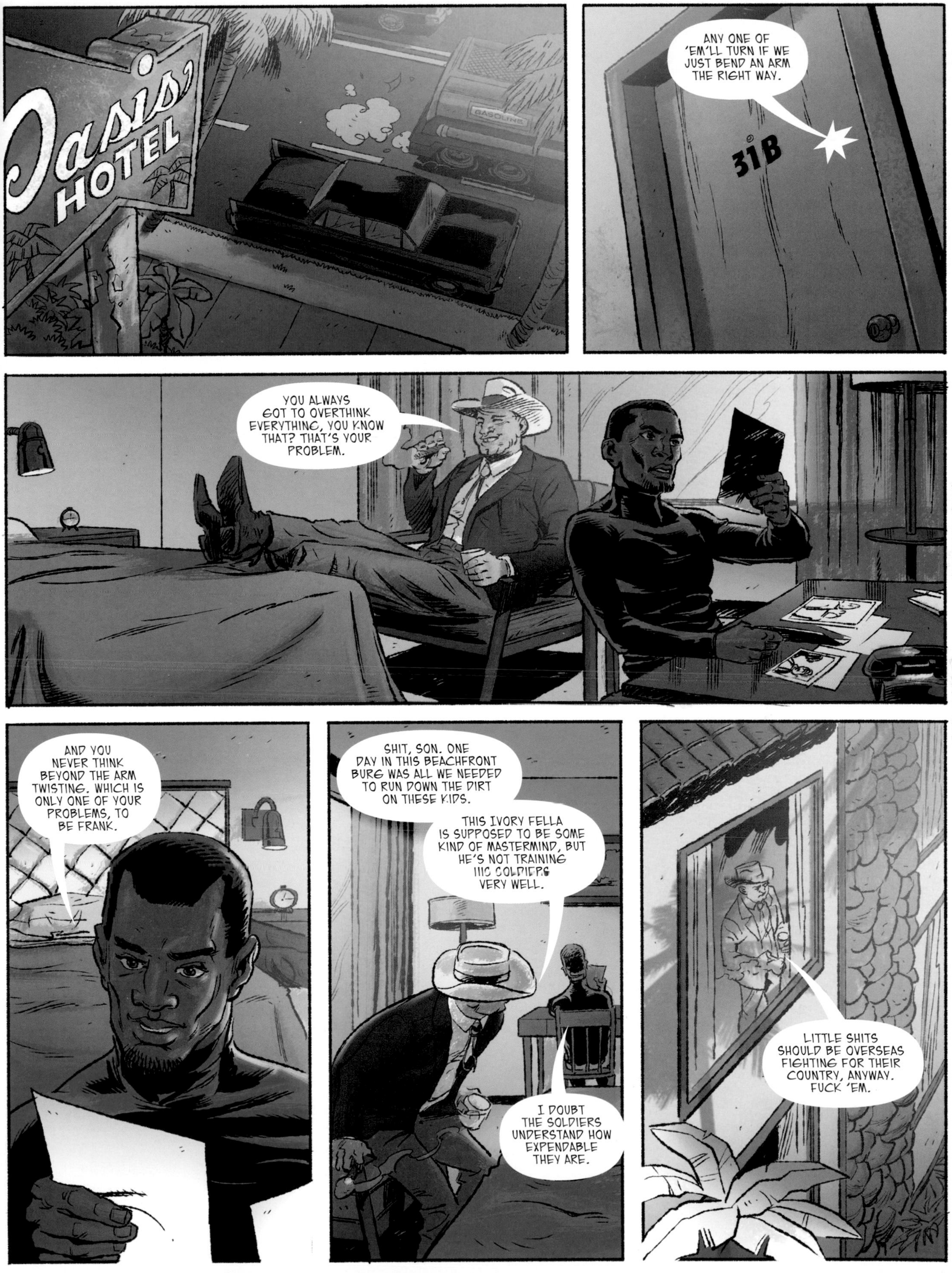

OASIS HOTEL
GASOLINE
ANY ONE OF 'EM'LL TURN IF WE JUST BEND AN ARM THE RIGHT WAY.
31B
YOU ALWAYS GOT TO OVERTHINK EVERYTHING, YOU KNOW THAT? THAT'S YOUR PROBLEM.
AND YOU NEVER THINK BEYOND THE ARM TWISTING. WHICH IS ONLY ONE OF YOUR PROBLEMS, TO BE FRANK.
SHIT, SON. ONE DAY IN THIS BEACHFRONT BURG WAS ALL WE NEEDED TO RUN DOWN THE DIRT ON THESE KIDS.
THIS IVORY FELLA IS SUPPOSED TO BE SOME KIND OF MASTERMIND, BUT HE'S NOT TRAINING HIS SOLDIERS VERY WELL.
I DOUBT THE SOLDIERS UNDERSTAND HOW EXPENDABLE THEY ARE.
LITTLE SHITS SHOULD BE OVERSEAS FIGHTING FOR THEIR COUNTRY, ANYWAY. FUCK 'EM.

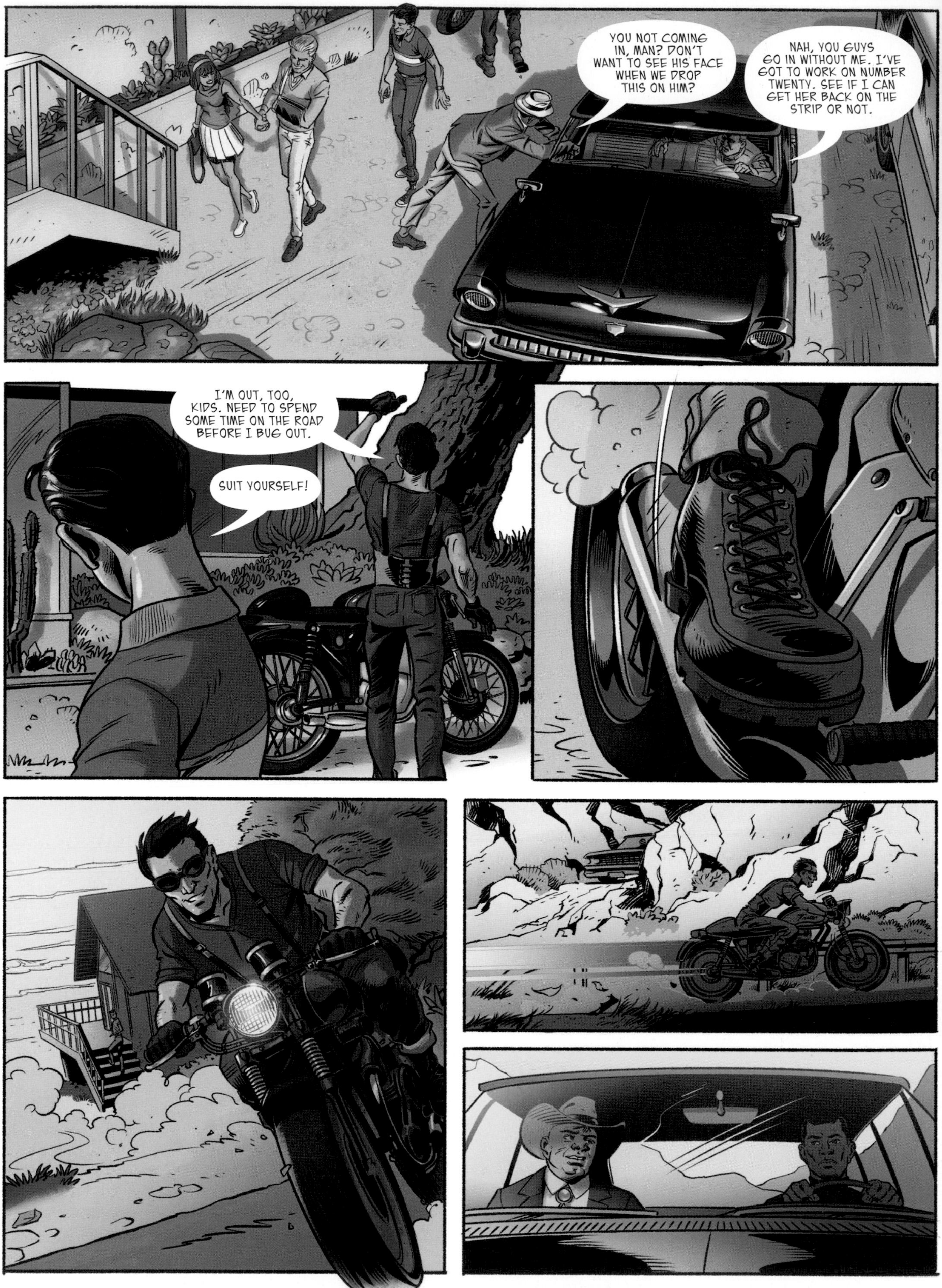
YOU NOT COMING IN, MAN? DON'T WANT TO SEE HIS FACE WHEN WE DROP THIS ON HIM?
NAH, YOU GUYS GO IN WITHOUT ME. I'VE GOT TO WORK ON NUMBER TWENTY. SEE IF I CAN GET HER BACK ON THE STRIP OR NOT.
I'M OUT, TOO, KIDS. NEED TO SPEND SOME TIME ON THE ROAD BEFORE I BUG OUT.
SUIT YOURSELF!

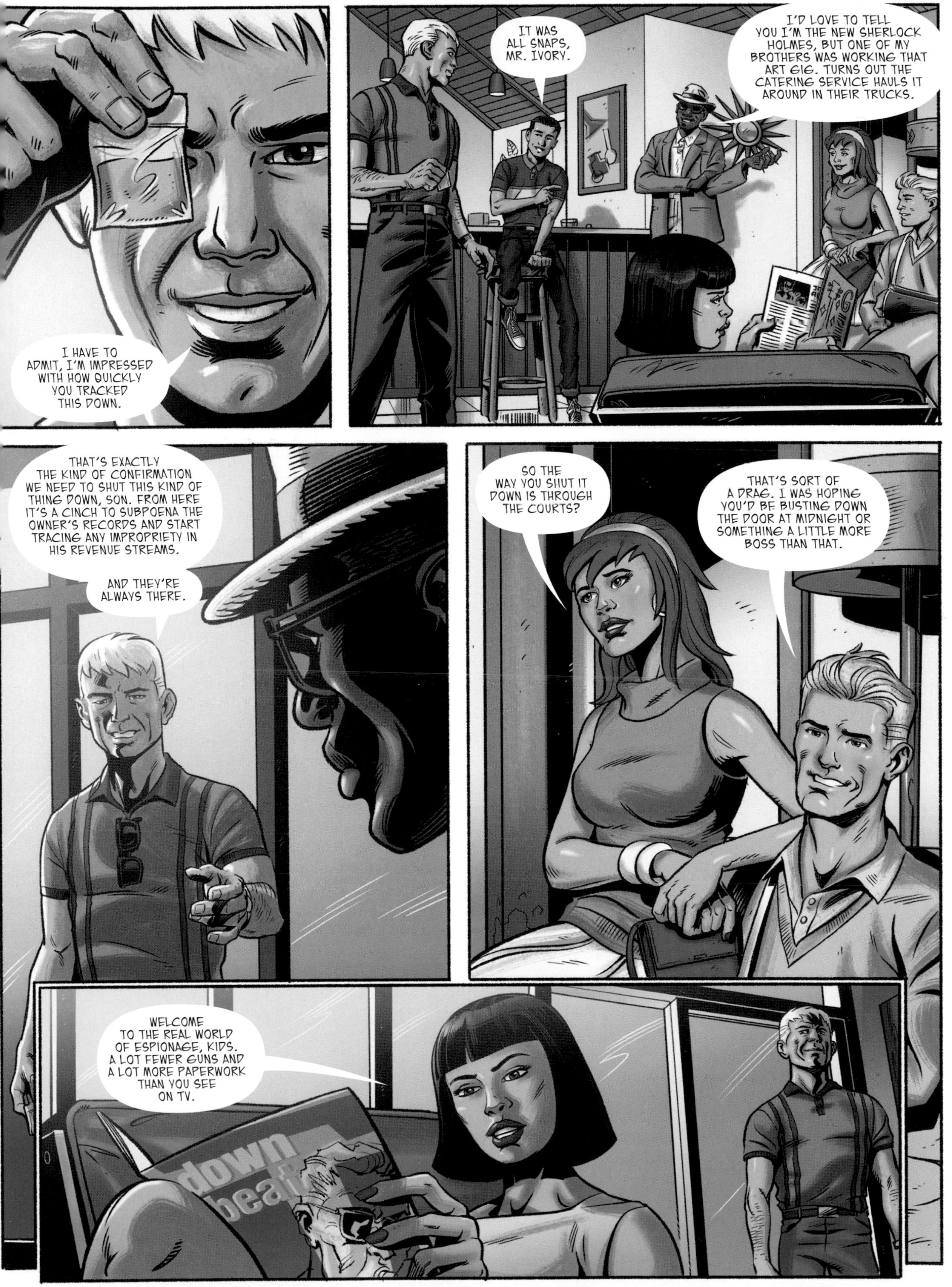
I HAVE TO ADMIT, I'M IMPRESSED WITH HOW QUICKLY YOU TRACKED THIS DOWN.
IT WAS ALL SNAPS, MR. IVORY.
I'D LOVE TO TELL YOU I'M THE NEW SHERLOCK HOLMES, BUT ONE OF MY BROTHERS WAS WORKING THAT ART GIG. TURNS OUT THE CATERING SERVICE HAULS IT AROUND IN THEIR TRUCKS.
THAT'S EXACTLY THE KIND OF CONFIRMATION WE NEED TO SHUT THIS KIND OF THING DOWN, SON. FROM HERE IT'S A CINCH TO SUBPOENA THE OWNER'S RECORDS AND START TRACING ANY IMPROPRIETY IN HIS REVENUE STREAMS.
AND THEY'RE ALWAYS THERE.
SO THE WAY YOU SHUT IT DOWN IS THROUGH THE COURTS?
THAT'S SORT OF A DRAG. I WAS HOPING YOU'D BE BUSTING DOWN THE DOOR AT MIDNIGHT OR SOMETHING A LITTLE MORE BOSS THAN THAT.
WELCOME TO THE REAL WORLD OF ESPIONAGE, KIDS. A LOT FEWER GUNS AND A LOT MORE PAPERWORK THAN YOU SEE ON TV.
down beat

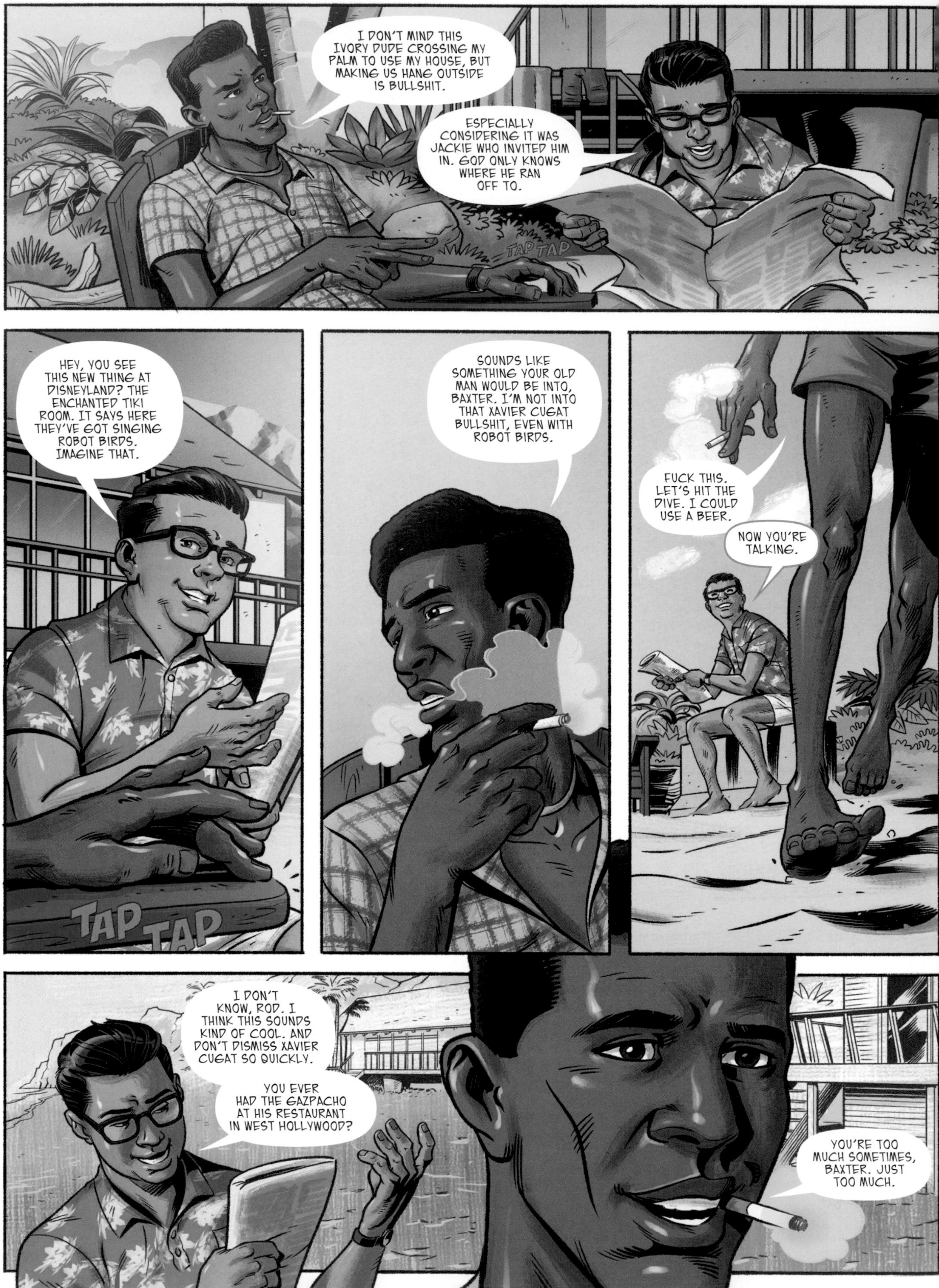

I DON'T MIND THIS IVORY DUDE CROSSING MY PALM TO USE MY HOUSE, BUT MAKING US HANG OUTSIDE IS BULLSHIT.
ESPECIALLY CONSIDERING IT WAS JACKIE WHO INVITED HIM IN. GOD ONLY KNOWS WHERE HE RAN OFF TO.
TAP TAP
HEY, YOU SEE THIS NEW THING AT DISNEYLAND? THE ENCHANTED TIKI ROOM. IT SAYS HERE THEY'VE GOT SINGING ROBOT BIRDS. IMAGINE THAT.
TAP TAP
SOUNDS LIKE SOMETHING YOUR OLD MAN WOULD BE INTO, BAXTER. I'M NOT INTO THAT XAVIER CUGAT BULLSHIT, EVEN WITH ROBOT BIRDS.
FUCK THIS. LET'S HIT THE DIVE. I COULD USE A BEER.
NOW YOU'RE TALKING.
I DON'T KNOW, ROD. I THINK THIS SOUNDS KIND OF COOL. AND DON'T DISMISS XAVIER CUGAT SO QUICKLY.
YOU EVER HAD THE GAZPACHO AT HIS RESTAURANT IN WEST HOLLYWOOD?
YOU'RE TOO MUCH SOMETIMES, BAXTER. JUST TOO MUCH.

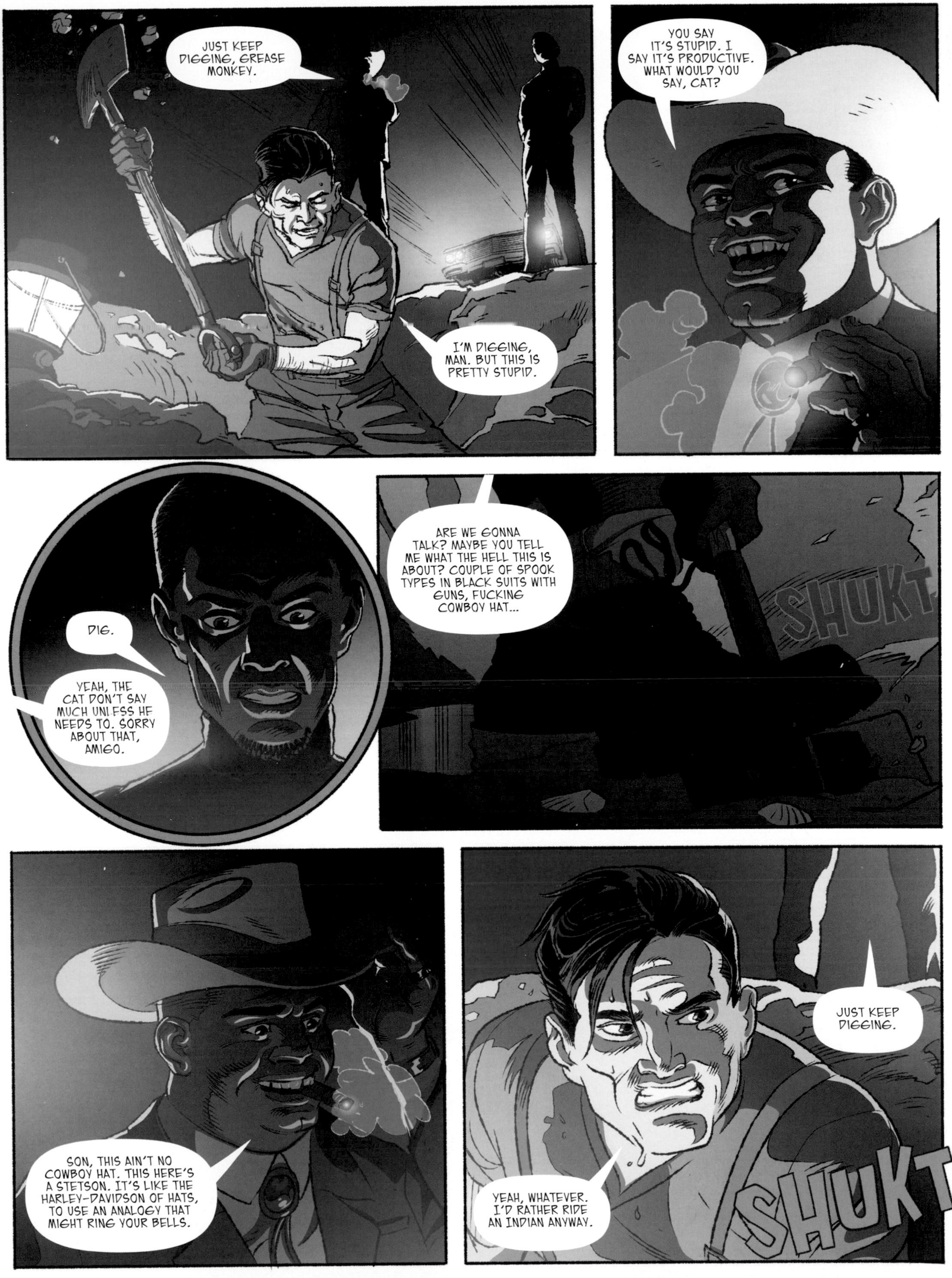
JUST KEEP DIGGING, GREASE MONKEY.
I'M DIGGING, MAN. BUT THIS IS PRETTY STUPID.
YOU SAY IT'S STUPID. I SAY IT'S PRODUCTIVE. WHAT WOULD YOU SAY, CAT?
DIG.
YEAH, THE CAT DON'T SAY MUCH UNLESS HE NEEDS TO. SORRY ABOUT THAT, AMIGO.
ARE WE GONNA TALK? MAYBE YOU TELL ME WHAT THE HELL THIS IS ABOUT? COUPLE OF SPOOK TYPES IN BLACK SUITS WITH GUNS, FUCKING COWBOY HAT...
SHUKT
SON, THIS AIN'T NO COWBOY HAT. THIS HERE'S A STETSON. IT'S LIKE THE HARLEY-DAVIDSON OF HATS, TO USE AN ANALOGY THAT MIGHT RING YOUR BELLS.
JUST KEEP DIGGING.
YEAH, WHATEVER. I'D RATHER RIDE AN INDIAN ANYWAY.
SHUKT

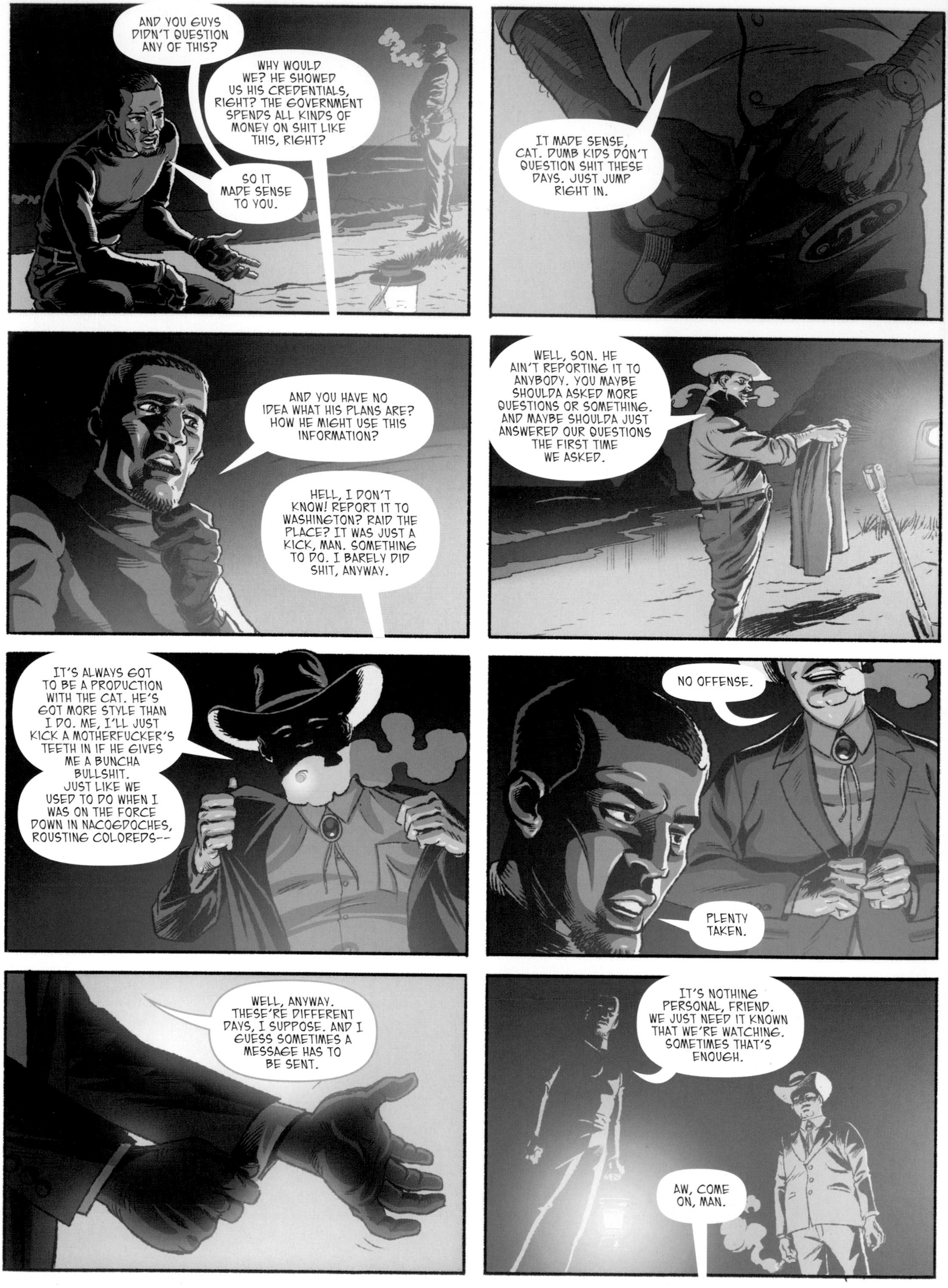
AND YOU GUYS DIDN'T QUESTION ANY OF THIS?
WHY WOULD WE? HE SHOWED US HIS CREDENTIALS, RIGHT? THE GOVERNMENT SPENDS ALL KINDS OF MONEY ON SHIT LIKE THIS, RIGHT?
SO IT MADE SENSE TO YOU.
IT MADE SENSE, CAT. DUMB KIDS DON'T QUESTION SHIT THESE DAYS. JUST JUMP RIGHT IN.
AND YOU HAVE NO IDEA WHAT HIS PLANS ARE? HOW HE MIGHT USE THIS INFORMATION?
HELL, I DON'T KNOW! REPORT IT TO WASHINGTON? RAID THE PLACE? IT WAS JUST A KICK, MAN. SOMETHING TO DO. I BARELY DID SHIT, ANYWAY.
WELL, SON. HE AIN'T REPORTING IT TO ANYBODY. YOU MAYBE SHOULDA ASKED MORE QUESTIONS OR SOMETHING. AND MAYBE SHOULDA JUST ANSWERED OUR QUESTIONS THE FIRST TIME WE ASKED.
IT'S ALWAYS GOT TO BE A PRODUCTION WITH THE CAT. HE'S GOT MORE STYLE THAN I DO. ME, I'LL JUST KICK A MOTHERFUCKER'S TEETH IN IF HE GIVES ME A BUNCHA BULLSHIT.
JUST LIKE WE USED TO DO WHEN I WAS ON THE FORCE DOWN IN NACOGDOCHES, ROUSTING COLOREDS--
NO OFFENSE.
PLENTY TAKEN.
WELL, ANYWAY. THESE'RE DIFFERENT DAYS, I SUPPOSE. AND I GUESS SOMETIMES A MESSAGE HAS TO BE SENT.
IT'S NOTHING PERSONAL, FRIEND. WE JUST NEED IT KNOWN THAT WE'RE WATCHING. SOMETIMES THAT'S ENOUGH.
AW, COME ON, MAN.

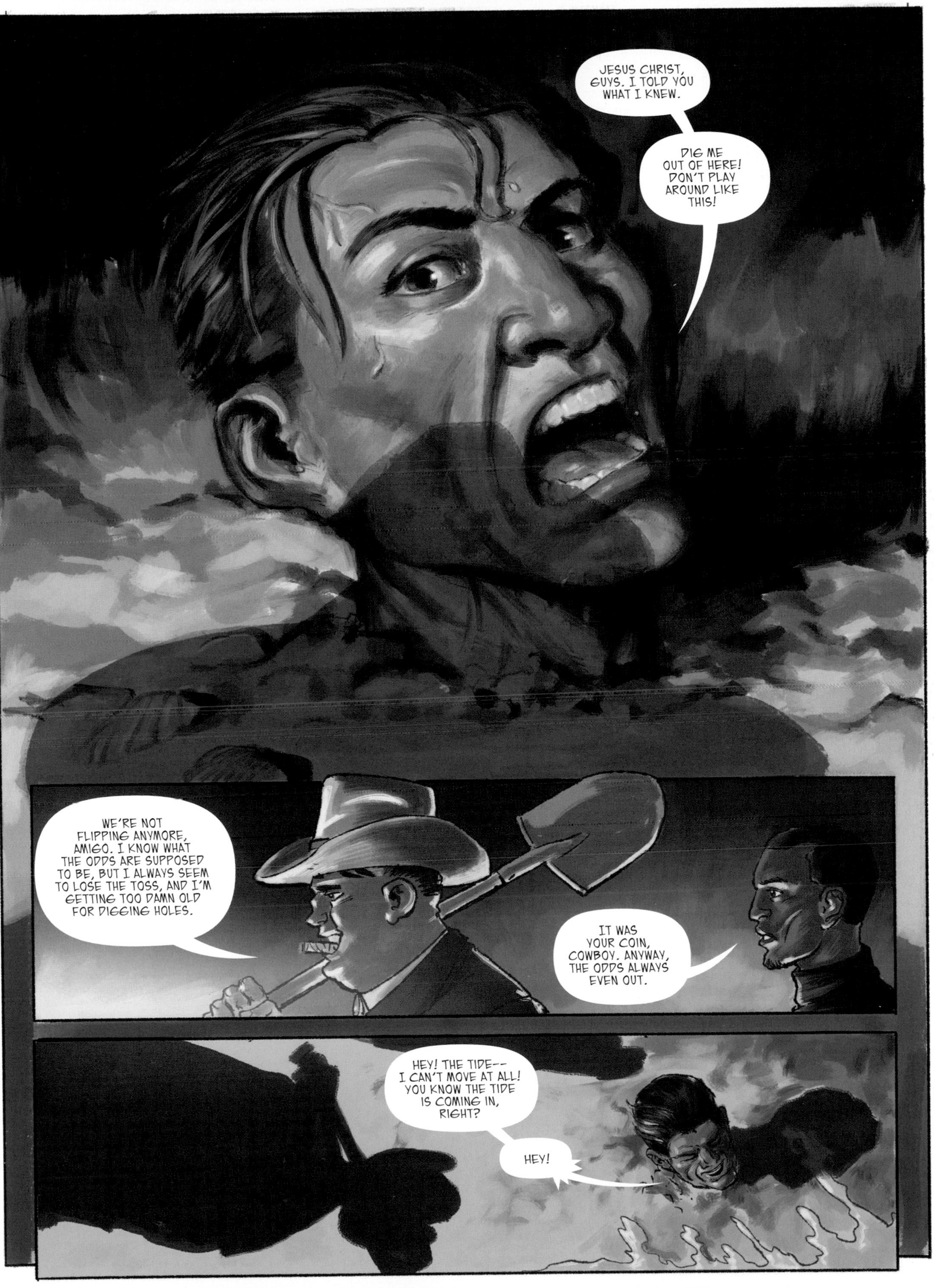
JESUS CHRIST, GUYS. I TOLD YOU WHAT I KNEW.
DIG ME OUT OF HERE! DON'T PLAY AROUND LIKE THIS!
WE'RE NOT FLIPPING ANYMORE, AMIGO. I KNOW WHAT THE ODDS ARE SUPPOSED TO BE, BUT I ALWAYS SEEM TO LOSE THE TOSS, AND I'M GETTING TOO DAMN OLD FOR DIGGING HOLES.
IT WAS YOUR COIN, COWBOY. ANYWAY, THE ODDS ALWAYS EVEN OUT.
HEY! THE TIDE-- I CAN'T MOVE AT ALL! YOU KNOW THE TIDE IS COMING IN, RIGHT?
HEY!

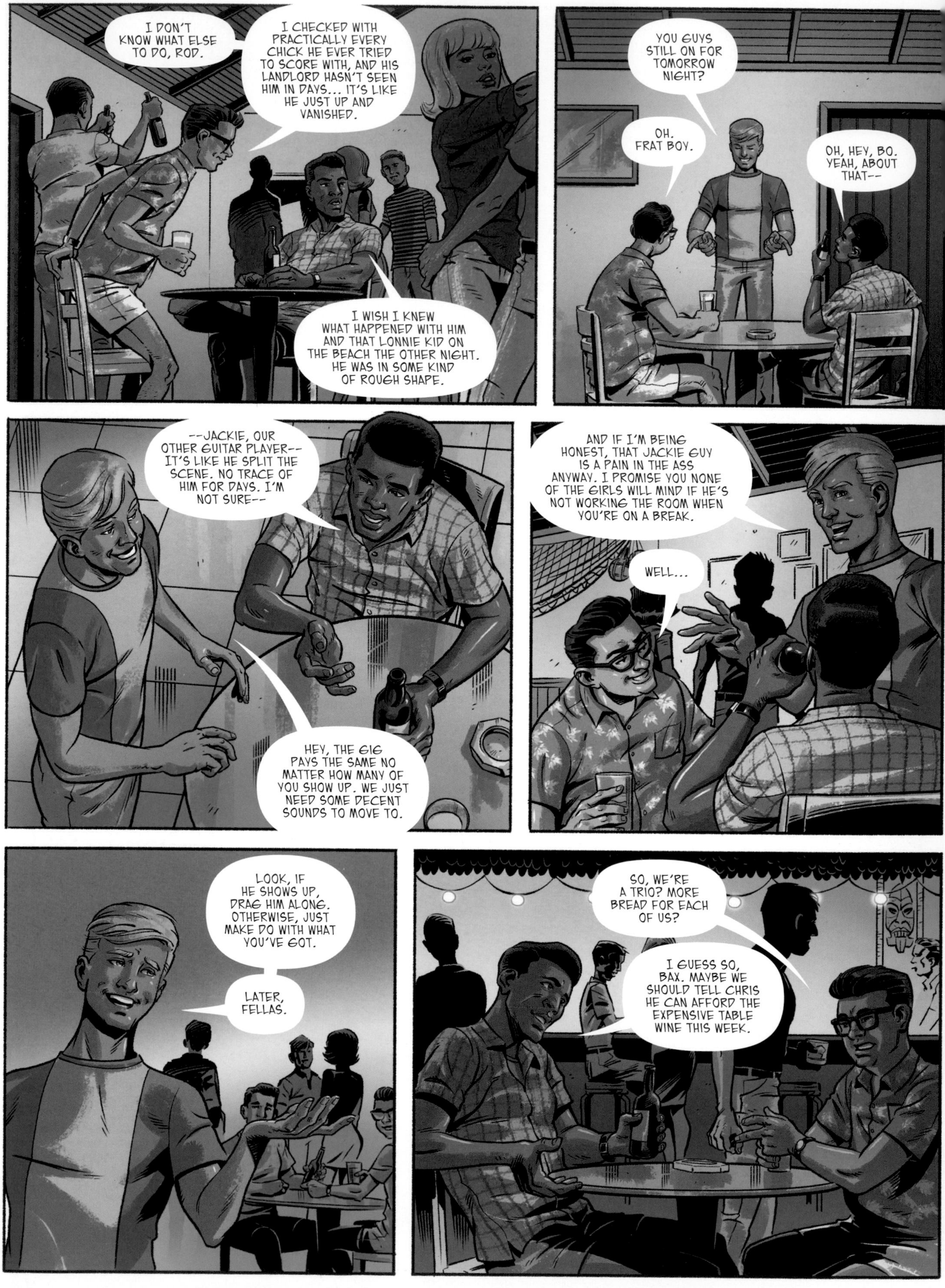

I DON'T KNOW WHAT ELSE TO DO, ROD.
I CHECKED WITH PRACTICALLY EVERY CHICK HE EVER TRIED TO SCORE WITH, AND HIS LANDLORD HASN'T SEEN HIM IN DAYS... IT'S LIKE HE JUST UP AND VANISHED.
I WISH I KNEW WHAT HAPPENED WITH HIM AND THAT LONNIE KID ON THE BEACH THE OTHER NIGHT. HE WAS IN SOME KIND OF ROUGH SHAPE.
YOU GUYS STILL ON FOR TOMORROW NIGHT?
OH. FRAT BOY.
OH, HEY, BO. YEAH, ABOUT THAT--
--JACKIE, OUR OTHER GUITAR PLAYER-- IT'S LIKE HE SPLIT THE SCENE. NO TRACE OF HIM FOR DAYS. I'M NOT SURE--
HEY, THE GIG PAYS THE SAME NO MATTER HOW MANY OF YOU SHOW UP. WE JUST NEED SOME DECENT SOUNDS TO MOVE TO.
AND IF I'M BEING HONEST, THAT JACKIE GUY IS A PAIN IN THE ASS ANYWAY. I PROMISE YOU NONE OF THE GIRLS WILL MIND IF HE'S NOT WORKING THE ROOM WHEN YOU'RE ON A BREAK.
WELL...
LOOK, IF HE SHOWS UP, DRAG HIM ALONG. OTHERWISE, JUST MAKE DO WITH WHAT YOU'VE GOT.
LATER, FELLAS.
SO, WE'RE A TRIO? MORE BREAD FOR EACH OF US?
I GUESS SO, BAX. MAYBE WE SHOULD TELL CHRIS HE CAN AFFORD THE EXPENSIVE TABLE WINE THIS WEEK.

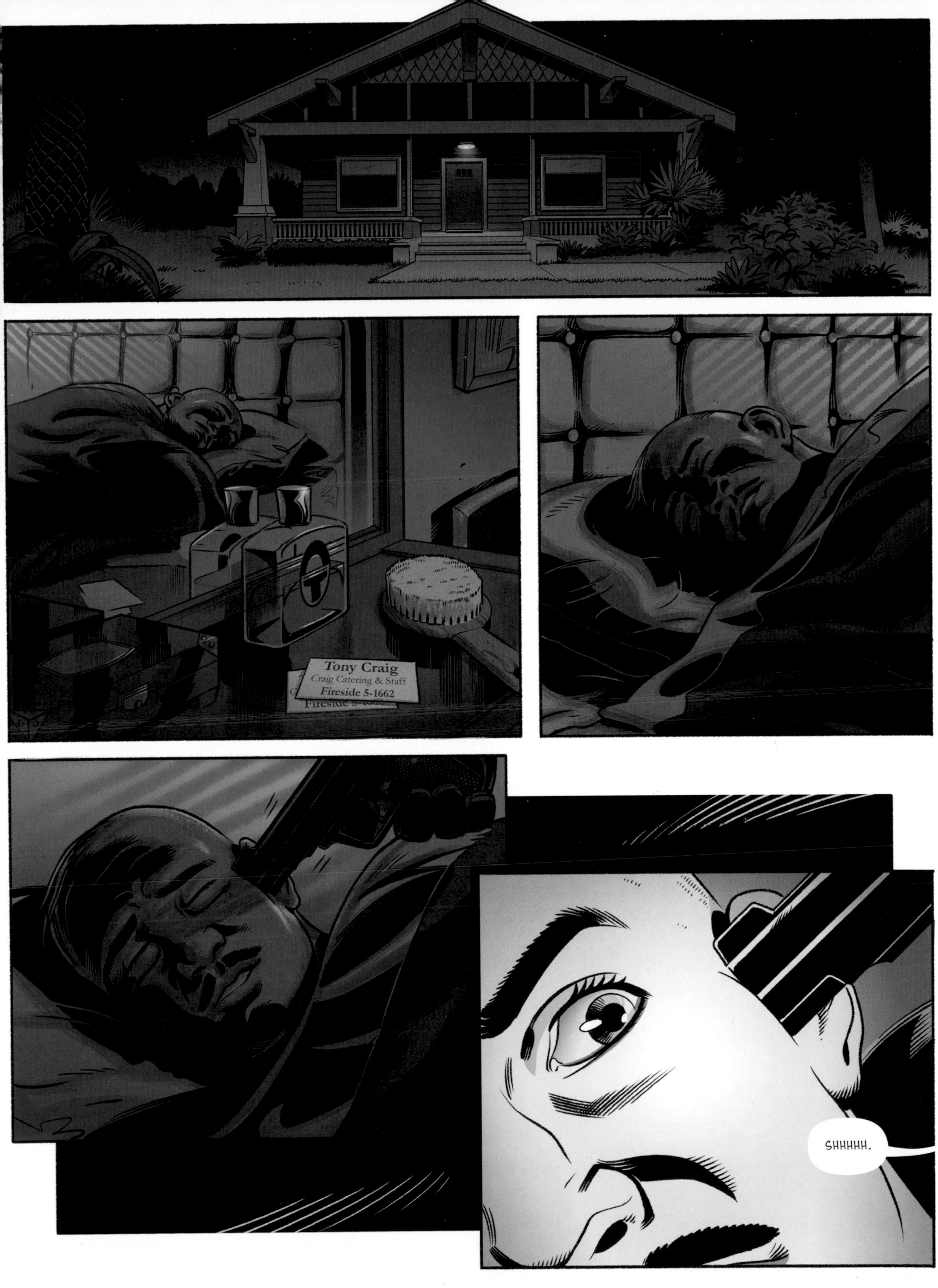
Tony Craig
Craig Catering & Staff
Fireside 5-1662
SHHHHH.

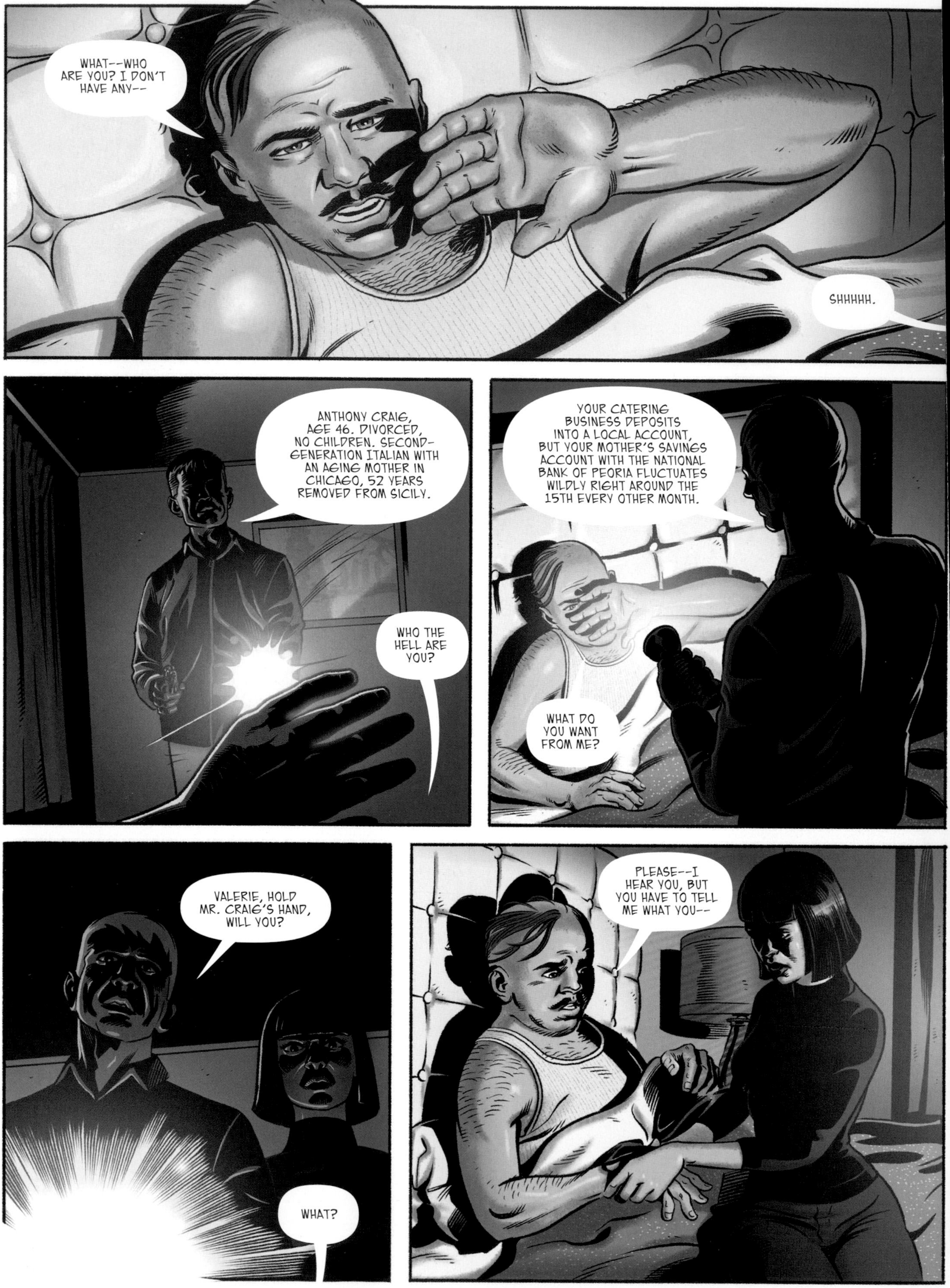
WHAT--WHO ARE YOU? I DON'T HAVE ANY--
SHHHHH.
ANTHONY CRAIG, AGE 46. DIVORCED, NO CHILDREN. SECOND-GENERATION ITALIAN WITH AN AGING MOTHER IN CHICAGO, 52 YEARS REMOVED FROM SICILY.
WHO THE HELL ARE YOU?
YOUR CATERING BUSINESS DEPOSITS INTO A LOCAL ACCOUNT, BUT YOUR MOTHER'S SAVINGS ACCOUNT WITH THE NATIONAL BANK OF PEORIA FLUCTUATES WILDLY RIGHT AROUND THE 15TH EVERY OTHER MONTH.
WHAT DO YOU WANT FROM ME?
VALERIE, HOLD MR. CRAIG'S HAND, WILL YOU?
WHAT?
PLEASE--I HEAR YOU, BUT YOU HAVE TO TELL ME WHAT YOU--

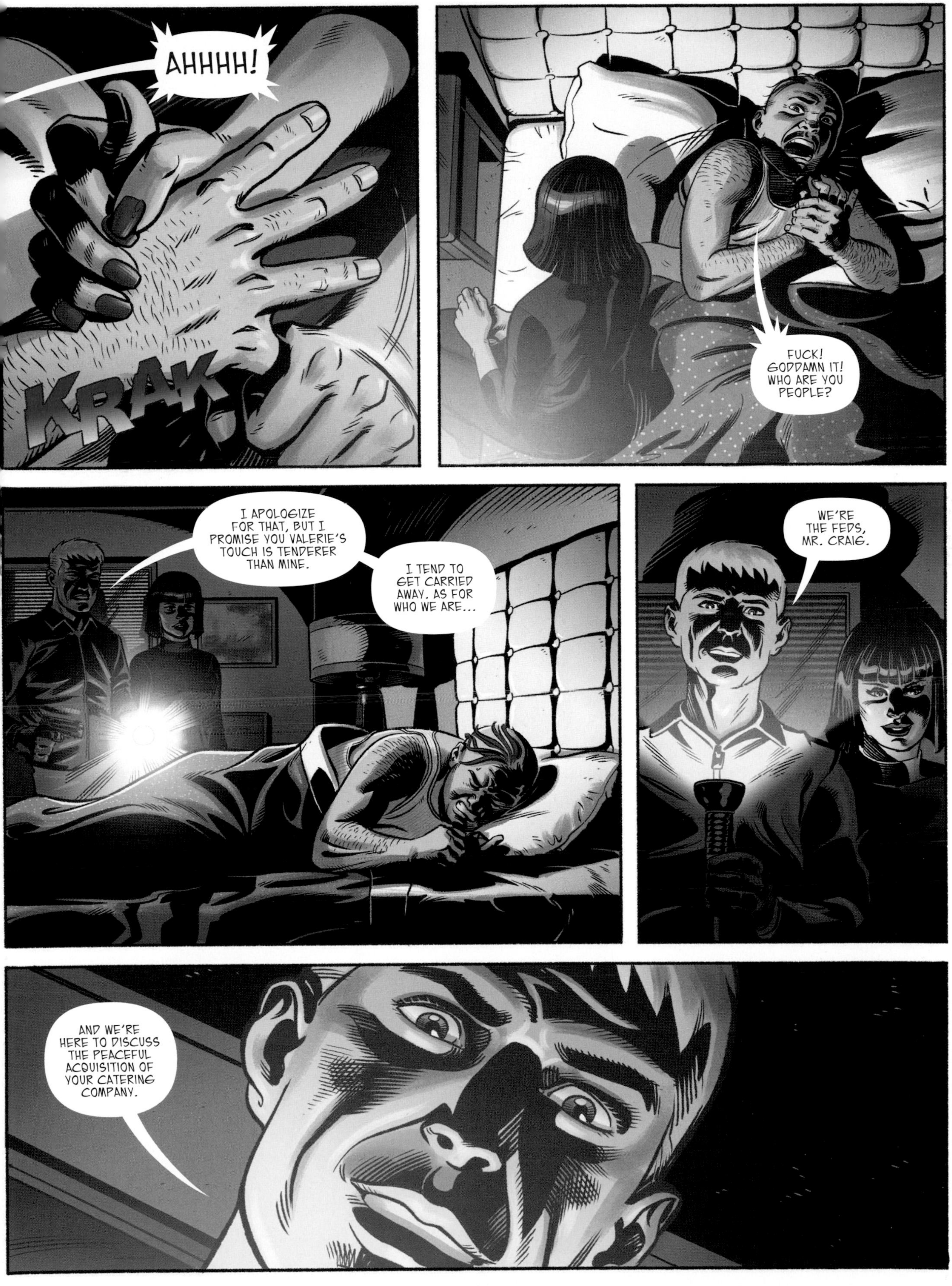
AHHHH!
KRAK
FUCK! GODDAMN IT! WHO ARE YOU PEOPLE?
I APOLOGIZE FOR THAT, BUT I PROMISE YOU VALERIE'S TOUCH IS TENDERER THAN MINE.
I TEND TO GET CARRIED AWAY. AS FOR WHO WE ARE...
WE'RE THE FEDS, MR. CRAIG.
AND WE'RE HERE TO DISCUSS THE PEACEFUL ACQUISITION OF YOUR CATERING COMPANY.

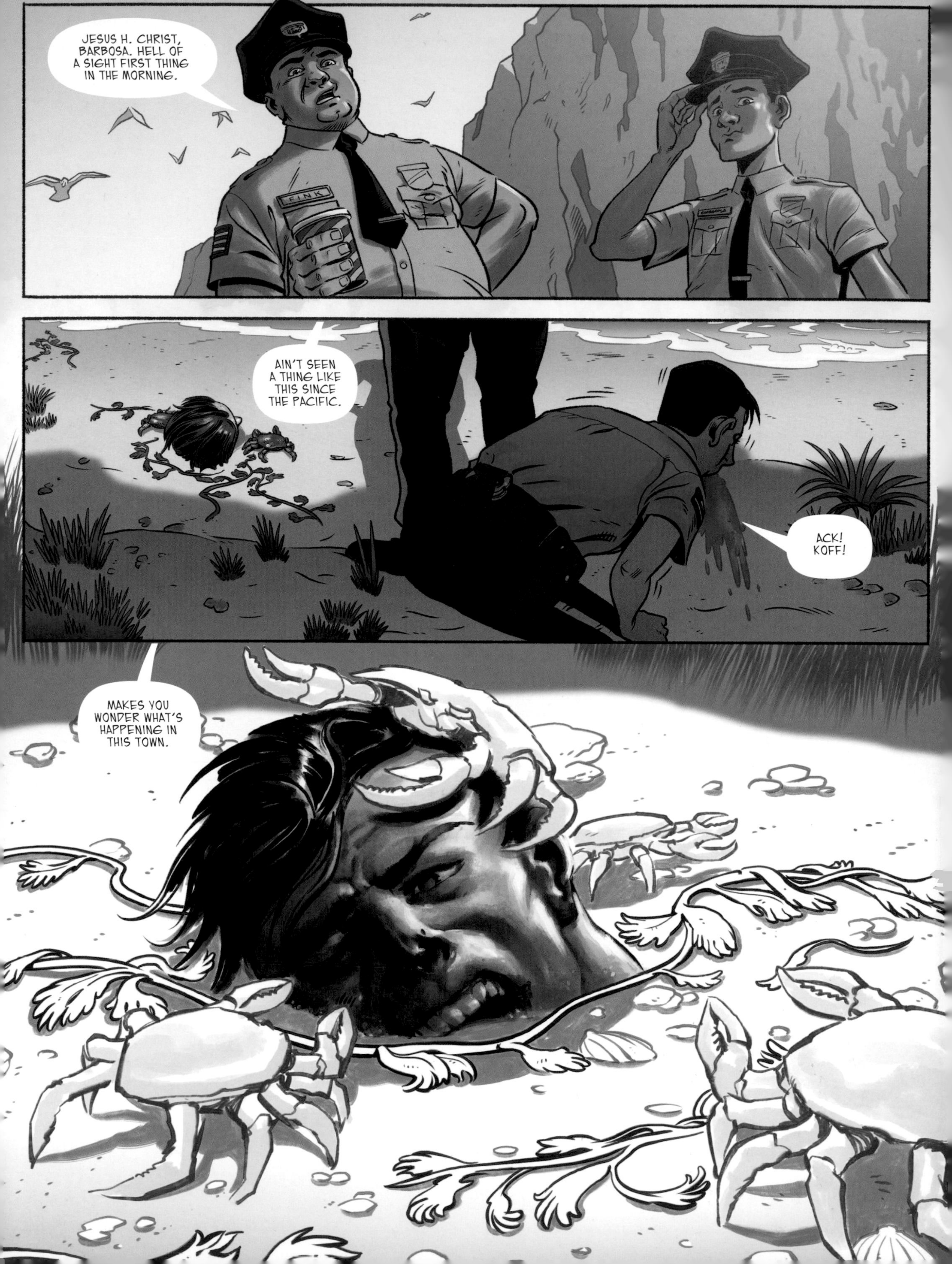
JESUS H. CHRIST, BARBOSA. HELL OF A SIGHT FIRST THING IN THE MORNING.
FINK
AIN'T SEEN A THING LIKE THIS SINCE THE PACIFIC.
ACK! KOFF!
MAKES YOU WONDER WHAT'S HAPPENING IN THIS TOWN.

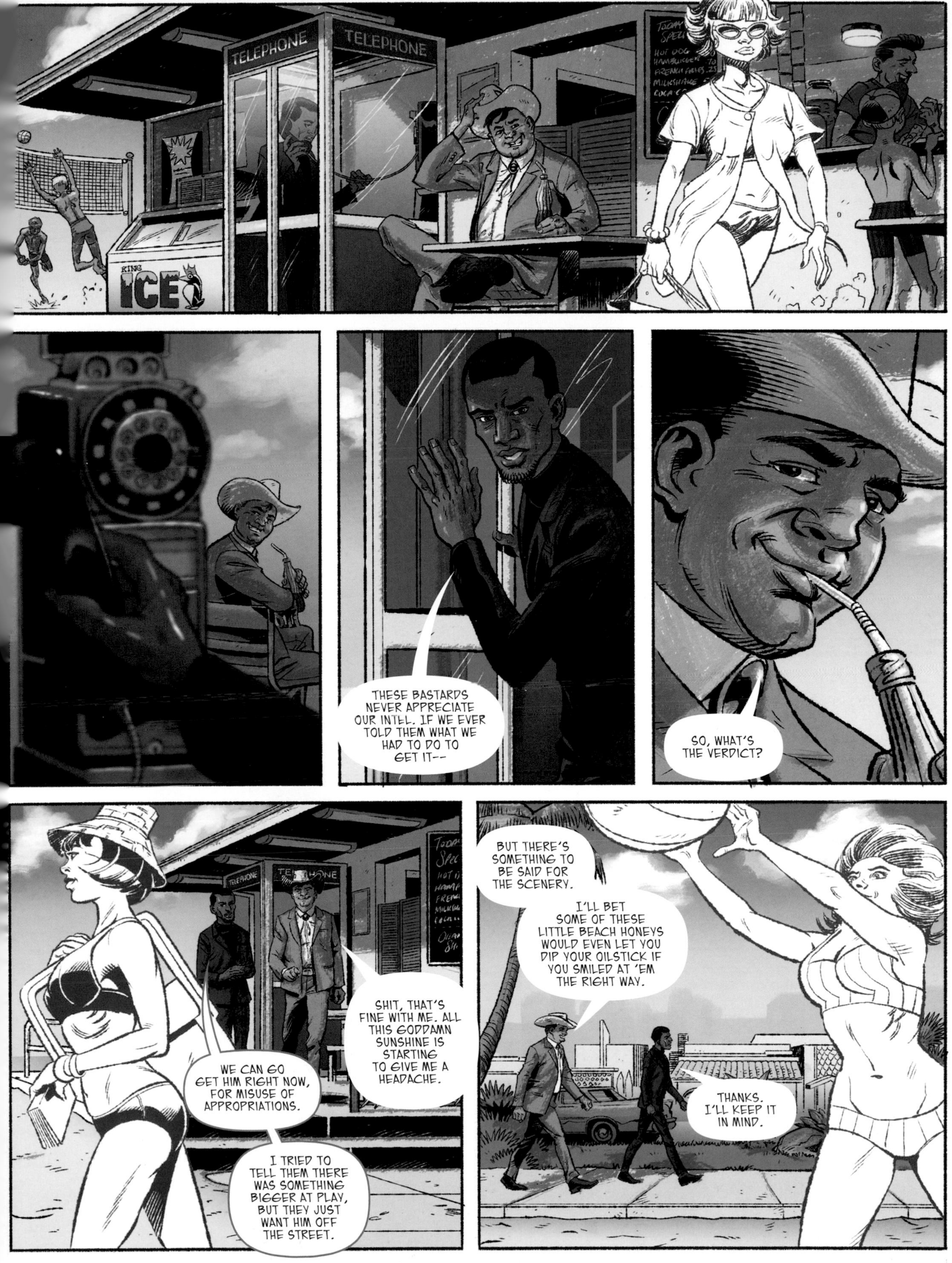
TELEPHONE
TELEPHONE
KING ICE
THESE BASTARDS NEVER APPRECIATE OUR INTEL. IF WE EVER TOLD THEM WHAT WE HAD TO DO TO GET IT--
SO, WHAT'S THE VERDICT?
WE CAN GO GET HIM RIGHT NOW, FOR MISUSE OF APPROPRIATIONS.
I TRIED TO TELL THEM THERE WAS SOMETHING BIGGER AT PLAY, BUT THEY JUST WANT HIM OFF THE STREET.
SHIT, THAT'S FINE WITH ME. ALL THIS GODDAMN SUNSHINE IS STARTING TO GIVE ME A HEADACHE.
BUT THERE'S SOMETHING TO BE SAID FOR THE SCENERY.
I'LL BET SOME OF THESE LITTLE BEACH HONEYS WOULD EVEN LET YOU DIP YOUR OILSTICK IF YOU SMILED AT 'EM THE RIGHT WAY.
THANKS. I'LL KEEP IT IN MIND.

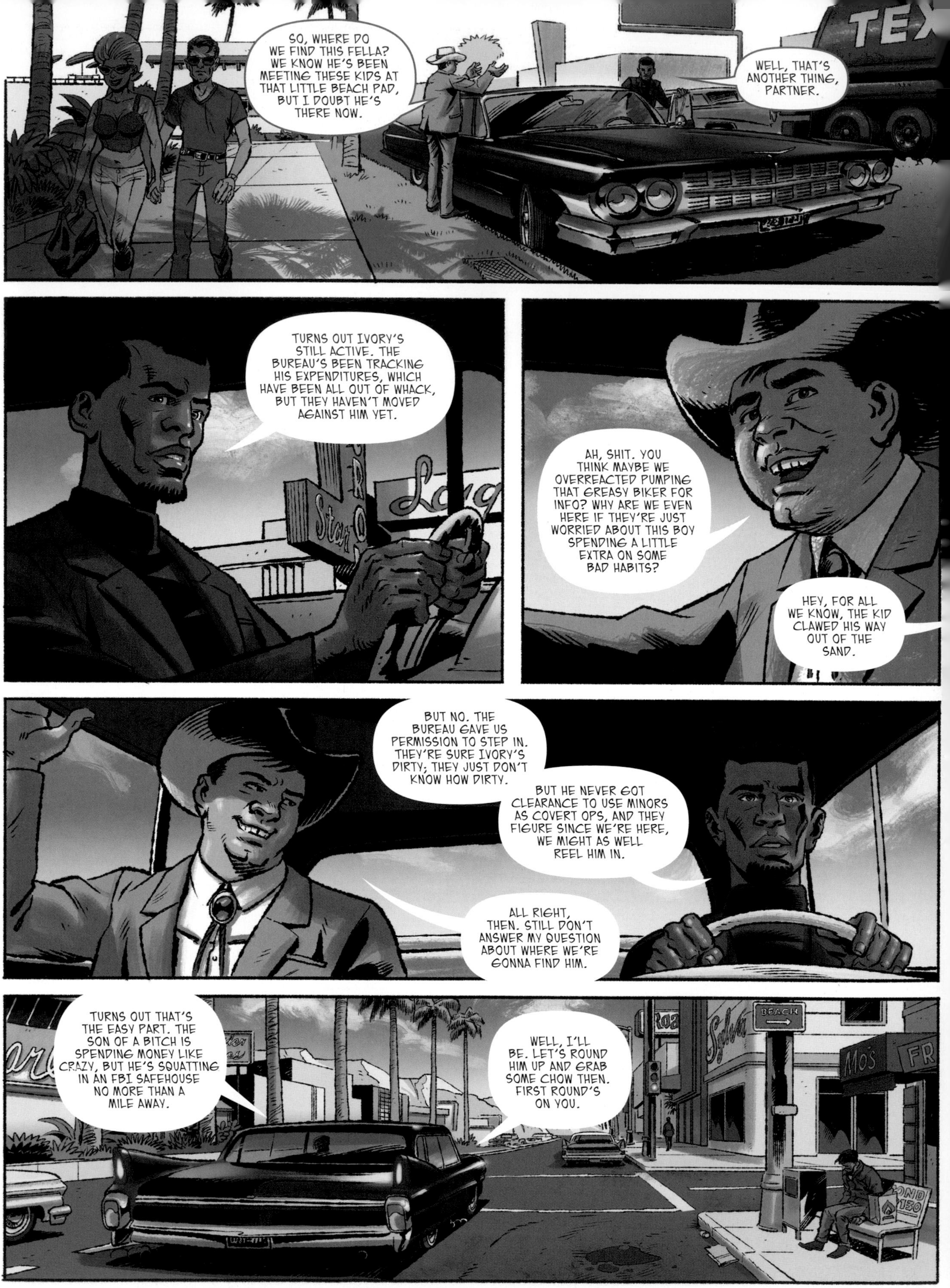

SO, WHERE DO WE FIND THIS FELLA? WE KNOW HE'S BEEN MEETING THESE KIDS AT THAT LITTLE BEACH PAD, BUT I DOUBT HE'S THERE NOW.
WELL, THAT'S ANOTHER THING, PARTNER.
TURNS OUT IVORY'S STILL ACTIVE. THE BUREAU'S BEEN TRACKING HIS EXPENDITURES, WHICH HAVE BEEN ALL OUT OF WHACK, BUT THEY HAVEN'T MOVED AGAINST HIM YET.
AH, SHIT. YOU THINK MAYBE WE OVERREACTED PUMPING THAT GREASY BIKER FOR INFO? WHY ARE WE EVEN HERE IF THEY'RE JUST WORRIED ABOUT THIS BOY SPENDING A LITTLE EXTRA ON SOME BAD HABITS?
HEY, FOR ALL WE KNOW, THE KID CLAWED HIS WAY OUT OF THE SAND.
BUT NO. THE BUREAU GAVE US PERMISSION TO STEP IN. THEY'RE SURE IVORY'S DIRTY; THEY JUST DON'T KNOW HOW DIRTY.
BUT HE NEVER GOT CLEARANCE TO USE MINORS AS COVERT OPS, AND THEY FIGURE SINCE WE'RE HERE, WE MIGHT AS WELL REEL HIM IN.
ALL RIGHT, THEN. STILL DON'T ANSWER MY QUESTION ABOUT WHERE WE'RE GONNA FIND HIM.
TURNS OUT THAT'S THE EASY PART. THE SON OF A BITCH IS SPENDING MONEY LIKE CRAZY, BUT HE'S SQUATTING IN AN FBI SAFEHOUSE NO MORE THAN A MILE AWAY.
WELL, I'LL BE. LET'S ROUND HIM UP AND GRAB SOME CHOW THEN. FIRST ROUND'S ON YOU.
BEACH

CRAIG KEPT BETTER RECORDS ON HIS HEROIN DISTRIBUTION THAN ON HIS CATERING RECEIPTS.

SO EVERYTHING RUNS THE WAY YOU THOUGHT IT DID?

BASICALLY. CRAIG WAS SLOPPY WITH HIS DISTRIBUTION, BUT WHEN IT CAME TO PURCHASING, HE RAN THROUGH SO MANY CHANNELS IT WOULD BE ALMOST IMPOSSIBLE TO CONNECT HIM WITH HIS SUPPLIER.

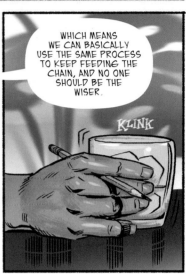

WHICH MEANS WE CAN BASICALLY USE THE SAME PROCESS TO KEEP FEEDING THE CHAIN, AND NO ONE SHOULD BE THE WISER.

KLINK

THIS IS QUITE A STEP UP FROM THE OPERATION IN THE VILLAGE, SCOTT. I HOPE WE CAN KEEP THIS ONE RUNNING WITHOUT LEAVING SO MANY CORPSES IN OUR WAKE.

THE OFFICIAL REPORT SAYS I SHUT THAT OPERATION DOWN AND PREVENTED MORE NEEDLESS DEATHS, VALERIE. YOU WERE A NAMELESS OPERATIVE. LET'S MAKE SURE IT ALL STAYS THAT--

KNOCK KNOCK KNOCK

WHO THE HELL COULD THAT BE?

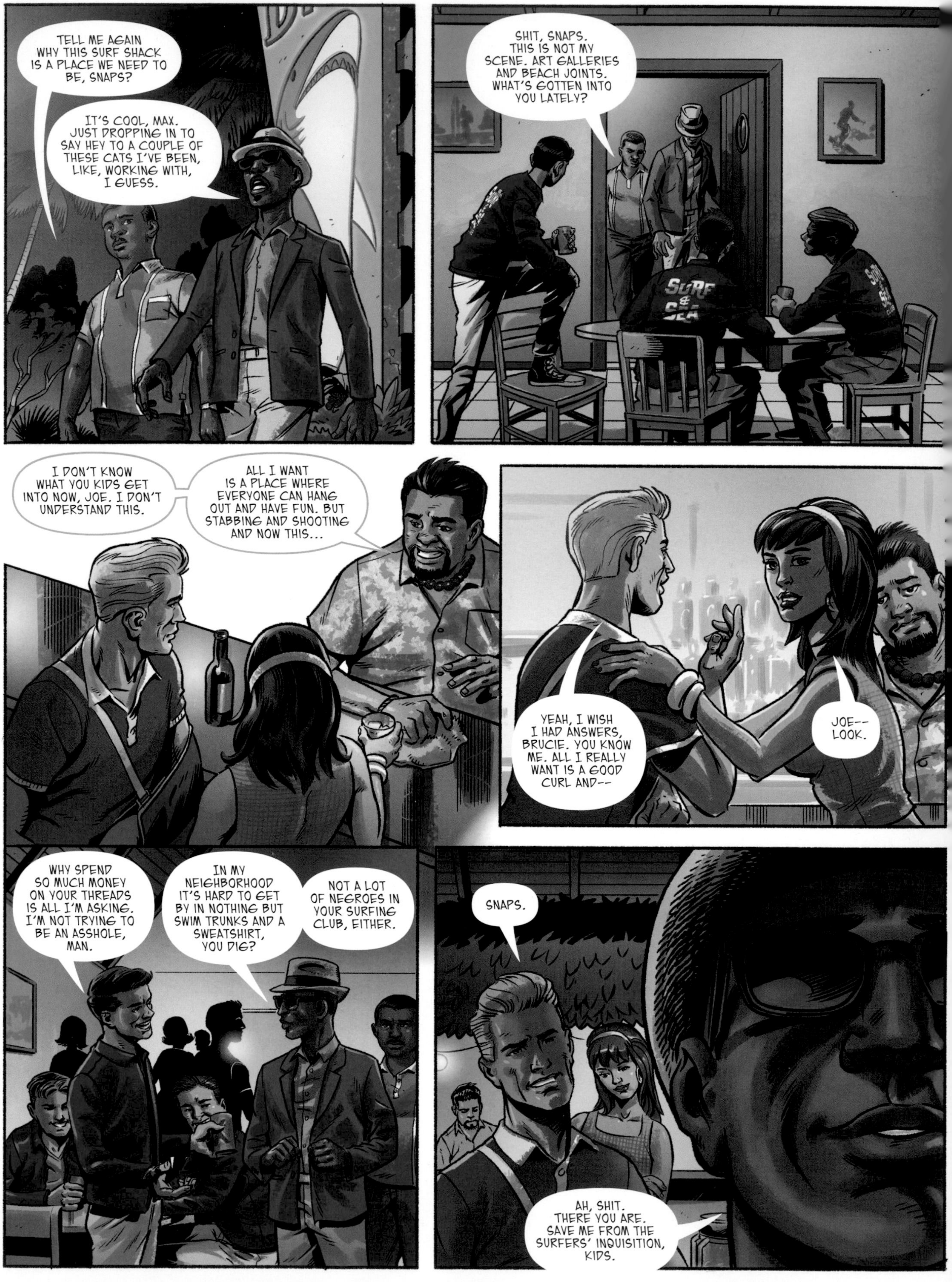
TELL ME AGAIN WHY THIS SURF SHACK IS A PLACE WE NEED TO BE, SNAPS?
IT'S COOL, MAX. JUST DROPPING IN TO SAY HEY TO A COUPLE OF THESE CATS I'VE BEEN, LIKE, WORKING WITH, I GUESS.
SHIT, SNAPS. THIS IS NOT MY SCENE. ART GALLERIES AND BEACH JOINTS. WHAT'S GOTTEN INTO YOU LATELY?
SURF & SEA
I DON'T KNOW WHAT YOU KIDS GET INTO NOW, JOE. I DON'T UNDERSTAND THIS.
ALL I WANT IS A PLACE WHERE EVERYONE CAN HANG OUT AND HAVE FUN. BUT STABBING AND SHOOTING AND NOW THIS...
YEAH, I WISH I HAD ANSWERS, BRUCIE. YOU KNOW ME. ALL I REALLY WANT IS A GOOD CURL AND--
JOE-- LOOK.
WHY SPEND SO MUCH MONEY ON YOUR THREADS IS ALL I'M ASKING. I'M NOT TRYING TO BE AN ASSHOLE, MAN.
IN MY NEIGHBORHOOD IT'S HARD TO GET BY IN NOTHING BUT SWIM TRUNKS AND A SWEATSHIRT, YOU DIG?
NOT A LOT OF NEGROES IN YOUR SURFING CLUB, EITHER.
SNAPS.
AH, SHIT. THERE YOU ARE. SAVE ME FROM THE SURFERS' INQUISITION, KIDS.

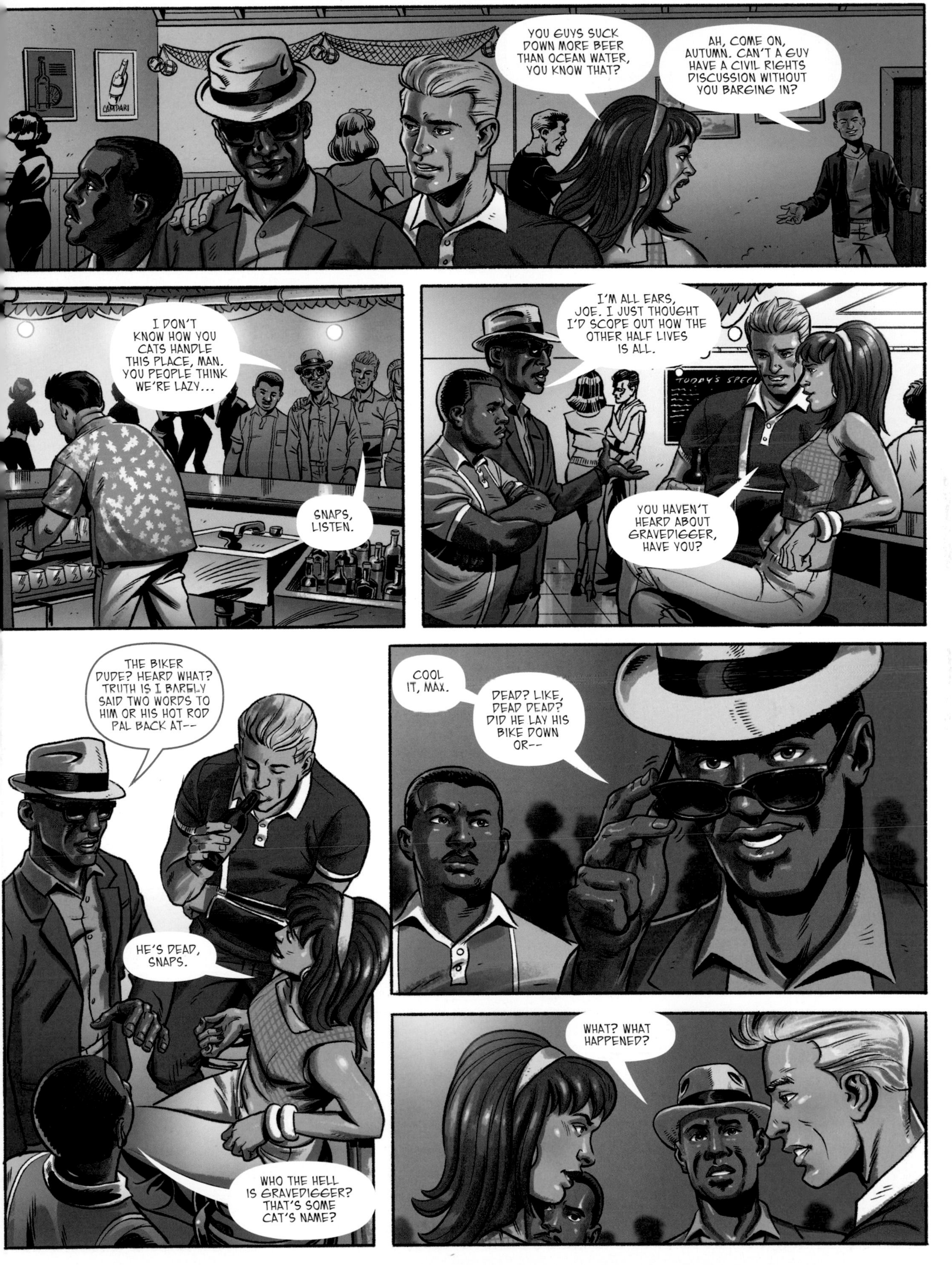

YOU GUYS SUCK DOWN MORE BEER THAN OCEAN WATER, YOU KNOW THAT?
AH, COME ON, AUTUMN. CAN'T A GUY HAVE A CIVIL RIGHTS DISCUSSION WITHOUT YOU BARGING IN?
I DON'T KNOW HOW YOU CATS HANDLE THIS PLACE, MAN. YOU PEOPLE THINK WE'RE LAZY...
SNAPS, LISTEN.
I'M ALL EARS, JOE. I JUST THOUGHT I'D SCOPE OUT HOW THE OTHER HALF LIVES IS ALL.
YOU HAVEN'T HEARD ABOUT GRAVEDIGGER, HAVE YOU?
THE BIKER DUDE? HEARD WHAT? TRUTH IS I BARELY SAID TWO WORDS TO HIM OR HIS HOT ROD PAL BACK AT--
HE'S DEAD, SNAPS.
WHO THE HELL IS GRAVEDIGGER? THAT'S SOME CAT'S NAME?
COOL IT, MAX.
DEAD? LIKE, DEAD DEAD? DID HE LAY HIS BIKE DOWN OR--
WHAT? WHAT HAPPENED?

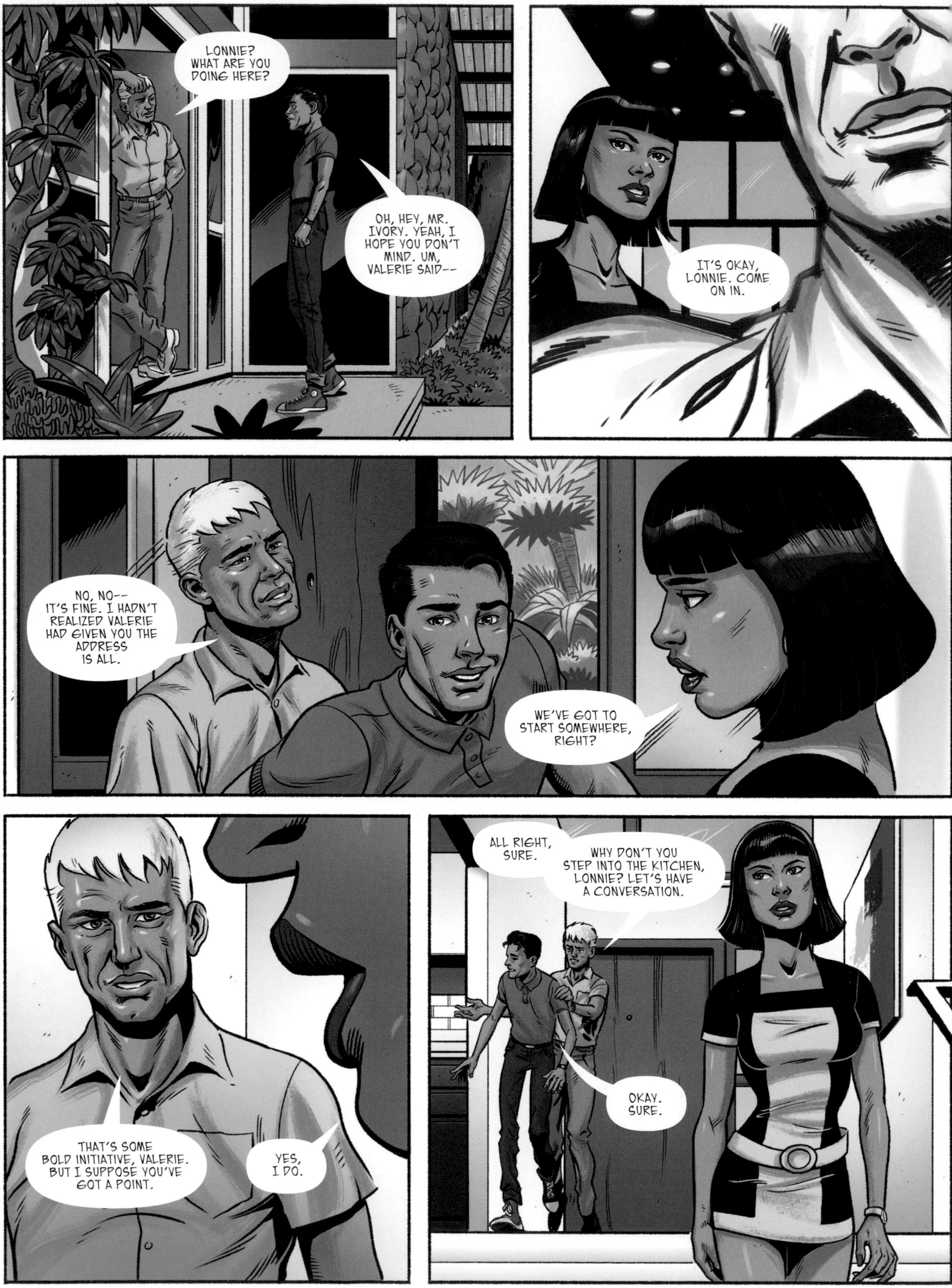
LONNIE? WHAT ARE YOU DOING HERE?
OH, HEY, MR. IVORY. YEAH, I HOPE YOU DON'T MIND. UM, VALERIE SAID--
IT'S OKAY, LONNIE. COME ON IN.
NO, NO-- IT'S FINE. I HADN'T REALIZED VALERIE HAD GIVEN YOU THE ADDRESS IS ALL.
WE'VE GOT TO START SOMEWHERE, RIGHT?
THAT'S SOME BOLD INITIATIVE, VALERIE. BUT I SUPPOSE YOU'VE GOT A POINT.
YES, I DO.
ALL RIGHT, SURE.
WHY DON'T YOU STEP INTO THE KITCHEN, LONNIE? LET'S HAVE A CONVERSATION.
OKAY. SURE.

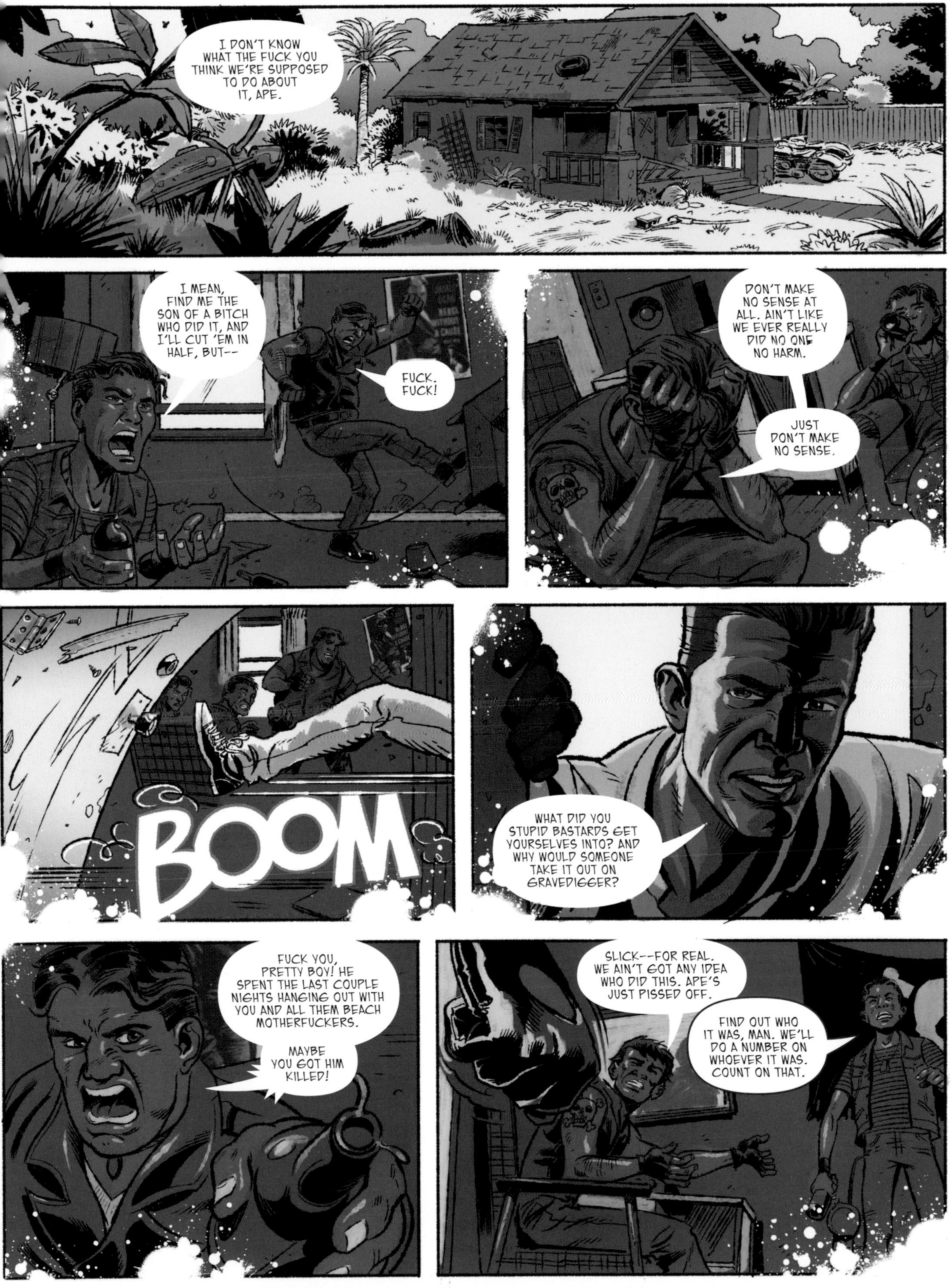

I DON'T KNOW WHAT THE FUCK YOU THINK WE'RE SUPPOSED TO DO ABOUT IT, APE.
I MEAN, FIND ME THE SON OF A BITCH WHO DID IT, AND I'LL CUT 'EM IN HALF, BUT--
FUCK. FUCK!
DON'T MAKE NO SENSE AT ALL. AIN'T LIKE WE EVER REALLY DID NO ONE NO HARM.
JUST DON'T MAKE NO SENSE.
BOOM
WHAT DID YOU STUPID BASTARDS GET YOURSELVES INTO? AND WHY WOULD SOMEONE TAKE IT OUT ON GRAVEDIGGER?
FUCK YOU, PRETTY BOY! HE SPENT THE LAST COUPLE NIGHTS HANGING OUT WITH YOU AND ALL THEM BEACH MOTHERFUCKERS.
MAYBE YOU GOT HIM KILLED!
SLICK--FOR REAL. WE AIN'T GOT ANY IDEA WHO DID THIS. APE'S JUST PISSED OFF.
FIND OUT WHO IT WAS, MAN. WE'LL DO A NUMBER ON WHOEVER IT WAS. COUNT ON THAT.

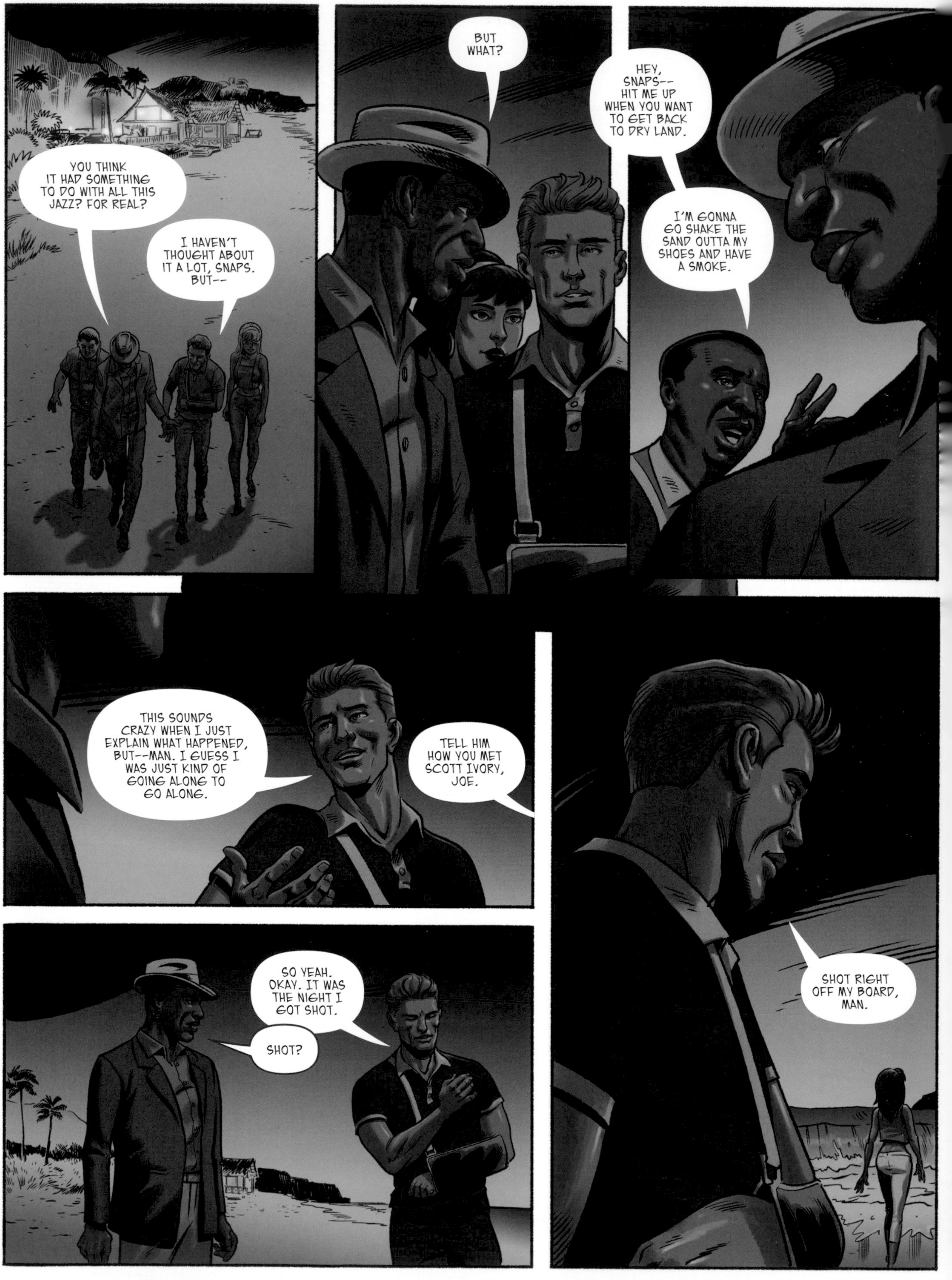
YOU THINK IT HAD SOMETHING TO DO WITH ALL THIS JAZZ? FOR REAL?
I HAVEN'T THOUGHT ABOUT IT A LOT, SNAPS. BUT--
BUT WHAT?
HEY, SNAPS-- HIT ME UP WHEN YOU WANT TO GET BACK TO DRY LAND.
I'M GONNA GO SHAKE THE SAND OUTTA MY SHOES AND HAVE A SMOKE.
THIS SOUNDS CRAZY WHEN I JUST EXPLAIN WHAT HAPPENED, BUT--MAN. I GUESS I WAS JUST KIND OF GOING ALONG TO GO ALONG.
TELL HIM HOW YOU MET SCOTT IVORY, JOE.
SO YEAH. OKAY. IT WAS THE NIGHT I GOT SHOT.
SHOT?
SHOT RIGHT OFF MY BOARD, MAN.

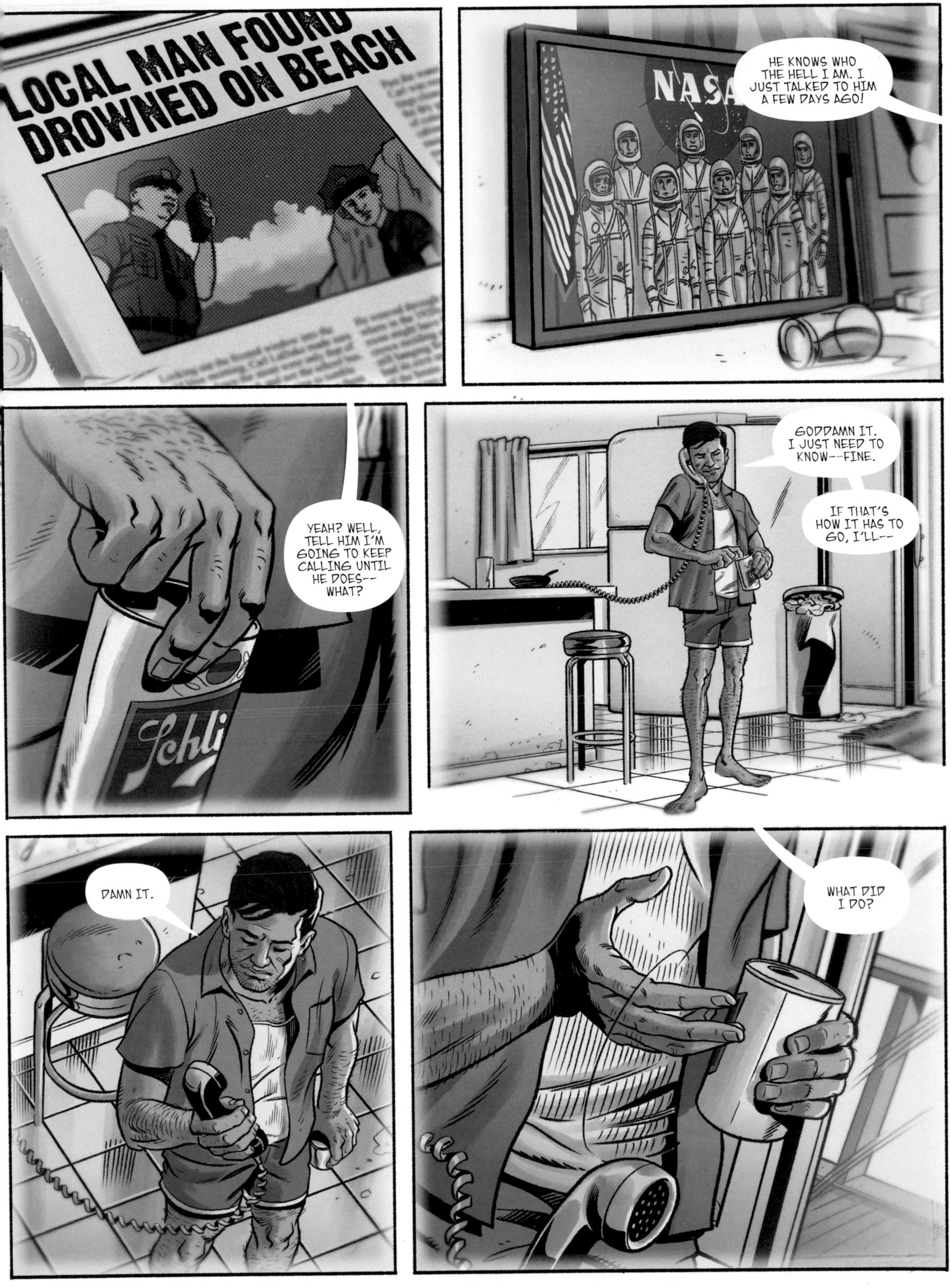
LOCAL MAN FOUND DROWNED ON BEACH
NASA
HE KNOWS WHO THE HELL I AM. I JUST TALKED TO HIM A FEW DAYS AGO!
YEAH? WELL, TELL HIM I'M GOING TO KEEP CALLING UNTIL HE DOES-- WHAT?
Schli
GODDAMN IT. I JUST NEED TO KNOW--FINE.
IF THAT'S HOW IT HAS TO GO, I'LL--
DAMN IT.
WHAT DID I DO?

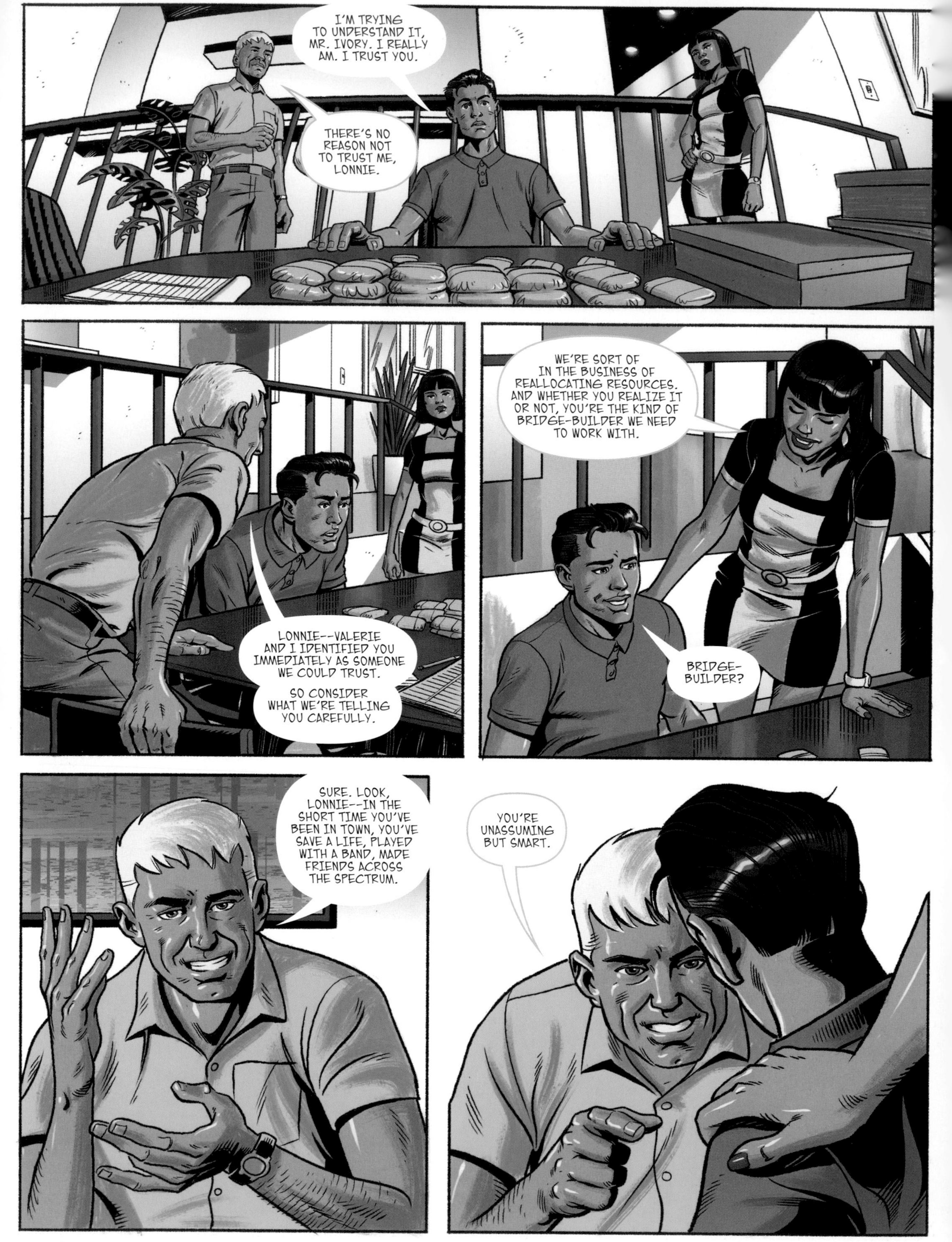
I'M TRYING TO UNDERSTAND IT, MR. IVORY. I REALLY AM. I TRUST YOU.
THERE'S NO REASON NOT TO TRUST ME, LONNIE.
LONNIE--VALERIE AND I IDENTIFIED YOU IMMEDIATELY AS SOMEONE WE COULD TRUST.
SO CONSIDER WHAT WE'RE TELLING YOU CAREFULLY.
WE'RE SORT OF IN THE BUSINESS OF REALLOCATING RESOURCES. AND WHETHER YOU REALIZE IT OR NOT, YOU'RE THE KIND OF BRIDGE-BUILDER WE NEED TO WORK WITH.
BRIDGE-BUILDER?
SURE. LOOK, LONNIE--IN THE SHORT TIME YOU'VE BEEN IN TOWN, YOU'VE SAVE A LIFE, PLAYED WITH A BAND, MADE FRIENDS ACROSS THE SPECTRUM.
YOU'RE UNASSUMING BUT SMART.

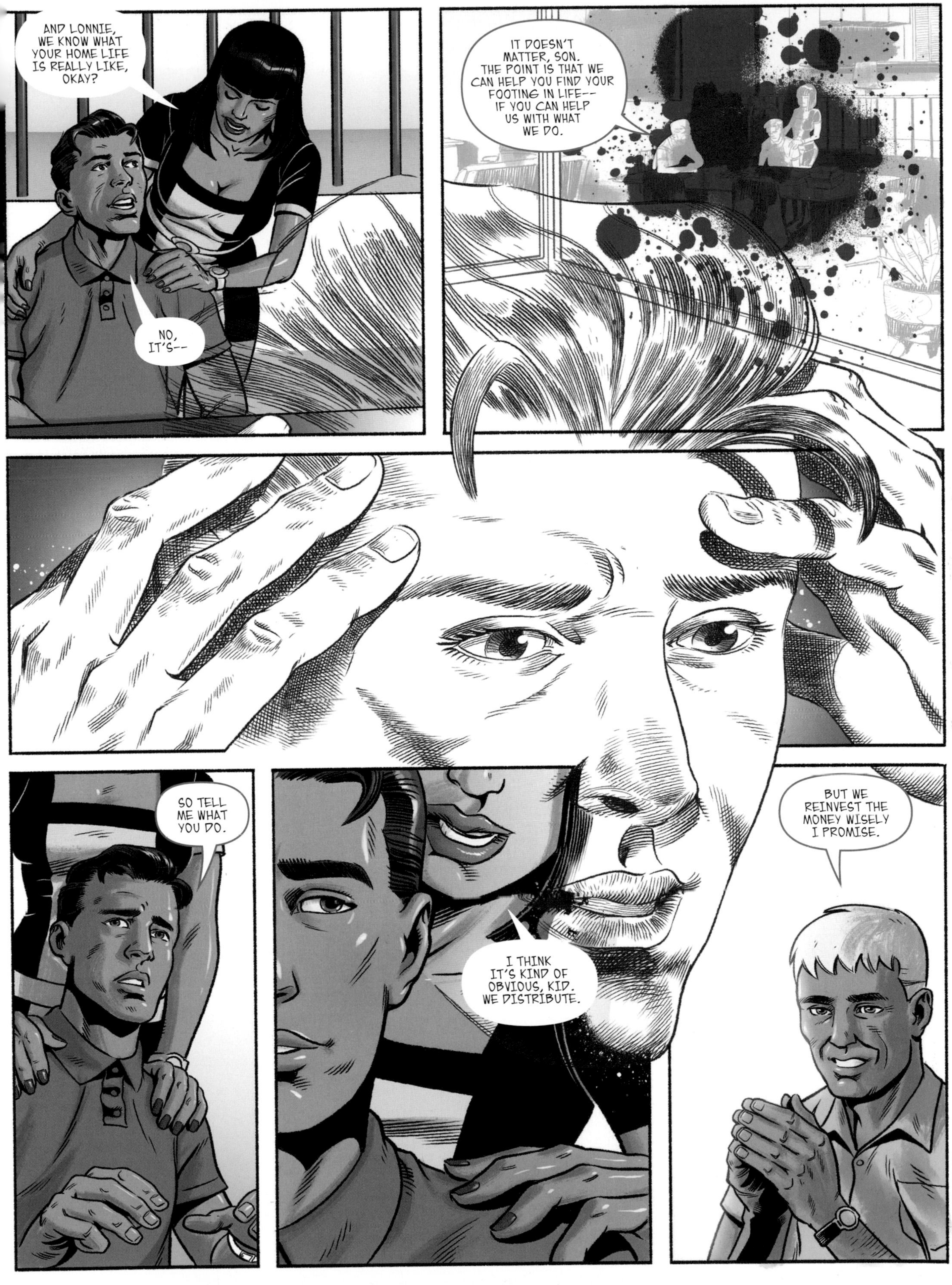
AND LONNIE, WE KNOW WHAT YOUR HOME LIFE IS REALLY LIKE, OKAY?
NO, IT'S--
IT DOESN'T MATTER, SON. THE POINT IS THAT WE CAN HELP YOU FIND YOUR FOOTING IN LIFE-- IF YOU CAN HELP US WITH WHAT WE DO.
SO TELL ME WHAT YOU DO.
I THINK IT'S KIND OF OBVIOUS, KID. WE DISTRIBUTE.
BUT WE REINVEST THE MONEY WISELY I PROMISE.

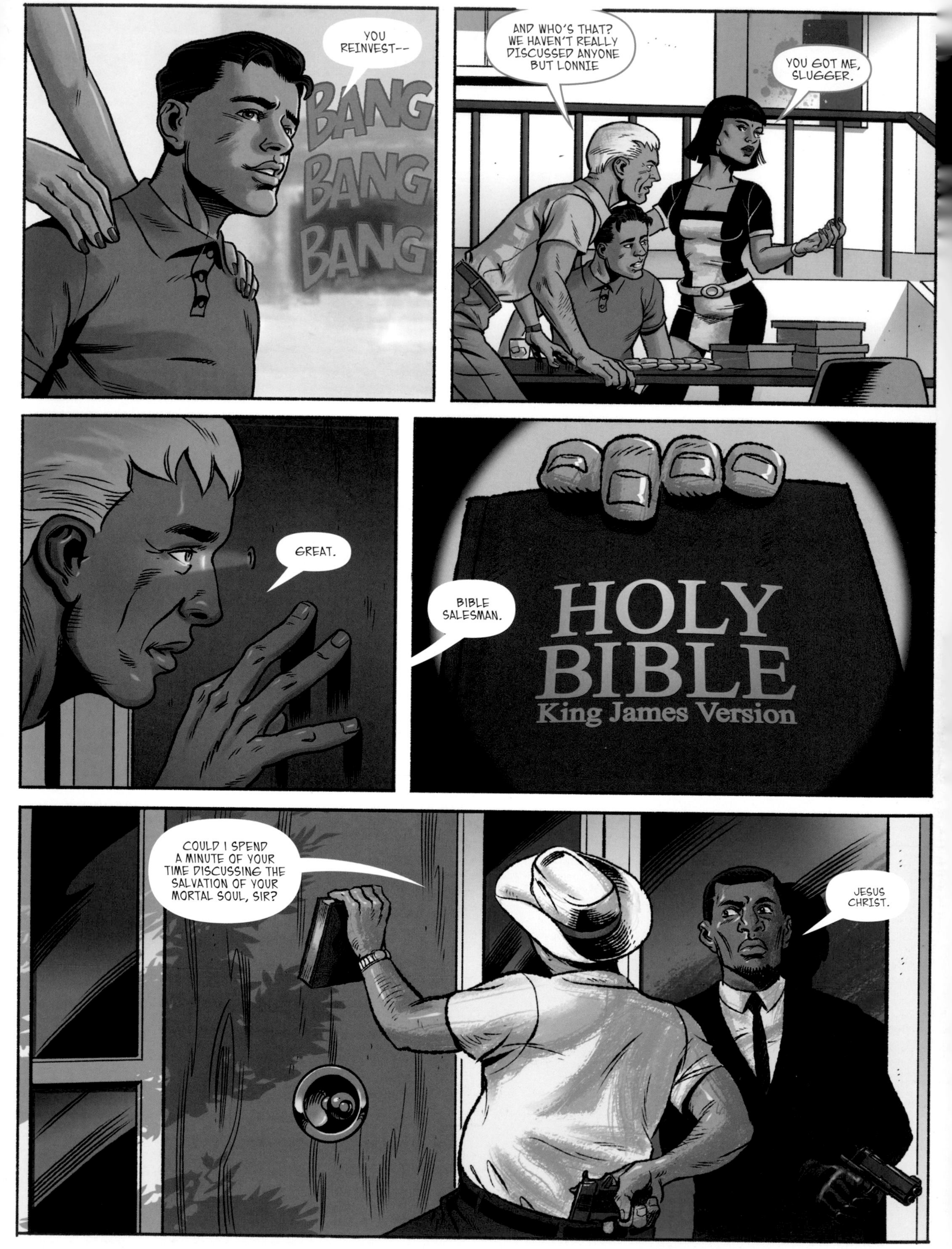
YOU REINVEST--
BANG BANG BANG
AND WHO'S THAT? WE HAVEN'T REALLY DISCUSSED ANYONE BUT LONNIE
YOU GOT ME, SLUGGER.
GREAT.
BIBLE SALESMAN.
HOLY BIBLE King James Version
COULD I SPEND A MINUTE OF YOUR TIME DISCUSSING THE SALVATION OF YOUR MORTAL SOUL, SIR?
JESUS CHRIST.

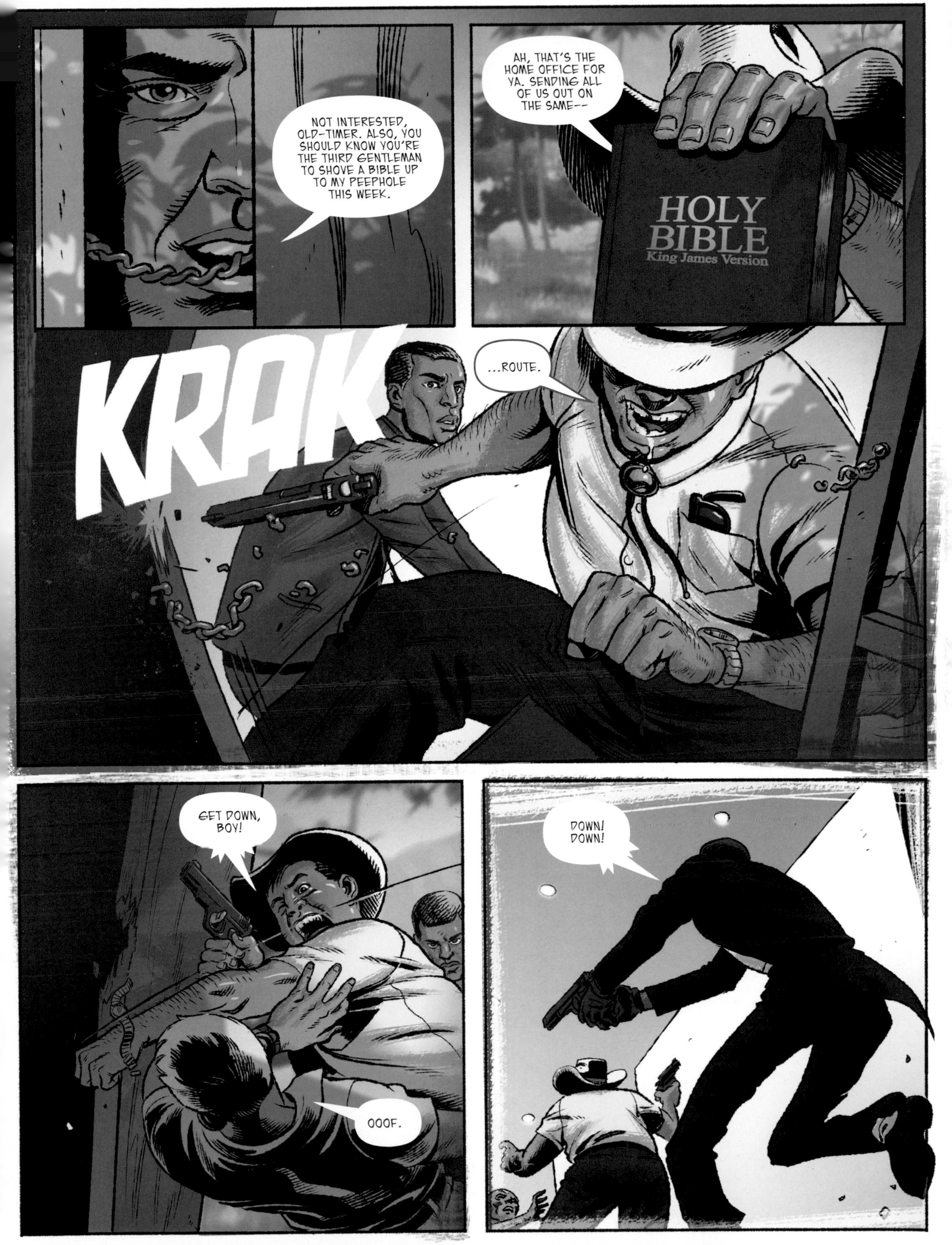
NOT INTERESTED, OLD-TIMER. ALSO, YOU SHOULD KNOW YOU'RE THE THIRD GENTLEMAN TO SHOVE A BIBLE UP TO MY PEEPHOLE THIS WEEK.
AH, THAT'S THE HOME OFFICE FOR YA. SENDING ALL OF US OUT ON THE SAME--
HOLY BIBLE King James Version
KRAK
...ROUTE.
GET DOWN, BOY!
OOOF.
DOWN! DOWN!

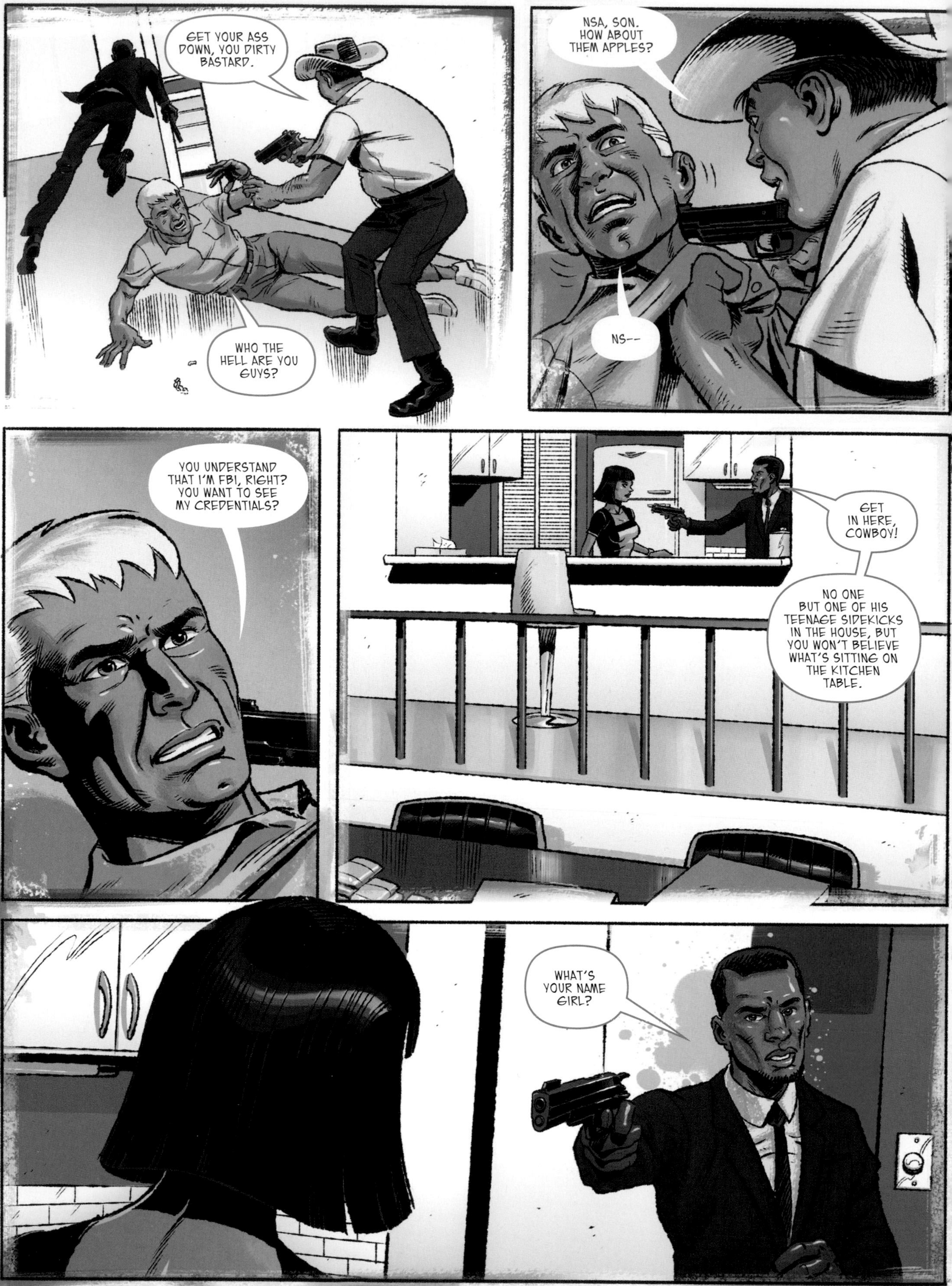
GET YOUR ASS DOWN, YOU DIRTY BASTARD.
WHO THE HELL ARE YOU GUYS?
NSA, SON. HOW ABOUT THEM APPLES?
NS--
YOU UNDERSTAND THAT I'M FBI, RIGHT? YOU WANT TO SEE MY CREDENTIALS?
GET IN HERE, COWBOY!
NO ONE BUT ONE OF HIS TEENAGE SIDEKICKS IN THE HOUSE, BUT YOU WON'T BELIEVE WHAT'S SITTING ON THE KITCHEN TABLE.
WHAT'S YOUR NAME GIRL?

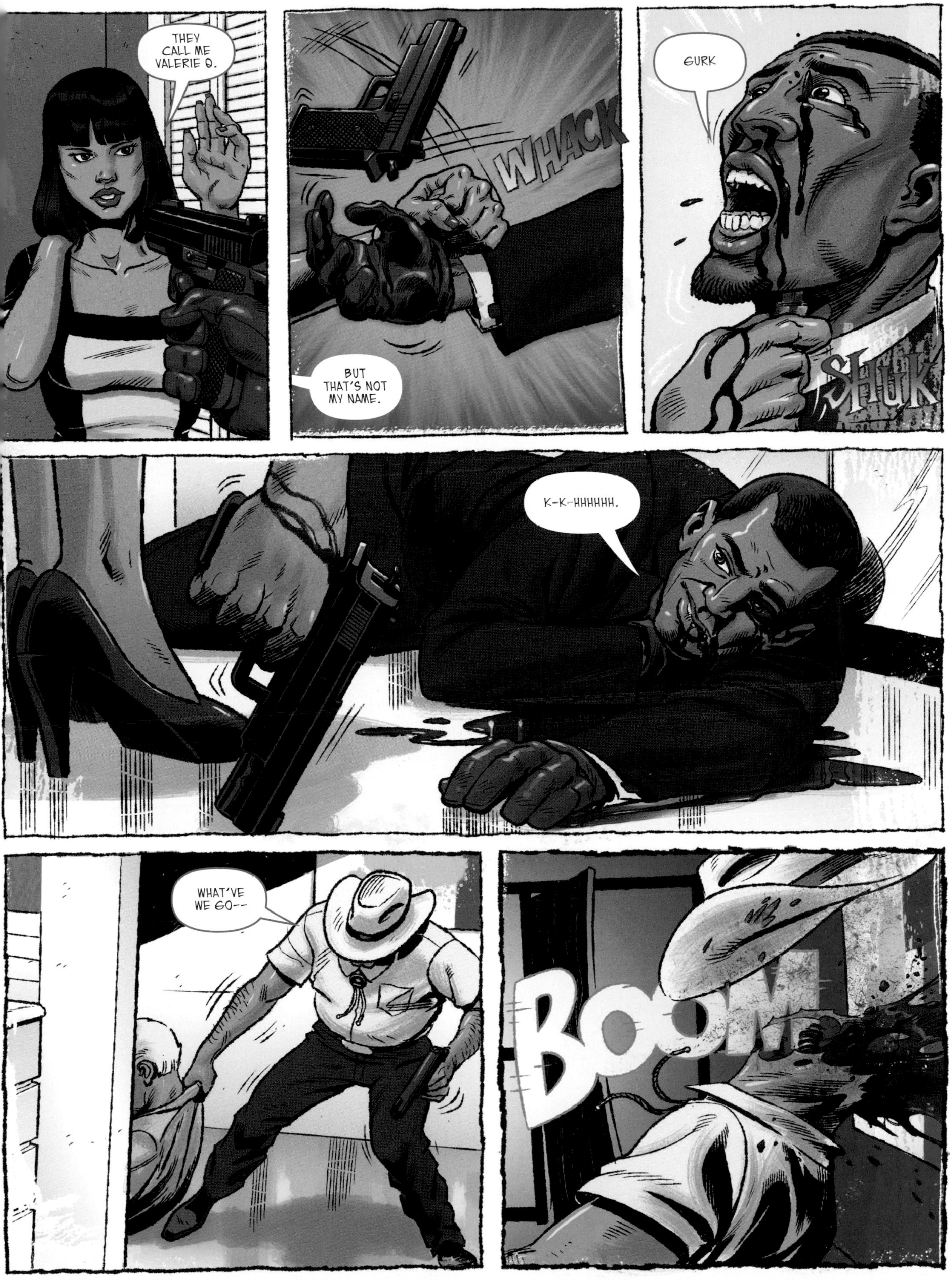
THEY CALL ME VALERIE Q.
WHACK
BUT THAT'S NOT MY NAME.
GURK
SHUK
K-K-HHHHHH.
WHAT'VE WE GO--
BOOM

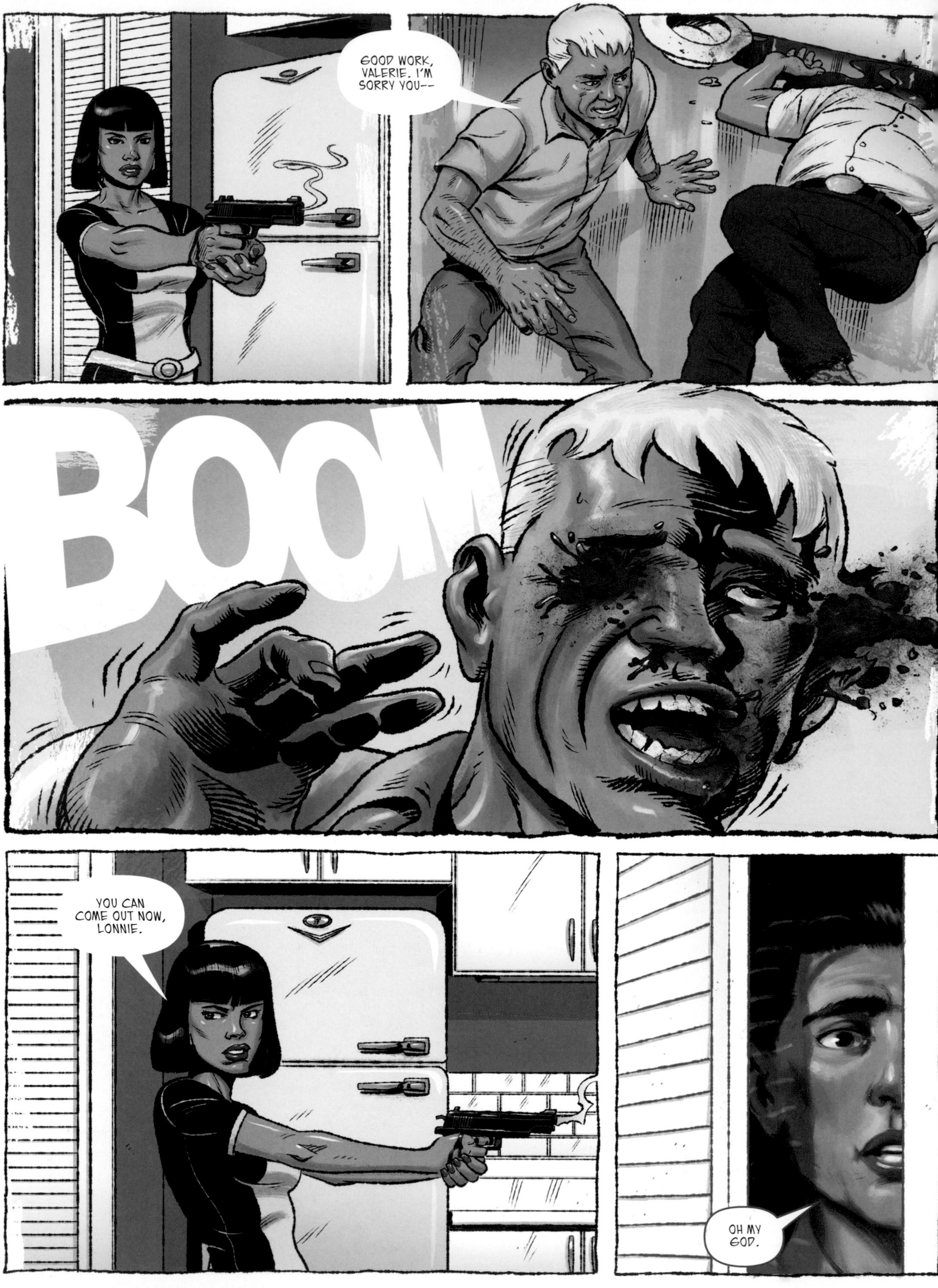
GOOD WORK, VALERIE. I'M SORRY YOU--
BOOM
YOU CAN COME OUT NOW, LONNIE.
OH MY GOD.

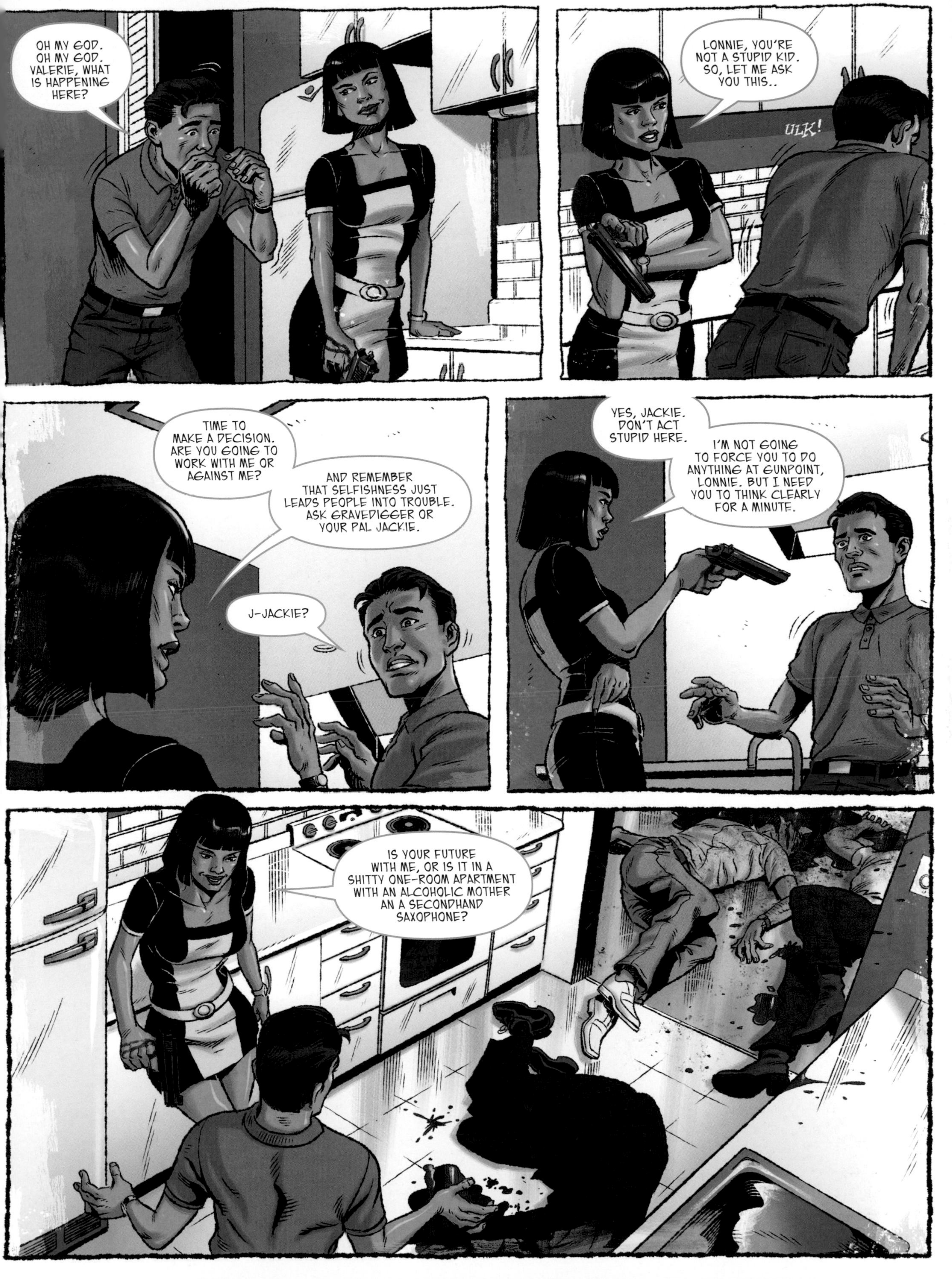
OH MY GOD. OH MY GOD. VALERIE, WHAT IS HAPPENING HERE?
LONNIE, YOU'RE NOT A STUPID KID. SO, LET ME ASK YOU THIS..
ULK!
TIME TO MAKE A DECISION. ARE YOU GOING TO WORK WITH ME OR AGAINST ME?
AND REMEMBER THAT SELFISHNESS JUST LEADS PEOPLE INTO TROUBLE. ASK GRAVEDIGGER OR YOUR PAL JACKIE.
J-JACKIE?
YES, JACKIE. DON'T ACT STUPID HERE.
I'M NOT GOING TO FORCE YOU TO DO ANYTHING AT GUNPOINT, LONNIE. BUT I NEED YOU TO THINK CLEARLY FOR A MINUTE.
IS YOUR FUTURE WITH ME, OR IS IT IN A SHITTY ONE-ROOM APARTMENT WITH AN ALCOHOLIC MOTHER AN A SECONDHAND SAXOPHONE?

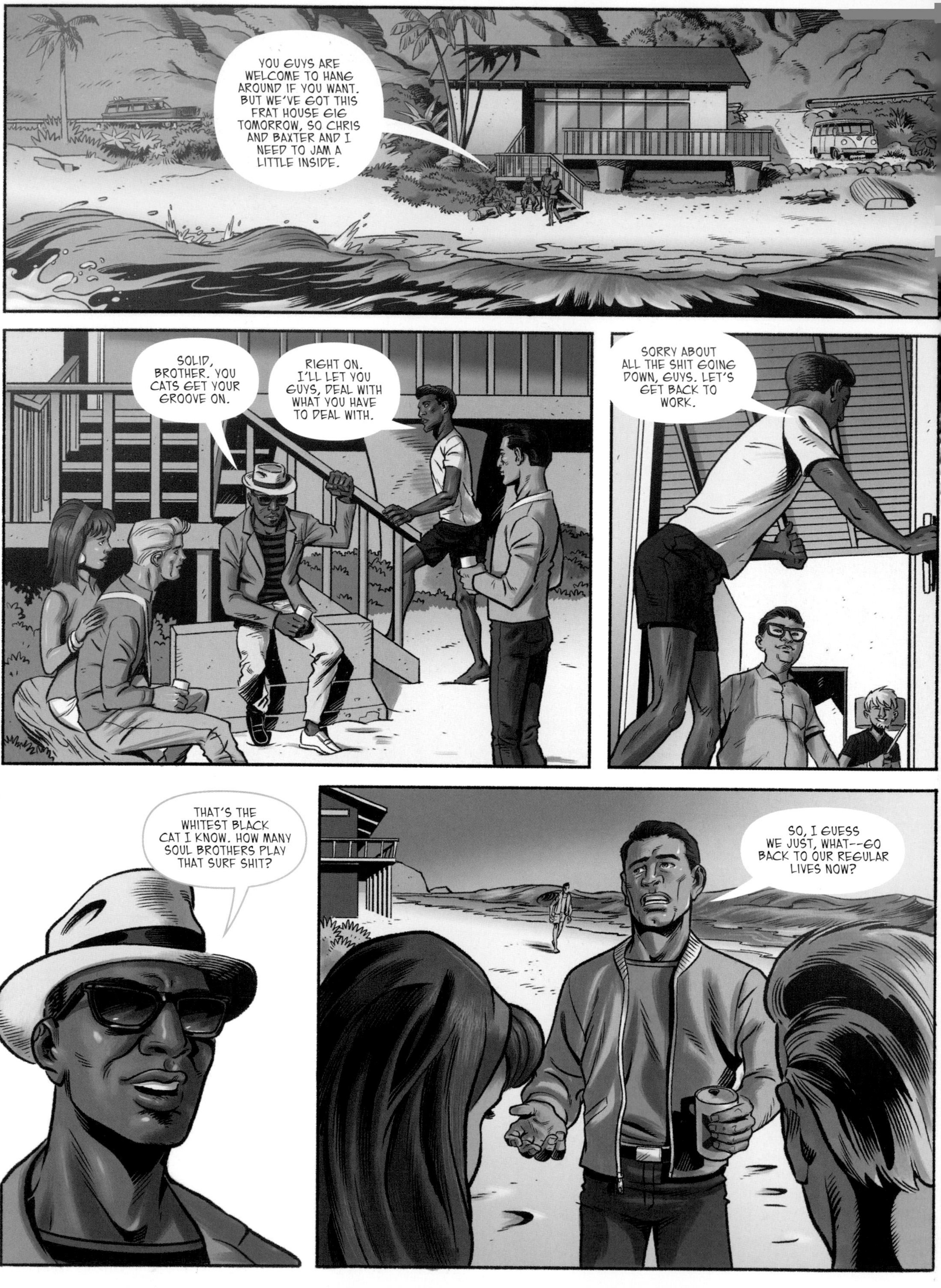
YOU GUYS ARE WELCOME TO HANG AROUND IF YOU WANT. BUT WE'VE GOT THIS FRAT HOUSE GIG TOMORROW, SO CHRIS AND BAXTER AND I NEED TO JAM A LITTLE INSIDE.
SOLID, BROTHER. YOU CATS GET YOUR GROOVE ON.
RIGHT ON. I'LL LET YOU GUYS, DEAL WITH WHAT YOU HAVE TO DEAL WITH.
SORRY ABOUT ALL THE SHIT GOING DOWN, GUYS. LET'S GET BACK TO WORK.
THAT'S THE WHITEST BLACK CAT I KNOW. HOW MANY SOUL BROTHERS PLAY THAT SURF SHIT?
SO, I GUESS WE JUST, WHAT--GO BACK TO OUR REGULAR LIVES NOW?

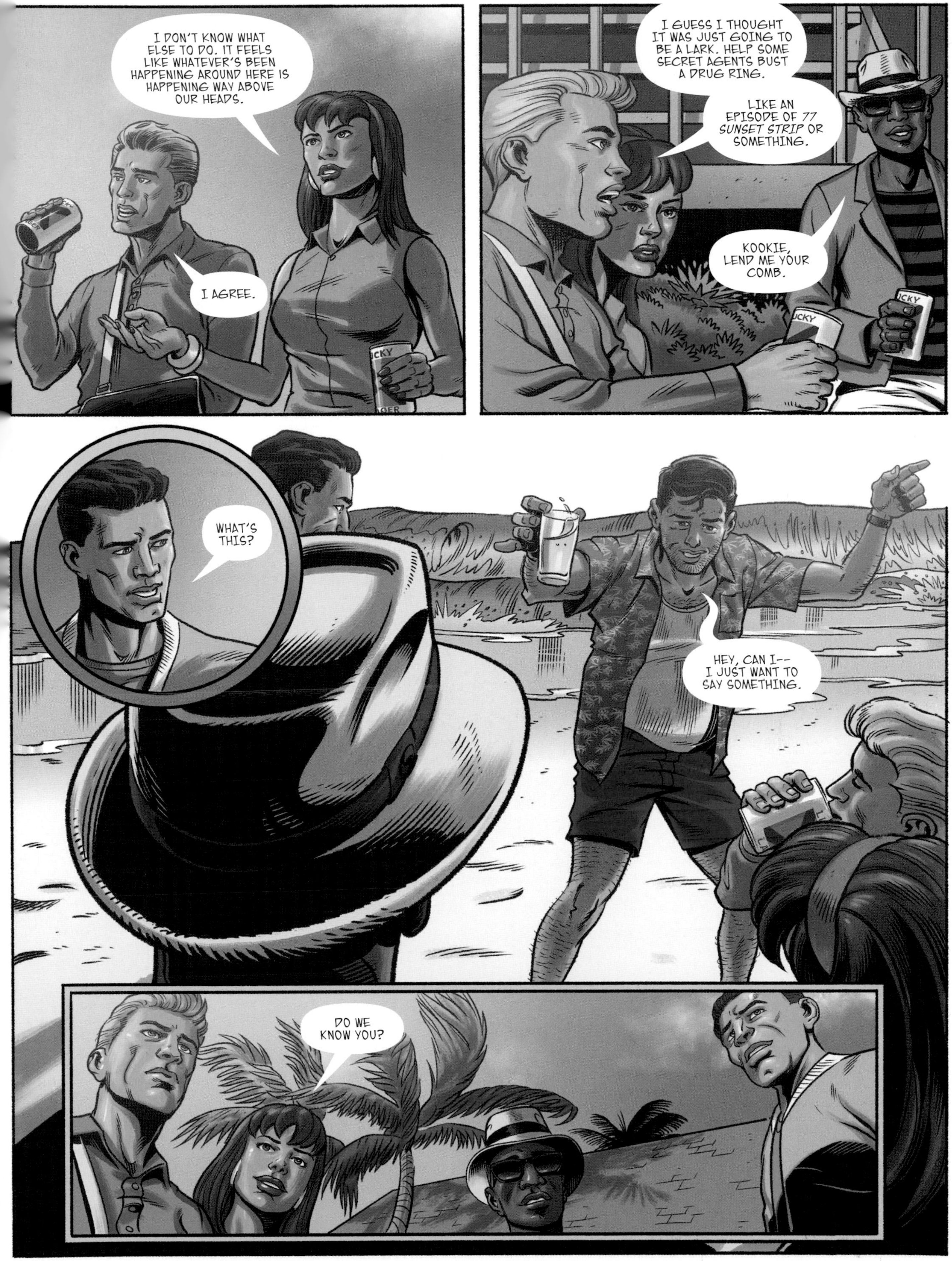
I DON'T KNOW WHAT ELSE TO DO. IT FEELS LIKE WHATEVER'S BEEN HAPPENING AROUND HERE IS HAPPENING WAY ABOVE OUR HEADS.
I AGREE.
I GUESS I THOUGHT IT WAS JUST GOING TO BE A LARK. HELP SOME SECRET AGENTS BUST A DRUG RING.
LIKE AN EPISODE OF *77 SUNSET STRIP* OR SOMETHING.
KOOKIE, LEND ME YOUR COMB.
WHAT'S THIS?
HEY, CAN I-- I JUST WANT TO SAY SOMETHING.
DO WE KNOW YOU?

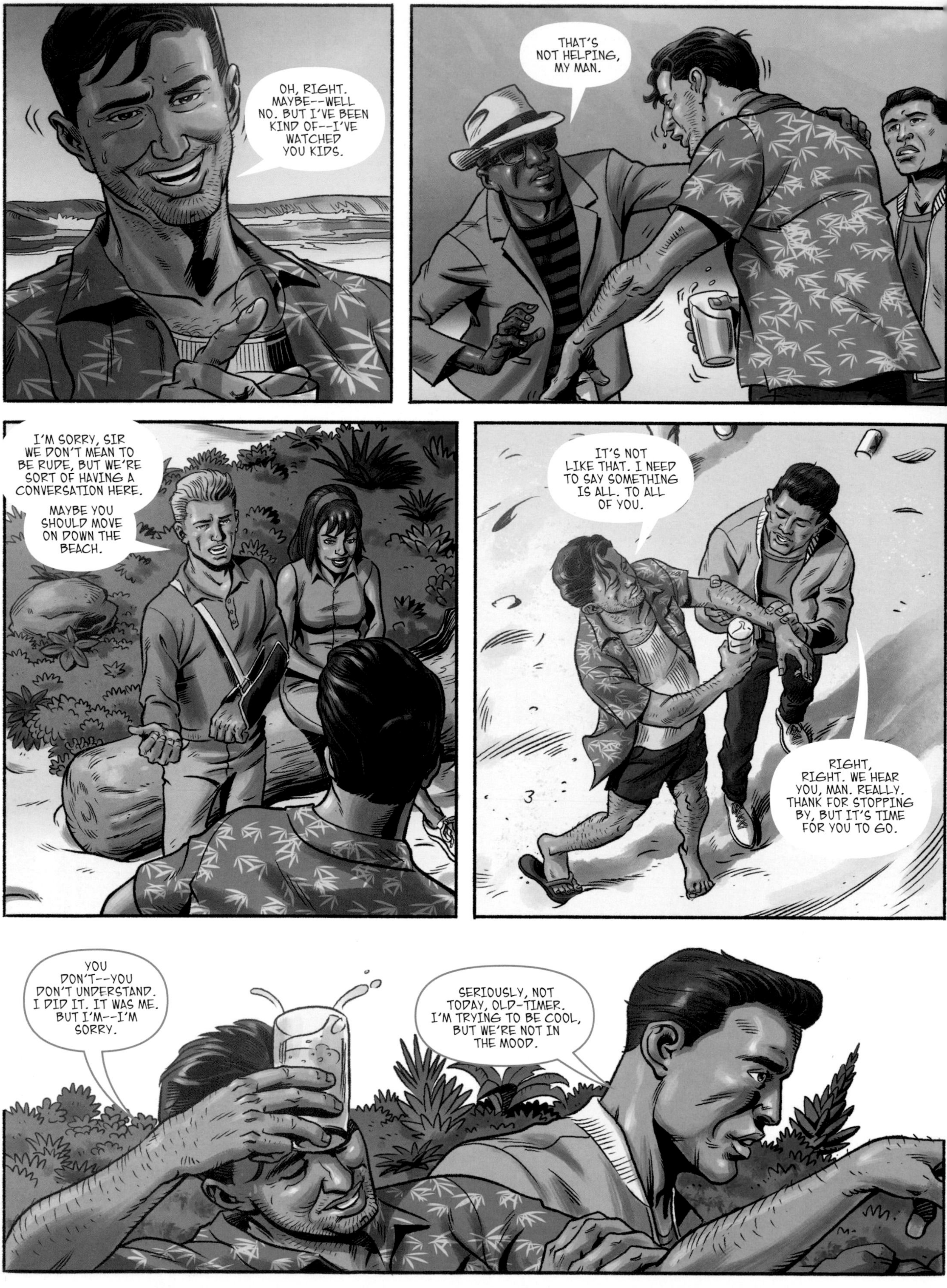
OH, RIGHT. MAYBE--WELL NO. BUT I'VE BEEN KIND OF--I'VE WATCHED YOU KIDS.
THAT'S NOT HELPING, MY MAN.
I'M SORRY, SIR WE DON'T MEAN TO BE RUDE, BUT WE'RE SORT OF HAVING A CONVERSATION HERE.
MAYBE YOU SHOULD MOVE ON DOWN THE BEACH.
IT'S NOT LIKE THAT. I NEED TO SAY SOMETHING IS ALL. TO ALL OF YOU.
RIGHT, RIGHT. WE HEAR YOU, MAN. REALLY. THANK FOR STOPPING BY, BUT IT'S TIME FOR YOU TO GO.
YOU DON'T--YOU DON'T UNDERSTAND. I DID IT. IT WAS ME. BUT I'M--I'M SORRY.
SERIOUSLY, NOT TODAY, OLD-TIMER. I'M TRYING TO BE COOL, BUT WE'RE NOT IN THE MOOD.

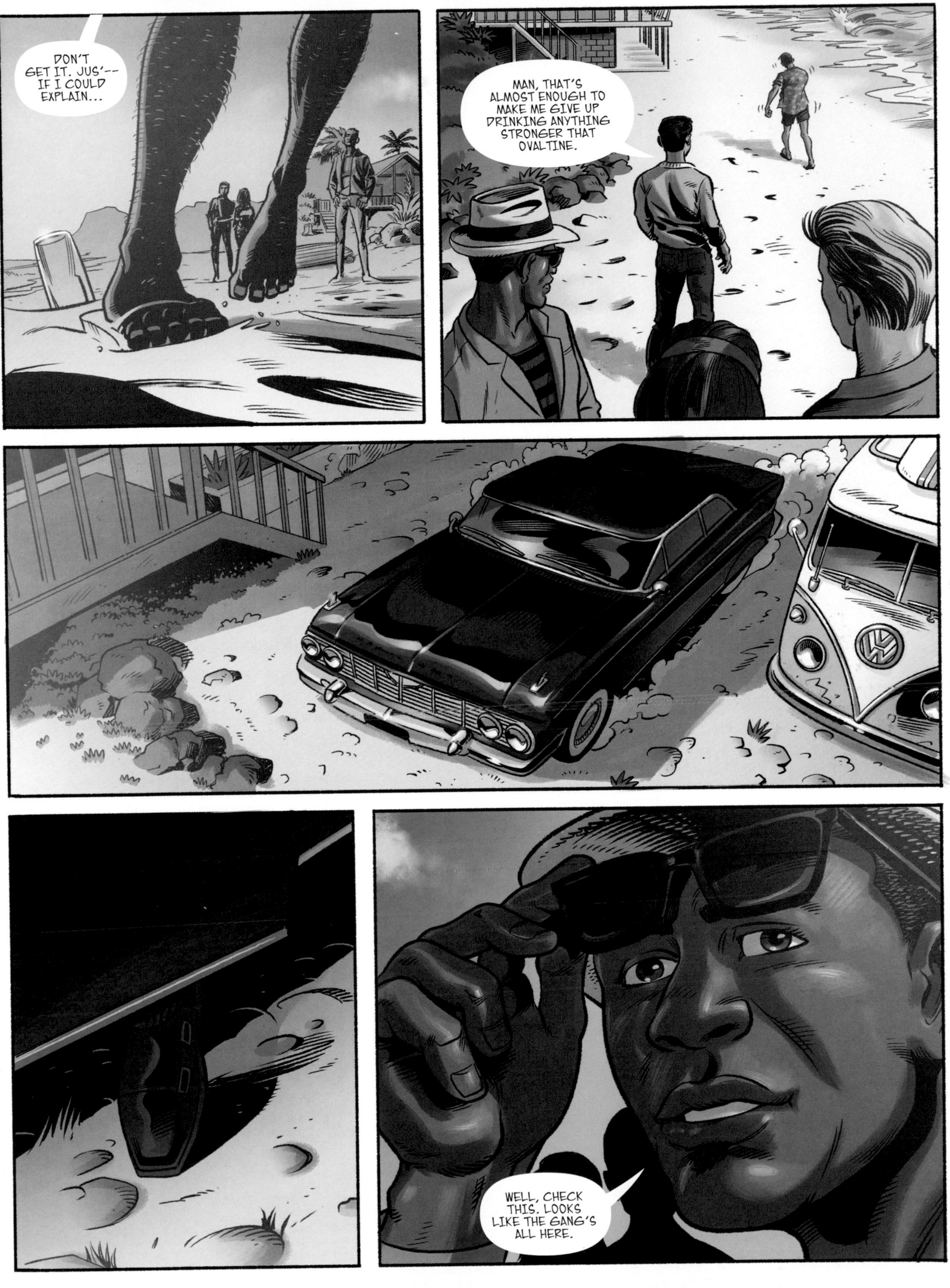
DON'T GET IT. JUS'-- IF I COULD EXPLAIN...
MAN, THAT'S ALMOST ENOUGH TO MAKE ME GIVE UP DRINKING ANYTHING STRONGER THAT OVALTINE.
WELL, CHECK THIS. LOOKS LIKE THE GANG'S ALL HERE.

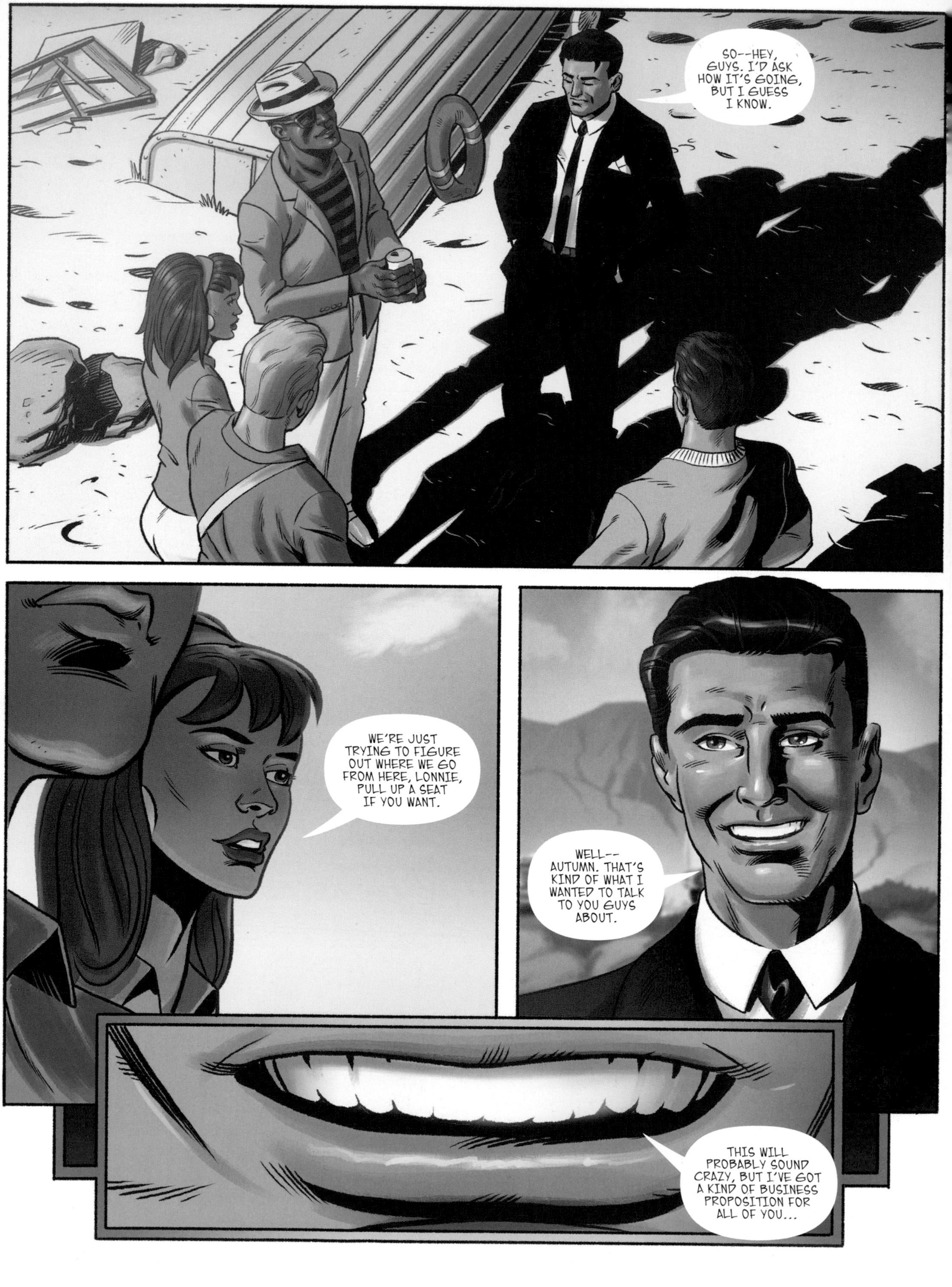
SO--HEY, GUYS. I'D ASK HOW IT'S GOING, BUT I GUESS I KNOW.
WE'RE JUST TRYING TO FIGURE OUT WHERE WE GO FROM HERE, LONNIE, PULL UP A SEAT IF YOU WANT.
WELL-- AUTUMN. THAT'S KIND OF WHAT I WANTED TO TALK TO YOU GUYS ABOUT.
THIS WILL PROBABLY SOUND CRAZY, BUT I'VE GOT A KIND OF BUSINESS PROPOSITION FOR ALL OF YOU...

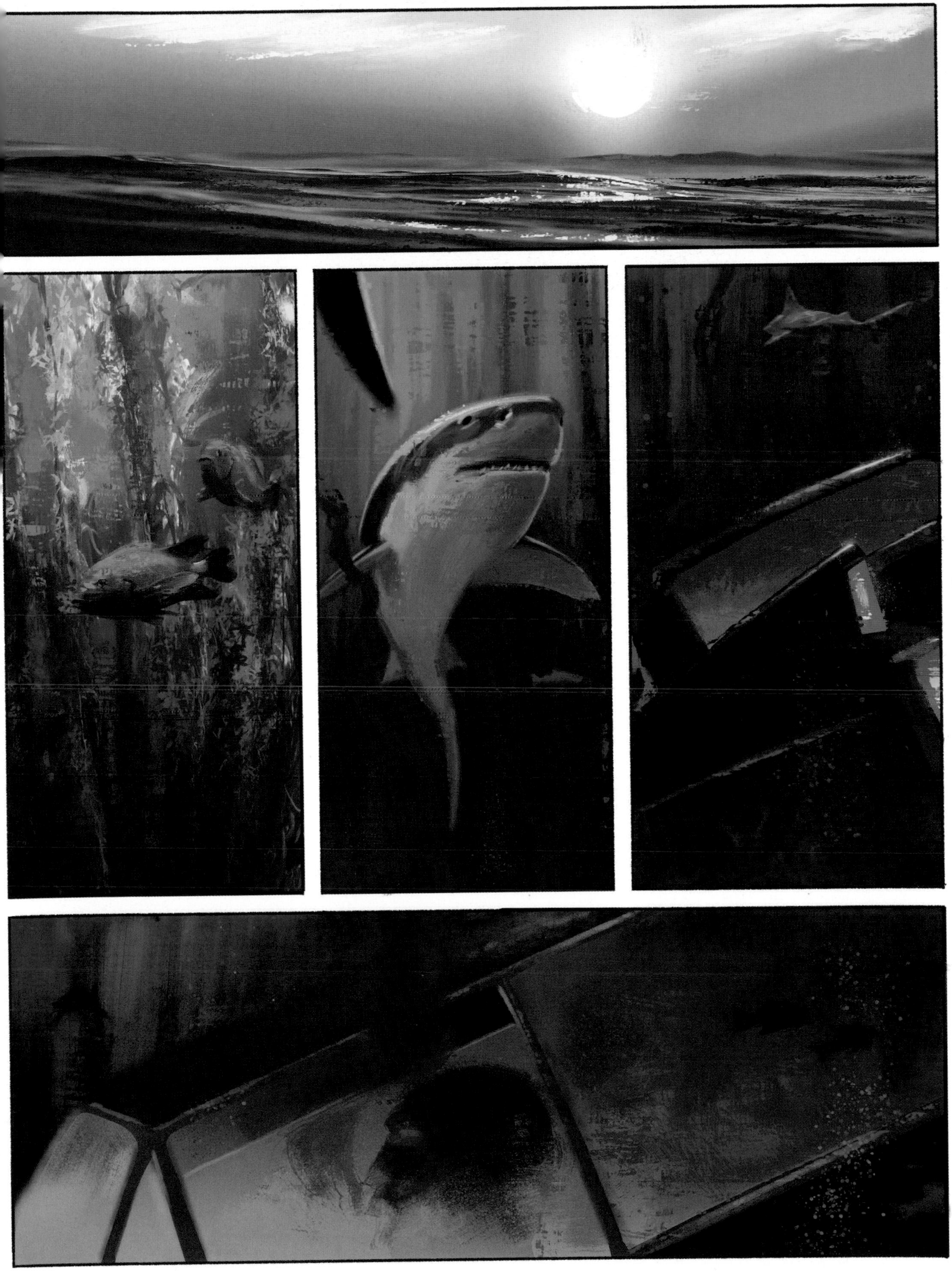

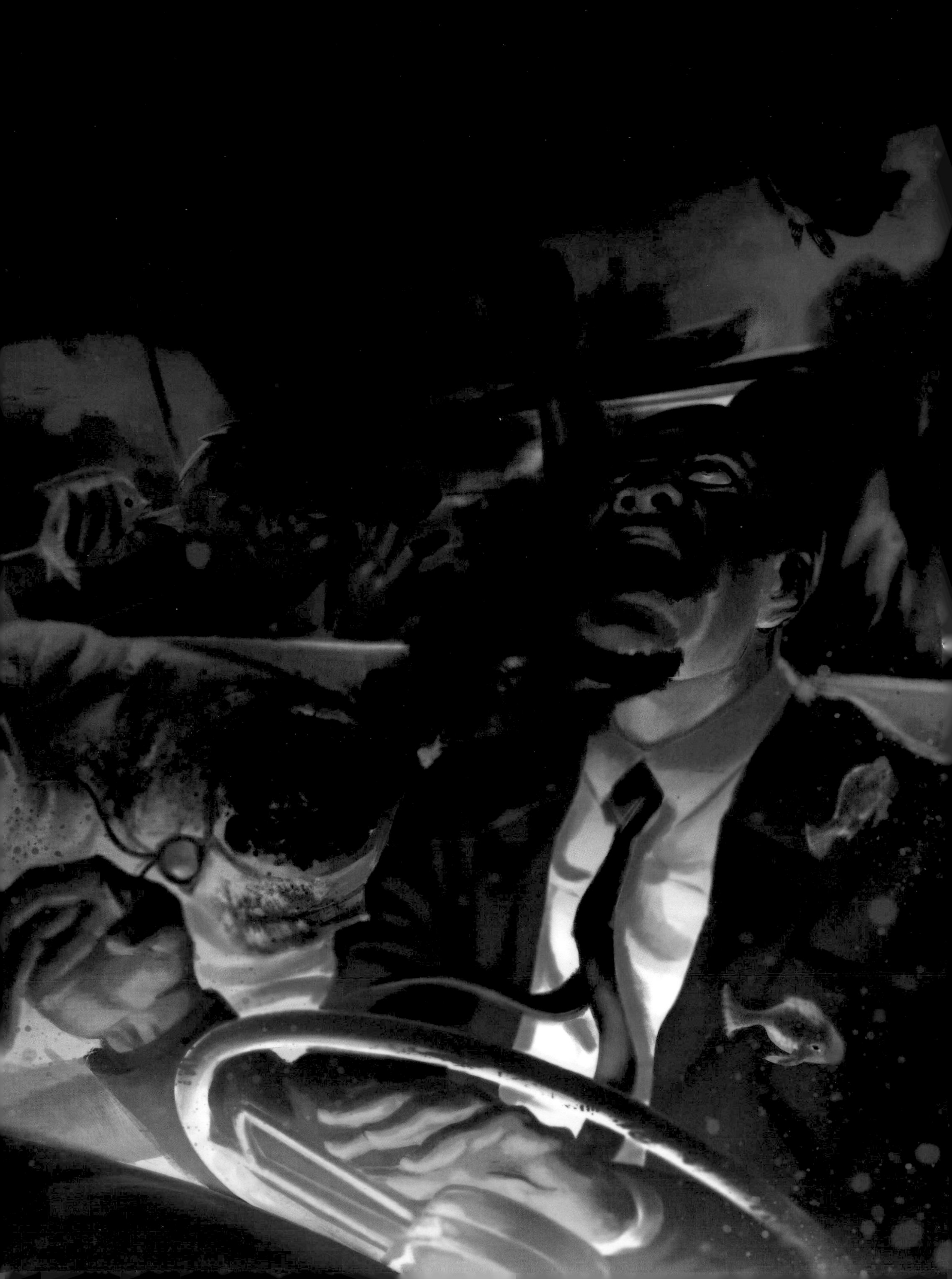

ENDLESS SUMMER

COVER GALLERY

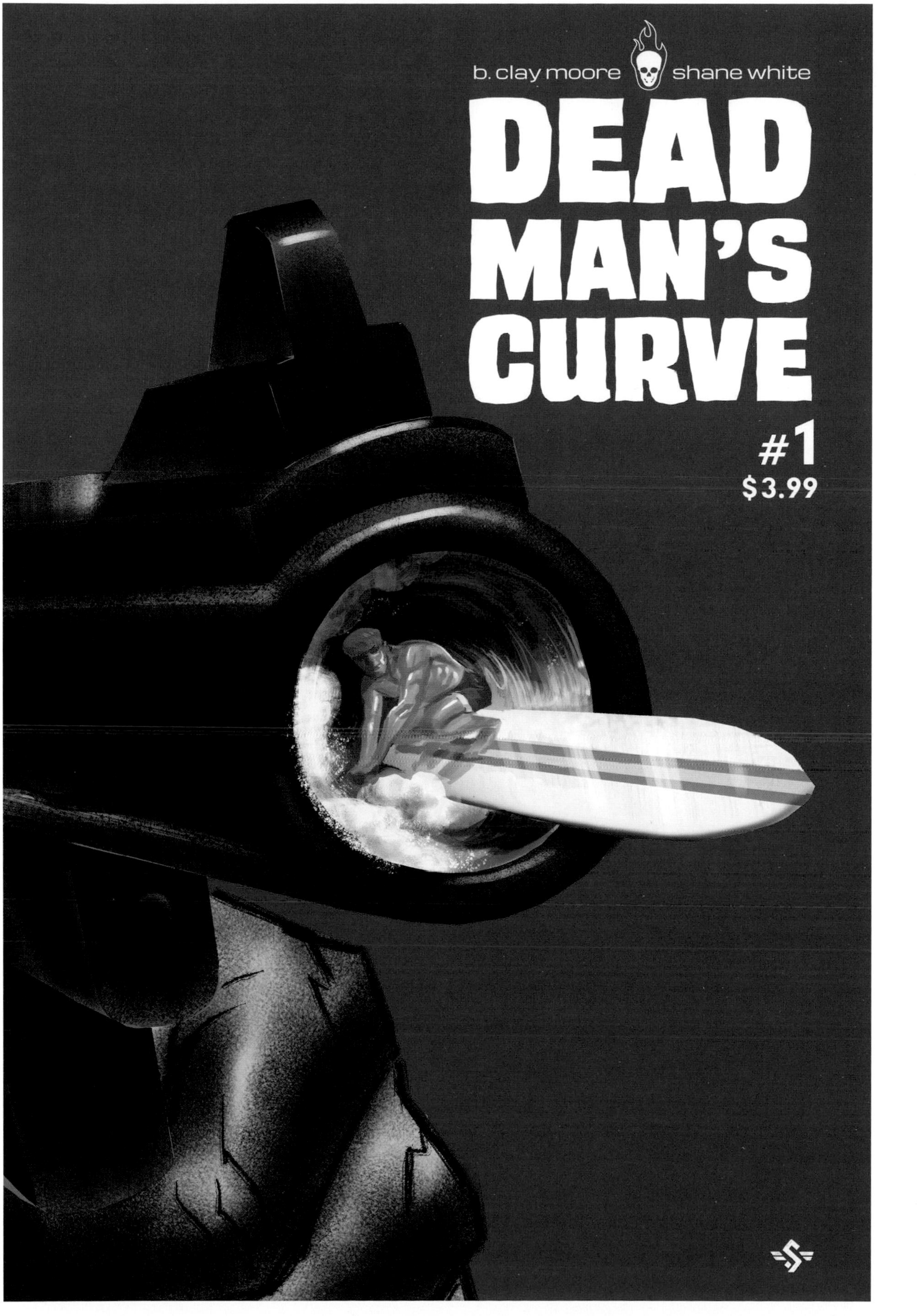
b. clay moore
shane white
DEAD MAN'S CURVE
#1
$3.99

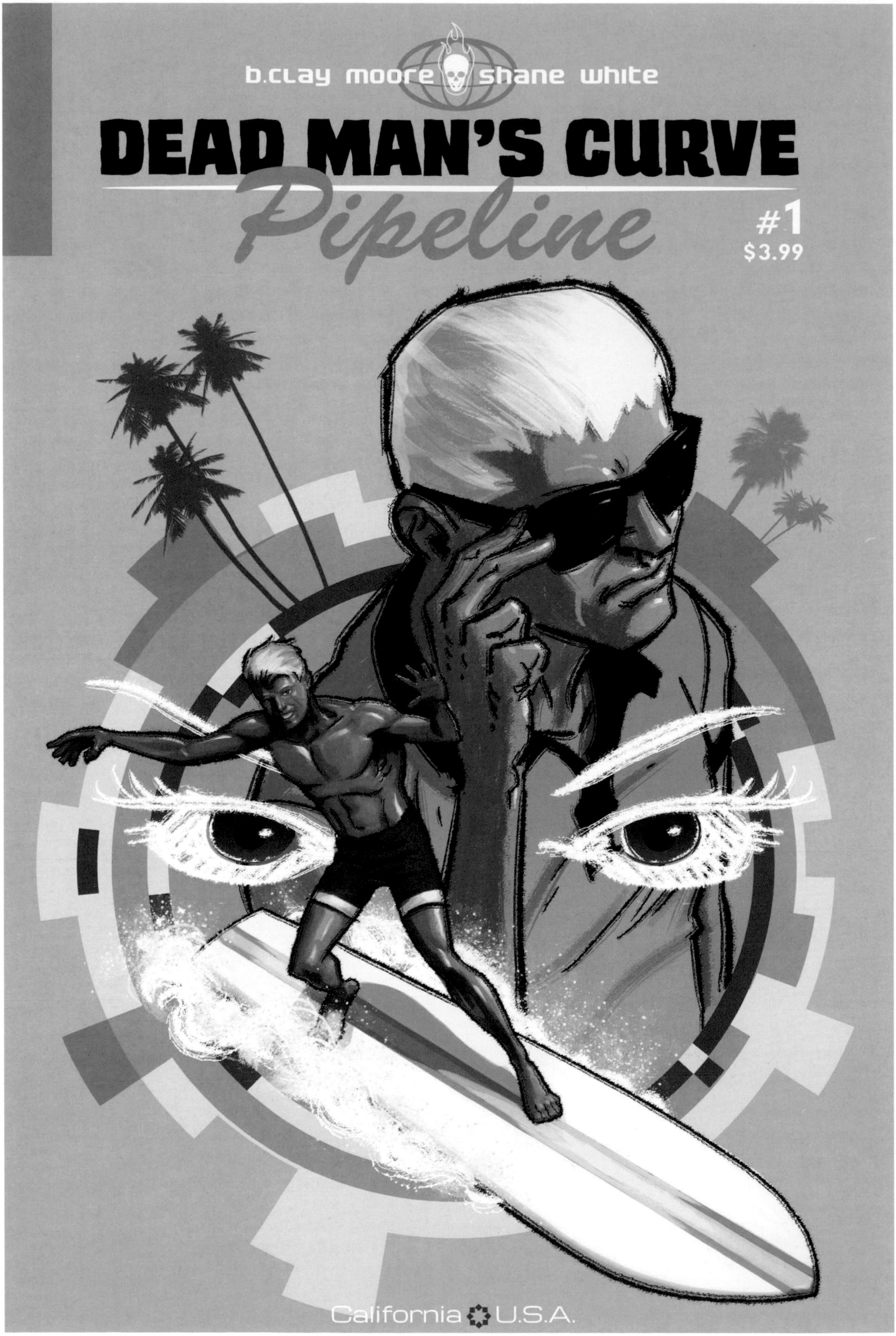
b.clay moore
shane white
DEAD MAN'S CURVE
Pipeline
#1
$3.99
California U.S.A.

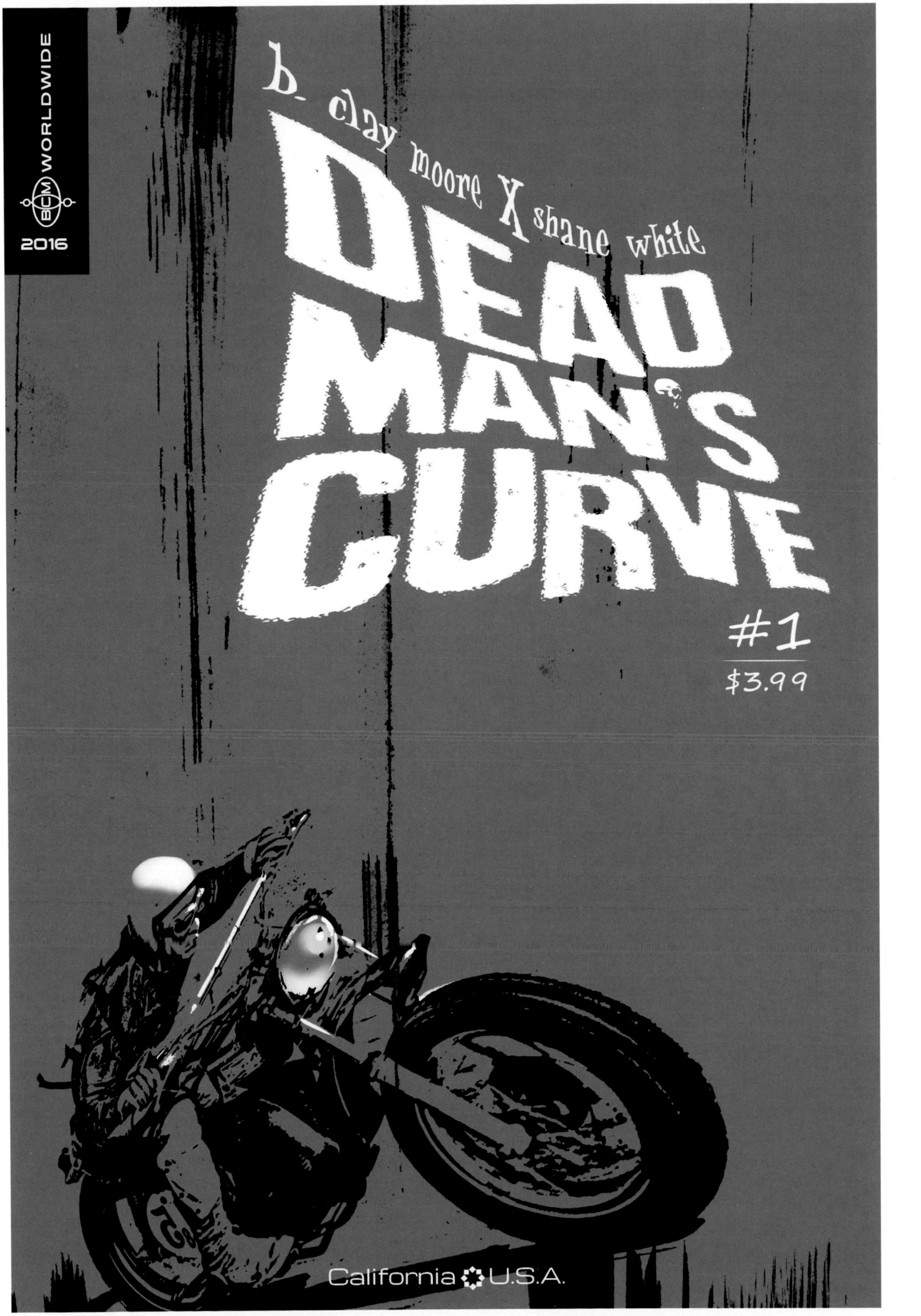

BCM WORLDWIDE
2016
b. clay moore X shane white
DEAD MAN'S CURVE
#1
$3.99
California U.S.A.

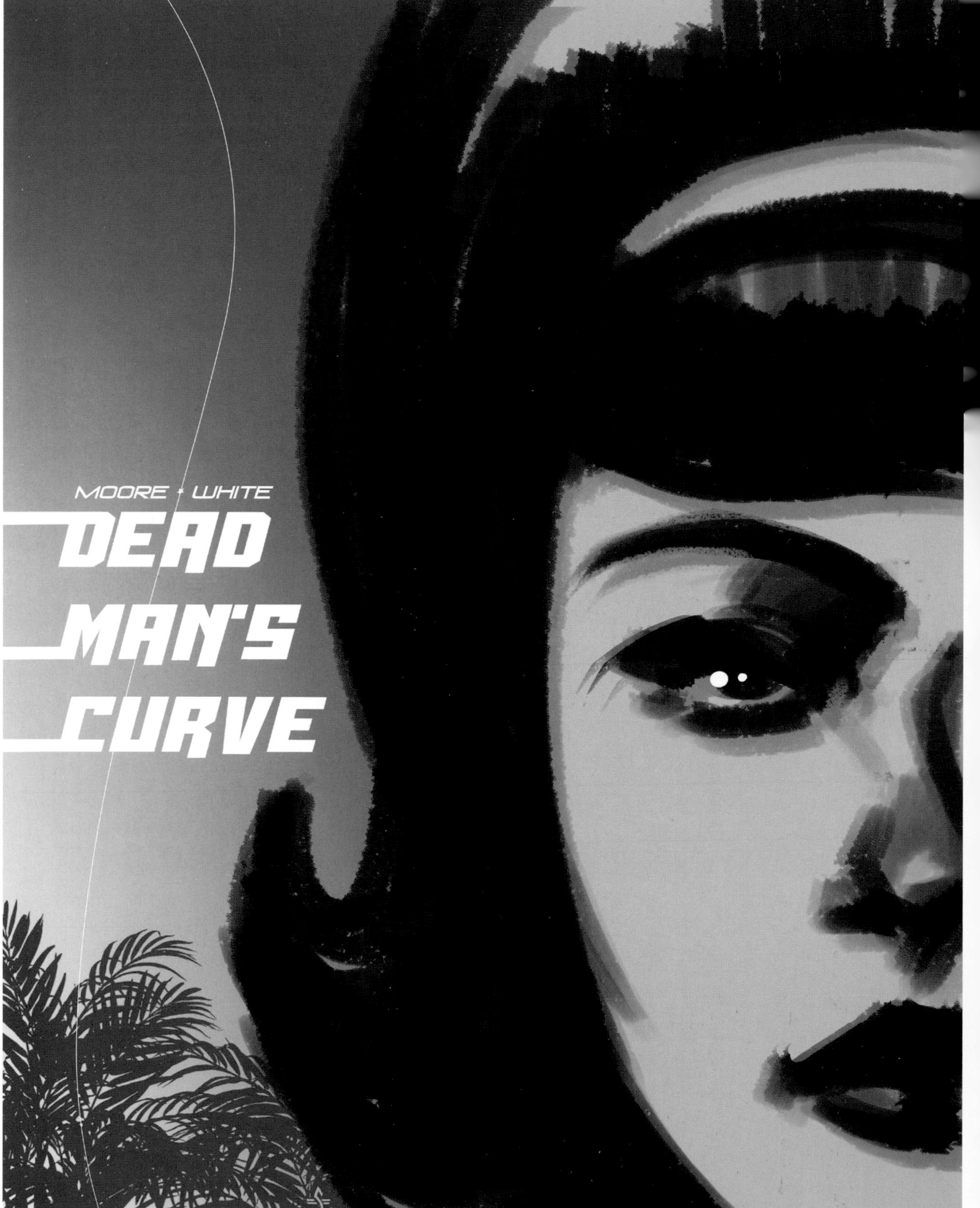
MOORE • WHITE
DEAD
MAN'S
CURVE

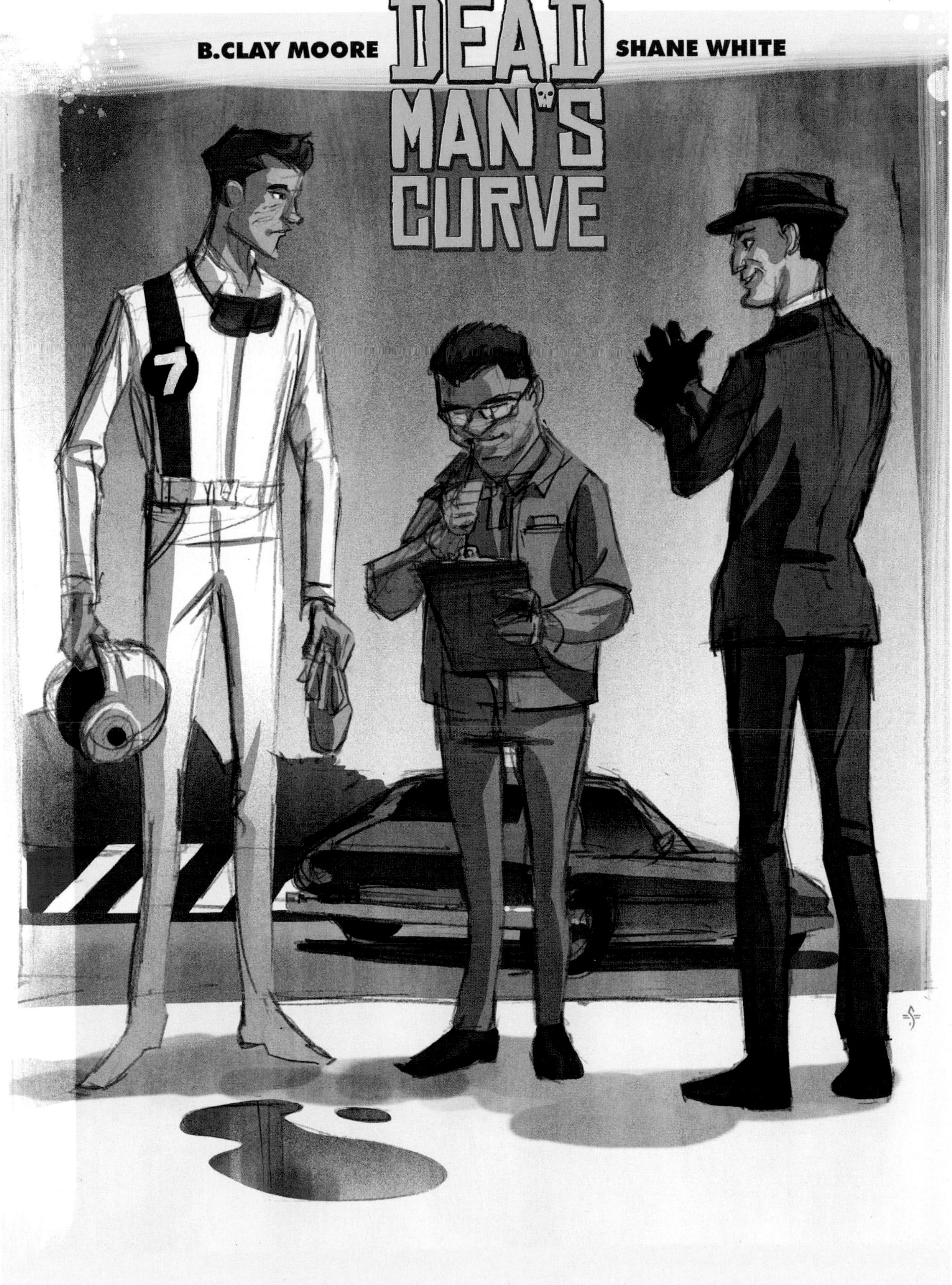
B.CLAY MOORE
DEAD MAN'S CURVE
SHANE WHITE
7

An Imprint of Insight Editions
PO Box 3088
San Rafael, CA 94912
www.insightcomics.com

Find us on Facebook:
www.facebook.com/InsightEditionsComics

Follow us on Twitter:
@InsightComics

Follow us on Instagram:
@insight_comics

Library of Congress Cataloging-in-Publication Data available.

ISBN: 978-1-68383-445-8

Publisher: Raoul Goff
VP of Licensing and Partnerships: Vanessa Lopez
VP of Manufacturing: Alix Nicholaeff
Editorial Director: Vicki Jaeger
Designer: Brooke McCullum
Editor: Mark Irwin
Associate Editor: Holly Fisher
Editorial Assistant: Elizabeth Ovieda
Production Editor: Elaine Ou
Production Associate: Andy Harper
Senior Production Manager, Subsidiary Rights: Lina s Palma

ROOTS of PEACE REPLANTED PAPER

Insight Editions, in association with Roots of Peace, will plant two trees for each tree used in the manufacturing of this book. Roots of Peace is an internationally renowned humanitarian organization dedicated to eradicating land mines worldwide and converting war-torn lands into productive farms and wildlife habitats. Roots of Peace will plant two million fruit and nut trees in Afghanistan and provide farmers there with the skills and support necessary for sustainable land use.

Manufactured in China by Insight Editions

10 9 8 7 6 5 4 3 2 1